THE HOUSE OF LORDS
AND THE
LABOUR GOVERNMENT
1964-1970

THE HOUSE OF LORDS
AND THE
LABOUR GOVERNMENT
1964-1970

———

JANET P. MORGAN

OXFORD

AT THE CLARENDON PRESS

1975

Oxford University Press, Ely House, London W. I

GLASGOW NEW YORK TORONTO MELBOURNE WELLINGTON
CAPE TOWN IBADAN NAIROBI DAR ES SALAAM LUSAKA ADDIS ABABA
DELHI BOMBAY CALCUTTA MADRAS KARACHI LAHORE DACCA
KUALA LUMPUR SINGAPORE HONG KONG TOKYO

ISBN 0 19 827191 3

© *Oxford University Press 1975*

*Printed in Great Britain
at the University Press, Oxford
by Vivian Ridler
Printer to the University*

R. H. S. C.
with thanks

FOREWORD

THIS is neither a study of Second Chambers in general nor an account of the complementary activities of the Upper and Lower Houses of Parliament in the later 1960s. It is merely a picture of the House of Lords—its members, their conventions and procedures—caught at a particularly interesting moment. For most of the time the Upper House is forgotten by those who write and think about British politics. An explorer who wishes to investigate this Lost World therefore relies very much on the advice of those who have gone before and on the goodwill of the indigenous inhabitants. Many people deserve especial thanks and, of these, some cannot be mentioned by name either here or in the text because much of their information was given in confidence. But the narrative shows how deeply I am obliged to them.

Some who can be identified include Professor Bromhead and Donald Shell, of the University of Bristol, and Gavin Drewry, of Bedford College, London, who explained how they had reconnoitred the Lords for their own books and articles. As they predicted, Mr. Reuter, and his staff of Doorkeepers, and Mr. William Stowell proved indispensable and discreet allies in the enterprise of selecting and intercepting Peers for interviews. Without demur, the Gentleman-Usher of the Black Rod, Admiral Sir Frank Twiss, and the Yeoman-Usher, Colonel Sayers, arranged for access to all parts of the House and for a seat in the Galleries. Lord Henley and Lord Amulree generously shared their own facilities and provided a room in which to work. The Librarian, Christopher Dobson, was equally kind.

Fortunately the Peers and those who serve them are interested and curious about their own role in public affairs and are ready to theorize about their House and themselves. For four years Peers and Peeresses helped with this inquiry, sometimes answering specific questions, often chatting and reminiscing informally. A hundred Peers, drawn from those who attend the House regularly, gave formal interviews from which the material for the typology (described in chapter 1) was derived. In addition, all those who make up the 'working House' were interviewed at some point,

except for those who are confused or otherwise incapable, and
about a third of the intermittent attenders were also asked for their
observations, together with a small number of those who hardly
attend at all.

It is therefore impossible to thank by name all those who were
so hospitable and frank. But I am very grateful to them all and to
those who encouraged them: Lord Carrington, Earl Jellicoe, and
Earl St. Aldwyn; Lord Shackleton, Lord Beswick, Lord Shepherd,
and Lord Strabolgi; Lord Henley and Lord Strang; Lord Champion and Lord Henderson; and Lord Saltoun.

It is the Clerks of the House, however, who perhaps have the
most thorough and detached understanding of the Lords and their
House. Not only did the Clerk of the Parliaments, Sir David
Stephens, and his staff in the Parliament Office make papers and
documents available, but several Clerks also scrutinized every draft
with clerkly care and patience. I am particularly indebted to Peter
Henderson in the Public Bill Office; to John Sainty and his suc-
cessor, Michael Wheeler Booth, in the Journal Office, and to their
Chief Assistant, Mr. Farrar; and to David Dewar and Michael
Davies in the Leader's Private Office.

Many civil servants, some of whom have at some time been
seconded to work in the Lords, have provided a shrewd commentary
on the affairs and effectiveness of the Upper House. Among these
I would like to thank particularly Roy Walker and David Martin,
who assisted the Leader of the House of Lords, and David Faulkner
and John Gunn. Like the Peers and the Clerks, they answered
questions of fact and offered opinions, but they do not, of course,
necessarily share the views expressed in the text.

Of the experienced academic observers, journalists, Ministers,
and Members of Parliament who gave a picture of the Lords as it
appears from the outside, the epitome was the late Richard Crossman, who was Leader of the House of Commons between 1966 and
1968 and who was one of the architects of the attempt to reform the
Second Chamber. His diaries and private papers have been extraordinarily helpful and have acted as a catalyst on the memories of
others who took part in that enterprise. I am extremely grateful
to him.

This book grew out of a doctoral thesis. It was transformed into
typescript by Mrs. Lyn Yates and her staff of secretaries, and by
Leofranc Holford-Strevens, who gave invaluable advice. I would

like to thank the staff of the Clarendon Press and of the Printer to the University for the care with which they have prepared this book. But most of all I would like to thank those who encouraged and supported this academic exercise—the Warden and Fellows of Nuffield College, Oxford, the President and Fellows of Wolfson College, Oxford, Lord Blake of the Queen's College, and Professor Max Beloff of All Souls College. It is to the Warden, D. N. Chester, and David Butler of Nuffield College that my deepest thanks are due.

J. P. M.

Nuffield College, Oxford
October 1973

CONTENTS

PART TWO

LIST OF TABLES IN APPENDIX

INTRODUCTION

MANY accounts of postwar British Parliamentary development neglect the House of Lords altogether; others give it only a passing glance. Apart from Professor Bromhead's study of the Lords between 1911 and 1957, a scattering of articles in professional journals and occasional periodicals, and Viscount Masserene and Ferrard's well-meant compilation, very little has been written about the functions and procedures of the Upper House. It is not surprising that students of modern British governmental machinery tend to be preoccupied with institutions that have an obvious impact on our political life and on each other. Compared with the House of Commons, the Cabinet, political parties at national and constituency level, pressure groups, trade unions, and the civil service, perhaps the House of Lords appears redundant and even absurd. Furthermore, it has awaited reform for so long that the uninformed assume that, if not dead, it must at least be moribund. But this assumption needs investigating. If the Lords do play a real part in our bicameral system it is odd that they are given so little attention; if, on the other hand, their power and influence are negligible, it is curious that the Lords have survived. There is certainly room to examine their deliberative and legislative role.

There are additional reasons for taking a fresh look at the Upper House. In 1964, as in 1911 and 1945, the party balance in the Lords was the reverse of that in the Commons. This provokes two questions. First, did Labour's legislation have a rough ride when it reached the Lords and did this lead to conflict between the two Houses? Secondly, what were the relations between the parties in the Lords when a minority Government faced an Opposition with an embarrassingly large majority? A study of the Lords' behaviour between 1964 and 1970 might suggest what ingenious methods of compromise they devised, and how all parties and the House itself handled an apparently precarious state of affairs.

In the House of Commons Labour had a majority of three in the General Election of October 1964 and increased it to a majority of a hundred in March 1966. In the House of Lords Labour Peers accordingly occupied the Government benches between 1964 and

1970 but as a party they were vastly outnumbered by the Conservatives. The most accurate figures show that, in mid 1968, 116 Labour Peers faced 351 Conservatives (with 41 Liberals and 554 Peers taking no party whip making up the rest of the House).[1] But while Labour Peers were hard pressed the Conservatives were in no less difficult a situation. They were obliged to give the Government a fair run, playing the constitutional game according to the rules by which Peers had played it since the sixteenth century, yet they sought to retain their credibility as an Opposition in the eyes of their own Backbenchers and in the larger world of Parliament and the politically informed. By frustrating the legislative programme Conservative Peers could help the Opposition in the Commons and maintain their own authority in the Lords, but at a price. The elected Government possessed the ultimate sanction of pruning the Lords' powers or abolishing them altogether.

At least these problems were not new. Roy Jenkins has shown how in the nineteenth century the Peers accepted measures proposed by Conservative Governments and rejected those of the Liberal Party, giving way to the elected Government 'only when the judgement of the nation has been challenged at the polls and decidedly expressed', an event 'so rare as practically to place little fetter upon our independence'.[2] The development of flourishing radical parties in the late nineteenth century required the Lords to behave more tactfully and, as Lord Lansdowne said on the passing of the 1906 Trades Disputes Bill,

> We are passing through a period when it is necessary for this House to move with very great caution . . . Conflicts, controversies may be inevitable, but let us, at any rate so far as we are able, be sure that if we join issue we do so upon ground that is as favourable as possible to ourselves.[3]

Nevertheless the crisis came over Lloyd George's budget, and the Lords were faced with a Parliament Bill designed by the Commons. The Peers spent the months before 1911 devising schemes to reform themselves but all their manœuvres failed. The diehards were defeated by the not unprecedented threat of the creation of new Peers to swamp the House. The 1911 Bill passed by 17 votes, 131 Content (81 Liberals, 37 Unionists, 13 Bishops) and 114 Not Content.

---

[1] Cmnd 3799, p. 5.   [2] M. Salisbury's letter to Earl Carnarvon, 20 Feb. 1871.
[3] *HC Debs.* (Fourth series), vol. 166, cols. 703-4. Quoted in Jenkins, p. 45.

The 1911 Act removed the Lords' power to reject 'Money Bills' as the Act defined them—this clause was never used. The powers of delay were reduced so that an ordinary Public Bill could become law despite the Lords if passed by the Commons in three successive Sessions, with not less than two years elapsing between Second Reading in the Commons in the first Session and the final passage of the Bill in the Commons in the third Session. Thus the Act allowed the Government to pass against Lords' opposition any legislation introduced in the first two Sessions of a five-year Parliament. (These emasculated delaying powers were used by the Lords on the Established Church (Wales) Bill and the Government of Ireland Bill, enacted in 1914 under the Parliament Act procedure.)

Though the Bill curbed the Lords' powers, the issue of the composition, functions, and limitations of a Second Chamber was still a matter of urgent dispute, but the outbreak of war prevented further action till 1917. In that year a Conference under the chairmanship of Lord Bryce made its report on the functions and changes appropriate to a reformed House,[4] of whose members three-quarters would be elected indirectly by M.P.s on a regional basis, with the remaining quarter chosen by a joint standing committee of both Houses, with a proportion of hereditary Peers and Bishops. However, members of the Conference could not agree and political circumstances made it expedient to drop the scheme.

Other proposals were made—and discarded—between the wars by Peers who continued to lament their awkward position *vis-à-vis* a House of Commons whose ultimate supremacy they found it hard to accept. Their discomfort was increased in 1929 when the Conservative Peers could not acknowledge that the minority Labour Government had a mandated right to insist on its legislative programme. The Opposition in the Lords put down wrecking amendments on such Bills as the 1930 Representation of the People (No. 2) Bill.

There had still been no further reform by the end of the Second World War, and with Labour's return to Government in 1945 the Conservative front bench in the Lords were once more in the uncomfortable role of a majority Opposition. At this point they adopted the explicit conventions of self-restraint that later on in 1964 were to provide a precedent. The 5th Marquess of Salisbury

[4] Cd. 9038.

explained to his fellow Conservative Peers in 1948 that some matters were 'outside our sphere'. In 1970 he reminisced:

> In 1945 we had to evolve a method of procedure. We had no previous experience and we had to make up our minds. The Conservative Peers came to the conclusion that where something was in the Labour Party manifesto we would regard it as approved by the country and we'd have Second Reading and amend it in Committee Stage. If they produced something that wasn't in the manifesto, we reserved the right to do what we thought best . . . We passed on Second Reading nearly all the nationalization bills—in the one case of the Iron and Steel Bill we went rather further as we didn't think they'd a justified demand. So we put in an amendment not to put it into force till after the Election. The Labour Party accepted that.

Such *ad hoc* tactics were equally awkward for the Labour Government in the Commons. Labour was pledged by the 1945 Election Manifesto not to allow the Lords to obstruct the legislative programme and in 1947 introduced a Parliament Bill to reduce the power of delay still further. An agreed reform proved impossible, for at an all-party Conference in 1948 the Conservatives could not approve Labour's proposals for a delaying period of less than one year from First Reading in the Commons—which would allow controversial legislation introduced in the fourth Session of a Parliament to be passed despite the Lords' opposition. Without agreement, therefore, the 1911 Act was used to pass the 1949 Bill.

This effectively reduced the period of delay to less than thirteen months, cutting from three to two the number of Sessions in which a disputed Bill must be passed by the Commons, and from three to two years the period of delay from Second Reading in the Commons. While trimming the powers of the Upper House, the 1949 Act did nothing to reconstitute its composition or recast its role.

A little progress was made in the next fifteen years. The White Paper published by the 1948 Conference[5] had discussed revisions of composition for a reformed House and further suggestions concerning the attendance of members were made in 1956 in the Report of the Select Committee chaired by Lord Swinton.[6] On some of these principles were based the subsequent changes of 1957 and 1958, when life peerages for men and women were introduced, with

[5] Cmd. 7380.
[6] Report by the Select Committee on the Powers of the House in relation to the attendance of its members, 24 Jan. 1956.

schemes for leave of absence and an attendance and expenses allowance. The Peerage Act of 1963, resulting from the work of joint Select Committees of both Houses, allowed hereditary Peers to renounce their peerages and admitted women Peers by succession. However, these were still only modifications of the existing state of affairs, far less inventive than the proposals for 'Lords of Parliament' recommended by the 1948 Conference.

Thus in 1964 the hereditary right to a seat in the Lords remained. Moreover, the Lords retained their powers to reject subordinate legislation, Private Bills, and Bills to confirm provisional Orders, of which there had been a vast increase since the war. Short though it was, the delaying power that they still possessed allowed the Peers to dislocate the Parliamentary time-table and at the end of a Parliament to force the loss of a Bill.

The problems the Lords faced in October 1964 were therefore very similar to those of 1911, 1929, and 1945. The Leader of the Conservative Peers, Lord Carrington, explained:

> If the Labour Leadership are reasonable, we let them get away with it. They know how far they can push us. Once we start using our veto, we're damaging the object of a Second Chamber. If the House of Lords is to work, we must show forbearance and commonsense.

Fifty years had not changed the Lords' dilemma. In 1910 Balfour told Lord Lansdowne that the Tory Peers were 'called upon to play a part at once so difficult and so delicate',[7] and although between 1964 and 1970 the question of their constitutional position was generally less urgent, sensitive and responsible Peers still saw the ambiguities of their position. This study examines the manner in which they sustained their difficult role.

As the 1966 Parliament wore on, underlying party tensions erupted and two episodes in particular provoked clashes between both parties and between the Upper and Lower Houses. These were the 1968 Southern Rhodesia (United Nations Sanctions) Order and 1969 House of Commons (Redistribution of Seats) Bill. They are discussed here in full for they also give the context of the attempt to secure an agreed reform of the House of Lords in 1968. It is only one of the ironies of this history that while a Government Bill to reform the Lords was welcomed by most of its potential victims in the Upper Chamber, it was the Commons that forced the

---

[7] Balfour's reply to Lansdowne, 13 Apr. 1910. Quoted in Jenkins, p. 39.

Government to abandon it. Moreover, the cabal of M.P.s who sabotaged the measure did so by exploiting the very procedural devices which the Commons proudly claimed gave the Government in that chamber control over business. The Lords lacked such devices and relied upon conventions of political decorum to smooth the passage of Government legislation. The self-restraint, rather than formal rules, that governed the Peers' behaviour is another important theme in this narrative.

The Parliament (No. 2) Bill was abandoned and once again the Lords in 1974 are left little changed, since 1910, in composition and formal powers. Nevertheless they are by this time remarkably well adjusted to their precarious position and accustomed to adapting themselves to the anomalies and anachronisms of their constitutional inheritance. In some respects 1964–70 was their twilight period, for they were uneasily aware of the Labour Party's readiness to attack a largely hereditary Second Chamber with its inherent Conservative majority, should there be the slightest provocation. But the account of these six years also shows the Lords' fundamental resilience. Throughout the century the possibility of abolition has hung over the Lords and conditioned their behaviour. Moreover, caution and self-control are second nature to a House accustomed to managing itself without a Speaker, for in the mid seventeenth century (the point at which, in contrast, the Speaker's authority to control the Commons had just begun to develop) the Lord Chancellor's formal powers to regulate order in the Lords began to pass to the House itself. In 1974 the Lords still run their business much on the lines of the eighteenth-century House of Commons, before the procedural reforms of the 1880s, and, especially when the Government party is in a minority in the Lords, collaboration between party managers is the only way of organizing proceedings. A hard-pressed Government cannot railroad business through. Conventional understandings also exist in the Commons but there it is deceptively easy to explain all conduct in terms of the demands of party conflict, and the operation of 'the usual channels' tends to pass unremarked. In the Upper House, party Leaders are obliged to co-operate and are more ready to refer openly to their arrangements. This account of Lords' business therefore indicates not only how the Lords have been able to adjust and survive but also exemplifies the delicate, unformulated mechanisms of the private world of Parliamentary management.

Self-restraint, hidden sanctions, and agreed conventions are three themes in this history and a fourth is the extreme individuality of members of the Lords. With a turnover less rapid than that of M.P.s, they paradoxically show less corporate spirit. The Peers seem to be less consciously obsessed with the House as an institution—there are 'House of Lords manners' but no 'House of Lords man'. Most Peers do not hang about their House but come, do their duty, and go away.

How they see that duty is another recurring theme. After all, Peers are not elected representatives but come at will, having inherited or accepted peerages. Some have a generalized idea of public service, others see their role as very much a political one (and it is interesting that since the sixteenth century a great part of the political work of the House has been done by Peers whose peerages have been expressly created for that purpose, to promote the fortunes of a particular monarch, party, or piece of legislation). In fulfilling their individual duty the Peers contribute to a collective operation, accepting the privileges and subtle disciplines of being 'among one's peers' in a Whole House greater than the sum of its parts, while retaining their idiosyncrasies and independence. Without corporate spirit (save when under attack), they are nevertheless intensely aware of their House as a Second Chamber of Parliament and preoccupied with its status in constitutional theory, whether as a supreme court of appointees checking the elected representatives, as a general ombudsman, or as a complementary amending and legislating chamber.

A symptom of this preoccupation is the traditional deep hostility between the two Houses. No doubt feelings of guilt nourish the Lords' jealous justifications for their privileges, powers, style of conducting business, and, not least important, their territory in the Palace of Westminster. Suspicious of Commons' encroachment, the Lords are fertile in proposing their own reforms; for their part, successive Governments in the Commons have been reluctant to introduce legislation that might strengthen the Upper House at the expense of the Lower.

Critics of bicameralism have argued that effective Second Chambers are meddlesome checks but that, ineffective, they are superfluous. This is still a topical question (New Zealand and Sweden have only recently abolished their Upper Houses) but in Britain studies of the House of Lords tend to be sidetracked into attacking its privileged composition rather than examining its usefulness as a Second Chamber, assisting the process of government or hindering the process of misgovernment. This history describes the Lords' role in the whole political arena, how they perform as an agent of government, and how they appear to the rest of the political world, to the Cabinet, the departments, and the House of Commons, to the Press, and the public. It is important to see how far the Peers' awareness of their political and public reputation is a constraint on their behaviour—for they have to be narcissistic in order to survive. Only by monitoring their own behaviour and remaining sensitive to their image in the world outside can they avoid infringing a web of sanctions, explicitly formulated or implicitly understood. This study, then, with its five themes, is thus an evolutionary parable: how the House of Lords, unreformed, has like the British Constitution adapted to the times.

PART ONE

1

THE WORKING HOUSE

A. *Innovations*

IN 1964 the principles on which the bulk of the members of the House of Lords took their seats followed a pattern maintained since very early times. True, the 1867 Appellate Jurisdiction Act, forced by the Wensleydale peerage case, had established the principle of judicial life peerages, and since 1958 men and women Life Peers had been introduced. More recently still, the 1963 Peerage Act permitted Scottish Peers and women Peers by succession to take their seats. (Holders of Scottish peerages had previously elected sixteen representative Peers for Scotland. Irish Peers lost their representation in 1922.) Otherwise the House was composed, as in medieval times, of hereditary Peers and those Bishops sitting as Lords of Parliament. The question of the composition of the Upper House, the rights of Peers to take a hand in government, and the likelihood of their turning up at Westminster had always bedevilled discussions of the role and powers of the Second Chamber, and abolition of this inherited privilege was a traditional part of Labour's programme.

In the light of these emotional and ideological criticisms, a great deal of work was done between 1964 and 1970 to provide a full picture of the composition and working membership of the Lords, as a background to proposals for reform. Statistical surveys were commissioned and, because the party Leaders in the Lords co-operated in submitting details of party affiliation, the figures set out in the 1968 White Paper are the most accurate available.[1] Occurring at the mid-point of this period, these analyses are a useful basis for examining what type of Peer came regularly to the House, his motives and ambitions, and his particular contribution. Moreover, a summary of the Lords' composition and of their party disposition illustrates some of the problems faced by the party Leaders in managing their Backbenchers during the years of Labour Government.

[1] Cmnd. 3799.

Because the House sat as a Court of Record the Lords' Journals have always been open to inspection and here Peers' daily attendances are recorded, based upon a note taken by the Clerks at the Table, assisted by the Doorkeepers noticing those Peers taking their seats in the chamber. Until very recently, attendances were listed in order of rank in the peerage. At the end of each Session the Clerk of the Journals prepares a more convenient alphabetical list of individual attendances for the whole Session. The Lords have been reluctant to publish this as a Parliamentary paper for it would provide ready ammunition for those who attack them as a chamber of absentees or backwoodsmen. The Sessional list was only made public in March 1969, when the list of attendances for each Session 1963–64 and 1967–68 was offered in reply to demands made in the Commons' discussion in the Committee stage of the Parliament (No. 2) Bill. Publication of these figures is now regularly sanctioned and, while the information can be obtained from a careful study of the Journals, Lords' Hansard, and other published sources, the published summaries show conveniently which Peers attend assiduously.

Attendance and Expenses Allowances

By 1964 the innovations of 1957, 1958, and 1963 were showing some results. The first changes in 1957 included arrangements for an attendance allowance for Peers. Payment of travelling expenses still depended on frequency of attendance (at least one-third of the sittings of the House or one of its committees or, in the case of Peers resident in Scotland, one-third of the sittings at which Scottish business is taken) but payment of the new attendance allowance did not depend upon how often a Peer took his place. Peers were entitled to claim, for every day they attended, up to three guineas a day for the reimbursement of their expenses and this sum, untaxed, was raised in November 1964 to four and a half guineas a day and in December 1969 to £6. 10s. (when the car mileage allowance and related travelling expenses were also raised). The *per diem* allowance is now (July 1973) £8·50 and it rests upon Peers themselves to submit a printed form, giving details of claims, which are administered by an unofficial committee of the Whips.

It is difficult to assess the effect of the scheme—a note in the *Table* in 1957 remarked: 'A first impression . . . is that it has very slightly raised the numbers attending in certain quarters of the

House.' Some elderly, retired Peers and some who succeed to a title and nothing more are now enabled to come when they might otherwise find it difficult. A typical comment came from a Conservative hereditary Peer who said:

It was too damned expensive. Then one of the Clerks told me I could claim my allowance even if I didn't come three days a week. So now it's quite easy and I can come whenever I'm interested and can pay for my fare and meals.

When the allowance was introduced there were some gibes about 'Chelsea pensioners', lodging in town during the week and spending their expenses allowance at the bar, but when the matter was mentioned among those who were interested in Lords' reform, it appeared that this 'underworld' numbers only a few. In fact other Peers find the allowance so negligible in relation to their other resources that they feel it too trivial to claim. Most, however, regard it as 'useful pocket-money', and while it does not provide a positive inducement to attend the House it certainly helps some Peers, old men with a small pension, younger men saddled with death duties, and Life Peers of little means who might otherwise be unable to accept a peerage and the responsibilities of attendance.

The Ministerial Salaries Consolidation Act 1965 gives details of the salaries of the Leader of the House and Chief Whip and the Leader of the Opposition and his Chief Whip. (A useful summary of the salaries paid to office-holders in the House of Lords and the most recently recommended increases can be found in the Report of the Committee on Top Salaries 1971.)[2] The 1968 Conference considered introducing salaries for Peers attending the House regularly and while this point was not thoroughly explored one or two official papers were prepared. (Lord Shackleton favoured the ingenious system of the Canadian Senate, described below on p. 183.) It was thought that not only do many Peers prefer a tax-free allowance (particularly the wealthy) but that their dignity would be offended were they offered salaries for their 'honorific' work. Moreover such a scheme would jar those M.P.s who regard the Lords as amateurs and the Commons as the professional House where salaries are appropriate.

[2] Cmnd. 4836.

Leave of Absence

The unpredictability of the Lords' attendance has always been open to attack and in 1957 the House also agreed to the Report of a Select Committee set up to inquire into the powers of the House in relation to the attendance of its members.[3] It was said that:

> In practice, the number of 'backwoodsmen' who have voted, even in the most numerous Divisions, has been very small; but the Government and the House have nevertheless thought it worthwhile, by the arrangements now made for leave of absence, to do something towards preventing their unexpected appearance in the House, and so refute the allegation that they might play a dangerously reactionary part in politics.

Briefly, the Committee explained that the House had no right

> either to prevent the attendance of any Peer who has received a Writ or to seek to whittle down the rights conferred upon him by his Writ and Patent, for instance, by seeking to prevent him from speaking or voting. In pursuance of its ordinary power to maintain order in debate, the House could clearly eject or suspend any of its members for disorderly behaviour, and on two occasions it has imposed the penalty of expulsion. But apart from this, the House has no power to exclude, wholly or partially, any Peer who is in receipt of a Writ.

The late Viscount Simonds was one of those who objected to any leave-of-absence scheme on the grounds that it would be *ultra vires*; and the fact that no Peer can be excluded from the House was to provide another argument against proposals for pruning membership in a reformed House. It has been alleged that conniving relations have managed to mislay the Writs sent to imbecile or dipsomaniac Peers but certainly the Lord Chancellor's Office is obliged to send them.

The scheme that was adopted in June 1958 and is set out in Standing Order 21 (now 22) is therefore not one that denies Peers who have not attended the House the right to do so in future, but one that allows them to apply for leave of absence, either for a single Session or for the remainder of a Parliament, if they wish. The numbers who have done so between 1964 and 1970 have been small and fairly constant; 5 or 6 per cent of Peers holding a Writ have applied for leave for a Session and 12 or 13 per cent for leave for a whole Parliament. A dozen or so Peers tend to change their minds and after applying for leave at the beginning of a Session decide to

---

[3] H.M.S.O., 24 Jan. 1956.

come after all; the Clerk of the Journals advises Peers who apply for leave not to take it if there is any likelihood of their turning up at all. In any case those who apply spontaneously are not the unpredictable backwoodsmen but a small core of conscientious Peers who are unlikely to attend, or those who live abroad, are going abroad, or know that their other duties will prevent their coming.

Under the revised Standing Order of June 1967, the Clerk of the Journals writes on the Lord Chancellor's behalf to all Peers who already take leave of absence, to all who have not attended in the previous Session, and to those who have come only to take the Oath, asking if they wish to take leave for the current Session. Those who do not reply are written to again and if they still do not signify their wishes they are automatically granted leave. However, the scheme is generally thought to be futile, for it is only those Peers who have no intention of attending the House anyway who ask for leave or allow themselves to be granted it and, moreover, any Peer can revoke his decision with a month's notice or even attend the House unannounced.[4]

Life Peerages

The innovations described above were intended to improve the working of the House by removing difficulties in the way of those who are willing to come and by acknowledging that some Peers do not wish to attend at all. The Life Peerages Act of April 1958 had a deeper purpose, to bring into Parliament men and women who might not wish to accept a hereditary title or to contest a seat in the Commons. This measure had been proposed on numerous occasions in the last hundred years, with little success until the passage of the 1876 Appellate Jurisdiction Act. The 1958 Act allowed the Crown to confer peerages, with the rank of a Baron, on men and women for life.

Hereditary women Peers had also had a long battle. After the passage of the 1919 Sex Disqualification (Removal) Act Lady Rhondda attempted to take her seat as a Viscountess in her own right, but was foiled by the arguments of lawyers in the Lords, notably the Earl of Birkenhead. Peeresses in their own right were eventually admitted under the 1963 Peerage Act.

[4] From time to time the ghostly backwoodsmen are still said to throng the House. For example, there was an unusually large vote on 28 Oct. 1971 when 509 Peers divided on the Motion that Britain should apply for Common Market membership. In reply to a question from Lord Maelor, an anti-Marketeer, on 10 Nov. 1971, Earl Jellicoe stated that perhaps thirty rare attenders had appeared. The Clerks put the estimate at about eighteen.

By June 1971 successive Prime Ministers had nominated 198 Life Peers, with a particularly large burst of creations in the early years of the Labour Government. There were, for example, 39 creations in 1964–5, 20 in 1965–6, and 51 between March 1966 and October 1968.[5] By November 1971 there had been 221 creations and of these Life Peers 31 had died since the Act was passed.

Peerages are offered on the recommendation of the Prime Minister of the day, but all honours are referred to an Honours Scrutiny Committee (of whose existence the public are officially unaware). During the Administrations of Harold Macmillan and Sir Alec Douglas-Home some hereditary peerages were created and some Peers advanced in degree, and while Home was Prime Minister the choice between a life peerage or hereditary peerage depended largely on the wishes of the recipient. Since Harold Wilson became Prime Minister in 1964 no new hereditary peerages have been created. (In answering a Parliamentary Question Edward Heath did not rule out further hereditary honours but during his 1970–74 Administration none were conferred.)

It is interesting to see how this patronage is used (Table 2),[6] and the records show that, in making their recommendations to the Queen, Prime Ministers have observed the convention of asking other party Leaders for suggestions. Indeed, as Leader of the Opposition, Hugh Gaitskell insisted on this principle before agreeing to the 1958 Act and Harold Macmillan felt that he was establishing the precedent by accepting the Opposition Leader's nominations without question. As he wrote in his memoirs:

I immediately saw Gaitskell and asked him whether he would send me any suggested names for the first list . . . I asked him about life peers. He is a little embarrassed—his party is again divided about this. (2 April 1958.)

However, after the Bill had successfully passed the House of Lords and received Royal Assent, I made another approach to him. After all the Socialist protestations regarding life peers—they would never touch it, etc., etc.,—he . . . produced five or six nominations. (1 July 1958.)[7]

The number of Opposition nominations that a Prime Minister accepts is a matter for him alone. Where Dissolution Honours are concerned, it is customary for the Leader of the Opposition to submit a list of names in order of preference, and although a Prime

[5] See appendix.   [6] See appendix.
[7] H. Macmillan, *Riding the Storm* (1971), p. 731.

Minister will confine his actual recommendations to a number he thinks appropriate he does not pick and choose among the list.

Successive Prime Ministers, particularly Wilson, have gradually increased the number of Life Peeresses and on occasion peerages are bestowed on the wives and widows of eminent men. Many Life Peeresses devote a great part of their lives to political activity and of the twenty-five created between 1958 and 1970 only two have chosen to sit as Crossbenchers.

Another principle on which life peerages have been conferred has been the deliberate strengthening of minority parties in the House. To boost the Labour ranks, Macmillan deliberately offered life peerages to members of that party while Wilson refrained from making Conservative creations, except in years when the Leader of the Opposition submitted Dissolution Honours (1964; 1966; a late nomination, Thorneycroft, in 1967; 1970). Wilson was generous with crossbench peerages but some of these are held by Labour sympathizers who prefer not to participate in party business in the House, in some cases (like Lords Aylestone, Hill, and Wigg) while they hold Government appointments outside it.

Liberal strength has also increased, though it is significant that Macmillan made no Liberal creations and was criticized for this in leading articles in the Press. For example, the Liberal Leadership suggested that Macmillan was generally hostile to their party and that his reluctance to make a particular nomination, that of Lady Violet Bonham Carter, an obvious candidate for the first Liberal life peerage, was a strengthening factor. The frosty attitude of the Liberal Leader, Jo Grimond, to the Upper House provided Macmillan with a convenient excuse. (It might also be thought that Grimond would find it awkward to plead for Lady Violet, his mother-in-law, but, according to an article in *The Times*, 26 July 1971, Grimond did eventually suggest her name to Wilson.) It was left to Wilson to nominate the first Liberal Life Peers. Lady Violet duly became Baroness Asquith; Lord Byers and Lord Wade were nominated at the same time.

According to a former Leader of the Lords, Gaitskell made it plain that those of his nominees who accepted life peerages were expected to attend the House regularly. At the beginning of the operation of the Act in 1958 an attempt was made to distinguish between 'working' and 'honorific' peerages by announcing life peerages separately from New Year and Birthday Honours, which were at that time largely hereditary. The batch nominated by Gaitskell are reputed to have been particularly energetic—and informed observers have said that even in 1970 they were still the driving force in the Labour Party in the Lords. Certainly Labour's long years in Opposition and their loss of the 1959 General Election provided a pool from which Gaitskell could propose a number of able and conscientious politicians. Wilson was perhaps less fortunate, for by 1964 fewer Labour M.P.s were anxious to leave the Commons despite the campaign of the Labour Leadership in the Lords to attract fresh recruits.

It has been suggested that a side-effect of abandoning hereditary honours has been to devalue the life peerage, since some eminent and preoccupied Life Peers see their title as purely honorific and come to the House only intermittently or not at all. But though not every Peer accepts a duty to come when he accepts a peerage, about eight out of ten do come regularly. Indeed, where attendance is concerned, figures set out in the White Paper on Lords' Reform show that a fair balance of activity is shared between Peers by succession and by creation (even allowing for the fact that the total number of created Peers includes hereditary Peers of first creation as well as Life Peers. A useful table (Table 3)[8] shows a total of 138 hereditary Peers attending more than $33\frac{1}{3}$ per cent of sitting days and 121 between 5 per cent and $33\frac{1}{3}$ per cent of the time, comparing well with totals of 153 and 95 created Peers. Certainly by 1970 it could not be said that the bulk of the work of the House was done exclusively either by created Peers or by hereditary Peers, and an examination of individual records for attendance and speaking supported the conclusion that Life Peers took their duties seriously. It also suggests that hereditary Peers had become more assiduous, stimulated by their new colleagues. According to a recent report prepared by a Committee of the Peers themselves:[9]

Of the greatly increased number of Peers attending the House each day (at present an average of 265 per day, compared with 140 in 1963 and 92 in 1955) . . . this increased attendance is mainly a reflection of the large creations of Life Peers in recent years . . .

The character of the House had also changed considerably

---

[8] See appendix. Frequent reference will be made to this table.
[9] The Tenth Report from a Select Committee on the Procedure of the House, 3 Aug. 1971. This document is based on a confidential report prepared in May 1971 by a Group appointed by the Leader of the House.

between 1964 and 1970. In an article[10] written in 1966 John Vincent analysed activity in the House, using as a measure interventions recorded in the index of Hansard for the Session beginning in October 1964. In terms of speeches, he was able to show that Life Peers and Peers of first creation had been more active than Peers by succession. By 1970, in a House 'far less dozy than ten years ago', senior Clerks remarked on the way that a large number of hereditary Peers had been provoked to speak regularly in debate and in Committee and, undoubtedly inspired by the challenge of created Peers, had helped to lift the House from 'the doldrums of the 1950s'.

Vincent's article looked at the House in 1964 and the progressive trend he discerned at that time continued during the later 1960s and early 1970s. He observed that those hereditary Peers who do attend a House 'conducted principally by new men' are presumably 'untypical in their adaptive capacity' and that such general and imperceptible self-selection causes both Life Peers and hereditary Peers to reinforce each other's influence in changing the character of the House. According to Vincent's analysis, the Peers' progressive attitude towards recent legislation on, for example, the abolition of capital punishment and laws affecting homosexuality, divorce, and abortion has been the result of co-operation between an older liberal aristocracy and some of the new 'politician' Peers. He supported this observation with analyses of voting and speeches. Conversations with Peers of all types show that in the early 1970s members of the Upper House do in fact pride themselves on a rational and liberal outlook, unconstrained by constituency or party ties. No doubt Life Peers (often newly liberated from the Commons and their electors) do encourage the Lords to act as an influential clerisy, advancing views very similar to those in *The Times* leaders of the day. Reciprocally, it is part of the style of the old, hereditary peerage to disregard mere conventional morality and this perhaps eggs on those created Peers who hesitate to use the freedom of the Upper House to promote permissive legislation and provocative debate. At any rate, the House of Lords has become a more lively place. As one shrewd young hereditary Peer observed:

 I never dreamt for a moment that my Conservative colleagues would wish to restore the death penalty. When unfamiliar people come down, they tend *not* to be reactionaries. If anything, we've got a *progressive* backwoods vote.

[10] *Parliamentary Affairs* (Summer 1966).

It is important to note, however, that in matters where the House may divide according to liberal versus reactionary opinion, Peers are very largely swayed by the attitude of the Leadership and, as a senior Clerk testified, if the Lords are skilfully managed, they may be persuaded to 'do anything'.[11] Furthermore, the forward-looking approach the Lords have shown since the mid 1960s owes a great deal to the liberal disposition of its three party Leaders, Lord Byers, Lord Jellicoe, and Lord Shackleton, who have all been prepared to co-operate on both the substance and handling of such legislation.

Life Peers, then, have made the House a more spirited place, but some problems have arisen both from increased attendance and the introduction of large numbers of newly created Peers at a rate faster than that to which the House has been accustomed. Some hereditary Peers have complained privately that Life Peers take too seriously the terms of the Writ of Summons to

be at the said day and place personally present with us and with the said Prelates Great Men and Peers to treat and give your counsel upon the affairs aforesaid . . .

and whatever the substance of this criticism the very making of the complaint is one symptom of new pressures in the House. Of course accommodation within and without the chamber is less ample and the list of Peers wishing to speak more crowded. In the words of the Peers' own Report, many of the new Life Peers

are ex-M.P.s or from local government, and approach their role as members of the House of Lords with a new professionalism which was largely unfamiliar to the House prior to the passage of the Life Peerage Act . . .

Some complaints have been heard of a new acerbity emerging in proceedings; but even if Peers are 'more pushy than they used to be' this cannot be ascribed to Life Peers alone. Their presence may act as a stimulus and bring to the surface polemical desires hitherto suppressed, making the Whole House more passionate. Altogether it seems that the Life Peers created since 1958 have acted not as sole agent but as a catalyst of change.

[11] 'Progressiveness' is not confined to social legislation, as the Divisions on the Southern Rhodesia (United Nations Sanctions) order 1968 and the 1971 E.E.C. debate suggest. See p. 148.

Disclaiming Peerages

In spite of this revitalization, it has been suggested that young and able Peers will shun the Upper House and choose a political career in the Commons, accelerating the decline of the Lords. The provisions of the 1963 Peerage Act, permitting any person succeeding to a peerage to disclaim it for life, gave them the opportunity. Ironically, it was an Opposition Amendment in the Lords, successfully moved by the Labour Peer, Lord Silkin, and passed by 105 to 25 votes, that brought the Act into immediate effect. Thus the Earl of Home and Viscount Hailsham were able to renounce their peerages in time to fight for the Conservative Leadership in 1963 and Home was permitted to become Prime Minister. Hogg returned to the Commons, and re-entered the Lords as Lord Hailsham of St. Marylebone, Lord Chancellor, in 1970.

Nevertheless by 1971 only eleven Peers had renounced their seats and, of these, four retained or returned to seats in the Commons, while one, Victor Montagu, sought unsuccessfully to return in 1964. Their number is so small that it is possible to look at each individual case and see what his motives were. In chronological order they are:

Viscount Stansgate (Anthony Wedgwood Benn), who at the time gave his Commons career as his reason.

Lord Altrincham (John Grigg) from distaste for the hereditary principle.

Earl of Home (Sir Alec Douglas-Home)—Commons career.

Viscount Hailsham (Quintin Hogg)—Commons career.

Lord Southampton (Charles Fitzroy) from an eighteenth-century reluctance to support 'an appropriate style of life'.

Lord Monkswell (William Collier)—radical distaste.

Lord Beaverbrook (Sir Max Aitken) out of respect for his father.

Earl of Sandwich (Victor Montagu)—Commons career.

Lord Fraser of Allandale (Sir Hugh Fraser)—filial respect.

Earl of Durham (Antony Lambton)—Commons career.

Lord Sanderson of Ayot (Dr. Alan Lindsay Sanderson)—retiring disposition.

The list shows that this part of the 1963 Act has in fact affected the Lords only as far as the contributions of significant individuals are concerned.[12]

---

[12] This is also true of the less well-publicized provisions that allowed Peeresses in their

In one case, that of the former Liberal M.P., Eric Lubbock, who in December 1970 faced the dilemma of either continuing to fight for a seat in the Commons or succeeding to the Barony of Avebury, his decision *not* to renounce the title gave him, he maintains, as influential a public platform in the Lords as the Commons had ever been. (Perhaps, for a Liberal, more so.)

However, well-informed Peers and Officials of the House observe that in future more of the young, intelligent hereditary Peers might be anxious to disclaim their peerages because the House of Commons is unarguably more attractive to an aspiring politician. Moreover, in the case of heirs who are already members of the Lower House, respect for their fathers' efforts in the Lords may still be outweighed by the deep contempt that the majority of M.P.s feel for the Upper House. This is a pity. The system that prevailed before the passage of the Peerage Act was objectionable, but those hereditary Peers who were obliged to make their political career in the Lords (and Lord Carrington is a good example of a Peer who succeeded to his title at an early age) contribute a great deal to the Lords' political effectiveness and as time progresses future renunciations might weaken the House.[13]

It is naturally impossible to establish how many men and women have declined to accept a peerage, though some famous examples come to mind in Winston Churchill, Harold Macmillan, G. B. Shaw, and R. H. Tawney. Others would be long-serving M.P.s who feel that they still have some useful life left in the Commons but would not refuse a future invitation. Discreet inquiries for the 1964-70 period show that, of those who admit to rejecting the honour, some refused the Prime Minister for reasons of principle (including Frank Cousins, John Freeman, Malcolm MacDonald, J. B. Priestley, Richard Titmuss, Kenneth Younger), others because they did not realize their political lives were to be shortened (Bessie Braddock, for example), and one (Cecil King) because, in the tradition of Press Lords, he wanted to be a Viscount.

own right to take their seats and admitted all Scottish Peers on the same terms as English and Welsh Peers, removing the long-standing grievance of those Scottish Peers who had been effectively disfranchised. The Irish Peers lost their representation in 1922 but still occasionally press their case. See Cmnd. 3799, p. 32, and *HL Debs.*, vol. 320, cols. 715-38.

[13] Of the two peerages that had been more recently disclaimed, by the summer of 1972, one was renounced by an M.P., Arthur Silkin, son of Lord Silkin who played a notable part in the passage of the 1963 Peerage Act. The other was that of Christopher John Reith, heir of Lord Reith.

Disregarding hearsay and modest confessions, however, it is clear that as a result of the statutory alterations of 1958 and 1963, the House of Lords is an increasingly attractive place to be, especially for those with no alternative political arena. At last some of its long-standing critics have been disarmed, for it is no longer a wholly masculine, largely hereditary chamber and, what is more, the party balance has also improved. However, the problems of party imbalance in the Upper House have by no means been solved, as the following description reveals.

B. *The Party Balance*

By 1968 the Conservatives' authority in the House of Lords was no longer undisputed. The effect of the large number of Labour creations that followed the passage of the 1958 Act, with Wilson's particular augmentations after 1964, is shown most strikingly in a chart prepared for the 1968 White Paper on Lords' Reform (Fig. 1).

The first two columns of 'Regular Attenders' show the balance between Conservative and Labour, and at the time of the White Paper it was estimated that there was a difference of only about thirty votes between them. If then the Conservatives refrained from strictly whipping their Backbenchers and if Labour had cross-bench support, Labour could conceivably win a Division. On the other hand, when numbers as small as 125 Conservatives and 95 Labour Peers are considered, thirty is a sizeable majority and, moreover, the Conservative Whips could without very much difficulty summon to Westminster a large number of infrequent attenders—represented in the column at the extreme left of the chart. While Labour's worry remained one of insufficient strength, the Conservative Whips had a lesser, but familiar problem, for they sometimes hoped that their supporters would not turn up in such large numbers that the Opposition would appear to be using 'over-kill'. (The Southern Rhodesia (United Nations Sanctions) Order was one such episode.)

It might also seem that the nineteen Liberals and fifty-two Crossbenchers would hold a balance between Conservative and Labour Peers, but in fact the Liberal group was minute and the Crossbenchers generally split. Subsequent chapters will describe the occasions when Liberal and crossbench tactics had a significant impact; in general this could not be relied upon. Many crossbench

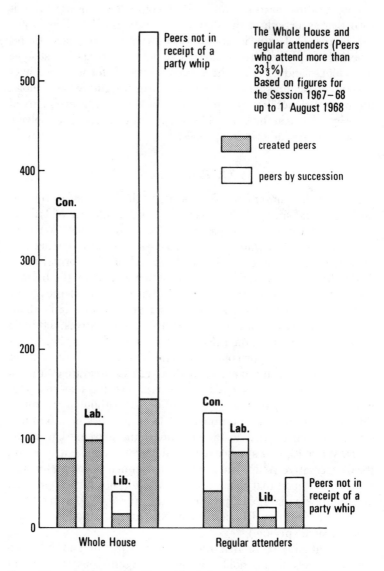

F IG. I. The party balance in the House of Lords, by attendance. *Source*: Cmnd. 3799, p. 7.

Peers are in fact predictable supporters of one or the other major parties and, of the largest group of all, the infrequently attending, non-affiliated Peers (represented by the tallest column), the majority are hidden Conservatives. Although it appears that the potential crossbench vote could swamp that of all other parties, this is unlikely ever to happen.

The chart shows that, among the Peers attending the House regularly, the party balance is less uneven but nevertheless unforeseeable. The party Leaders' problems are compounded when the tall shadow of the potential Whole House is taken into account. However, it was certainly the influx of created Peers that alleviated the previous distorted situation. This is best illustrated by the other chart in the White Paper, that of party balance by nature of peerage (Fig. 2).

The chart shows that Labour created Peers evidently take their responsibilities most seriously of all (it has been described as a retirement job on half-pay for Labour politicians). At the other extreme, the furthest right-hand column of crossbench Life Peers have the highest proportion of non-attenders and from these too come the large group of created Peers who attend only up to a third of the time. Many of these created Crossbenchers are the eminent men and women known as 'Peers of occasional excellence' who come to make infrequent but influential contributions to debate.

Whenever crossbench Peers are considered, it is important to remember that official figures do not distinguish between undeclared Conservatives, Crossbenchers in general, and the most zealous Crossbenchers of all, those who take the notice of information or 'non-whip' issued by Lord Strang to those uncommitted Crossbenchers who request it. There were in 1964 125 Peers on his list (though these included at least thirty who came rarely or not at all and even some who had not yet made their maiden speech even though they had been members of the House for some years).[14]

Crosschecking with the table of attendance (of which further sections are reproduced in the appendix as Table 4) shows that very few created Peers never attend at all—only forty-one in 1967–68 (and this includes Peers of first creation). Such non-attending created Peers would be the very old, the very busy, those residing abroad, or those like Lord Robens whose appointments at that time disqualified them from participation in proceedings. Altogether the

[14] See p. 98.

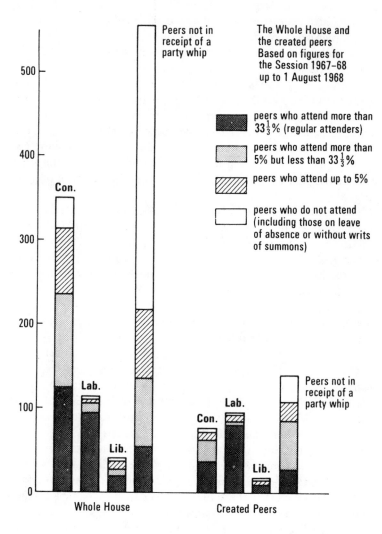

F IG. 2. The party balance in the House of Lords, by nature of Peerage. *Source*: Cmnd. 3799, p. 6.

figures bear out the conclusion that the introduction of life peerages has done much to revitalize the House and correct the party imbalance there, and they give a counter-argument to allegations that the Lords are 'one-sided, hereditary and absentee', as Churchill once described them.

Nevertheless it is a curious assembly where a quarter of the members never turn up at all. Although Officials in the Whips' Office suggest that they can usually guess within twenty votes the outcome of a Division, in principle the likelihood of Peers' attending or voting is still unpredictable. Not only is the outcome of a controversial issue difficult to foresee with any accuracy, but the oddities of the House, with its preponderance of Crossbenchers, its insistence on the independence of its members, and the vagaries of its party distribution, mean that the Life Peerages Act has by no means removed the thorns in the party Leaders' paths. Moreover, the figures and charts illustrate Peers' attendance; they do not take account of the Peers' behaviour in debate and Division. To explore this, it is necessary to ask how they see their fundamental obligations to party, to the country, and to their House.

c. *Types of Peer*

Tables and percentages give a quantitative picture of the House; a different sort of analysis is needed to give a qualitative impression. A simple typology of the Lords based not on party, length of service, nature of peerage, or profession but on the characteristics of Peers' personalities and their outlook on the world helps the outsider to see the Lords in more immediate and human terms. Though unsophisticated and inevitably imprecise, such a classification nevertheless reveals a good deal about the motives and ambitions of those who take part in the business of the Upper House.

Peers are curious about their House and themselves and are ready to theorize about their role in public affairs. Still, an investigation based largely upon interviews must be designed with rigour and common sense and it is just as important to explain how a representative sample of Peers has been defined as it is to assemble their remarks into significant and honest evidence.

In 1970, 1,063 Peers were entitled to take their seats and, though it is clearly impossible to interview them all, a statistical sample of about a hundred is manageable. There is little point in drawing this from all Peers entitled to sit—including those who never attend at all—for a study seeking to describe the conduct of the House over a particular period of time and the behaviour of individuals and groups within it. The Peers in the statistical sample are therefore taken from 'the working House' of those who attend more than a third of the time, carefully selected to give weight in due proportion to important categories of Peers. It is absurd to try to construct a microcosm of the House but some broad correspondence has been established between features of the Whole House and the sample. Party and type of peerage are important, so an appropriate balance is kept between interviews with Conservative, Labour, Liberal, Crossbenchers, and other Peers, and between hereditary Peers and those of first creation, Law Lords and Bishops. The sample also includes fair numbers of Peers of each sex and of varying age and length of service and there are other significant controls—whether a Lord belongs to groups like those of the lawyers, trade unionists, military Peers, Scots, or the 'amenity lobby', for instance.

The 'working House' from which the sample is derived is that of the Session beginning in November 1967 and sitting until the end of July 1968. This is particularly useful because Lords' attendances in that Session have been analysed by party affiliation and type of peerage as evidence to the Inter-party Conference on Lords' reform. Moreover, the Session falls conveniently in the middle of the period of the Labour Administration of October 1964 to June 1970. It is also a Session well after the 1966 General Election when in Lords and Commons Labour was firmly established as the governing party. A later Session might have special attributes because of the imminence of a Dissolution and the Government's visibly declining fortunes.

The 1967–68 Session is also ideal from the point of view of legislative business. Plenty of work was at that point coming up from the Commons and business was also fairly typical in items both of some controversy and of lesser importance. As well as major issues like the 1968 Commonwealth Immigration Bill, the 1968 Southern Rhodesia Order, the Theft Bill, Transport Bill, Countryside Bill, and Town and Country Planning Bill, there were innumerable Questions about matters like S.E.T. and the Third London Airport at Stansted, along with a large volume of routine business.

From this Session the sample was taken, and from extended interviews a set of portraits emerge. Without prior assumptions, but with their own remarks as a guide, Peers can be said to cluster into types which, for convenience, can be called 'Apprentices', 'Innocents', 'Adventurers', 'Legalists', 'Politicians', and 'Elder Statesmen', titles which are sufficiently apt to convey an immediate impression of the idiosyncrasies of the different groups. Such classifications and the assignment of Peers to each one are necessarily arbitrary but they have been broadly endorsed by a representative number of Peers, by the party Leaders, and by senior Clerks, so that while they claim no anthropological precision, they do give some insight into the contribution that Peers of varying character make to their assembly.

It is important to remember that these observations are those of the Lords themselves, advanced at the time of their 'twilight period' of uncertainty about their reputation, function, and destiny. Some of their comments are shrewd and realistic but others are absurd, illustrating the gap between political actuality and some Peers' interpretations of it. It will be instructive to compare the Lords' own descriptions of their role, their activities, and of each other, with the accounts that follow in later chapters.

The 'Apprentices'

Out of the full sample it is logical to begin with the five Apprentices, none of whom has been sitting for longer than three years. Three are young hereditary Peers; two are middle-aged, and of these one is a hereditary and one a Life Peer. The Life Peer sits with Labour, two of the younger men with the Conservatives, and the other two on the cross benches.

The Life Peer is the most critical of the way the House is run and, familiar with the Commons, he feels that the Lords misuse their expertise and are poorly publicized. Like the others, though, he finds it a warm and tolerant House, despite his awe of many fellow Peers.

Only the longest-serving (three years) of the five can recall instances where he feels he influenced opinion or successfully amended a Bill, but now this Peer feels sufficiently encouraged to sit on a Public Bill Committee.[15] The other Apprentices are still pondering on their maiden speeches and only speculating on the contribution they can make to the House. Two of the younger ones

---

[15] These are miniature Committees of the House, used on a limited scale, and are described in chapter 2.

see it as a duty for hereditary Peers to report to the House the prevailing opinions of their various worlds—in their own examples,
transmitting the current grievances of the young, of scattered
Scottish tenants, or of small manufacturers.

Their discussions of party affiliation are guarded, and the Life
Peer, a Labour supporter, admits that though he naturally follows
his Leader's directions, he would not hesitate to vote against his
front bench if his conscience so directed. All five emphasize the
freedom of the Lords but even the Crossbenchers confess reliable
sympathy with one party or another, and all feel it is reasonable to
follow the Whips' advice. This group seem especially vulnerable
to the moral and personal suasion that is so important in the Lords,
and a lead given by respected Elder Statesmen will strongly influence
the way they vote.

The Apprentices' attitudes to other Peers are equally tentative
and cautious but when they eventually learn the manners of the
Lords all feel they will find a role there. They already seek to
proselytize and with what is perhaps the uncritical enthusiasm
of newcomers they are anxious to tell the public of the scope of the
Lords' work. Finding themselves 'near the centre of political action'
(though the Life Peer does suspect this might be self-delusion) they
speak of their eagerness to explain political issues to neighbours,
customers, and fellow students.

Their approach is, in the words of one of the younger men, that
'the best way to go about things . . . is not to push too hard, be
openly friendly to people without pushing yourself forward . . .'
Aware of their inexperience, this group does not discern or will
not yet presume to comment on the tactics of Frontbenchers, whom
they see as remote and expert figures. Though the 'new men' can
recall dramatic episodes they cannot analyse the behaviour of the
House or the strategy of its Leaders.

Apprentices are keen to learn the ways of the House, but at the
beginning much of their value is as a reassurance to its older members that the House occasionally receives infusions of fresh blood—
that it is still attractive to those who have been successful in other
walks of life, or appeals to hereditary Peers who are still young or
who come from an unusual or ordinary profession. (Ordinariness
is as important to an assembly criticized for being unrepresentative
as youth is to a chamber where two-thirds of the members are over
sixty-five.) The appeal of the Apprentices to the older Peers is

reflected in the delight with which longer-serving colleagues speculate on how the newcomers will turn out. There is a good deal of talk about the way a new acquisition 'promises to be good front-bench material' and, where a self-assertive import from the Commons is concerned, of how 'this House tames people. Even the wildest or crustiest Life Peers settle down . . .'

Undoubtedly senior Peers enjoy teaching the customs of the place. What is more, older members are often familiar with the political or professional histories of new recruits or, particularly in the case of hereditary Peers, remember their fathers or kinsmen. Apprentices are made to feel welcome and in their turn serve as a stimulus to the House, as long as the introduction of new Peers is not so fast that the process of assimilation becomes uncomfortable.

The 'Innocents'

Some Apprentices never blossom into Frontbenchers but grow up into Innocents, a group who *enjoy* the House, attach little importance to the Whips, and indulge what is basically a dilettante interest. They do feel that their presence is important. As one remarks, 'the whole idea of this House is to represent the rational voter . . .', an observation which itself reveals what a senior Clerk describes as 'the pathetic self-delusion' of the great number of Peers who hold this view. Innocents see the value of the House in its deliberations—'you hear a lot of frightfully good stuff in here'—and they are not enthusiasts for reform. Three of the four in the sample are Peers by succession and all want to retain the hereditary peerage, doubting that any sort of elected Second Chamber would work. Nevertheless they admire the Life Peers and are intimidated by their eminent colleagues, while regretting that the House seems in consequence less dignified nowadays and speeches 'less natural'. As one Innocent observes ruefully, 'Today Life Peers, especially professors and people, read a brief and then go away'.

One Innocent sits on the Liberal benches, two on the cross benches, and the third is a hereditary Conservative

because I usually find my party has the interests of the country at stake . . . Labour Peers tend to vote with their party because the majority are Life Peers and if a man's a Life Peer (mind you, I only presume this) created by his P.M. or his party, to vote against the party would be rather a dirty thing to do. But I can tell you, some fathers are made Peers and then their sons change sides . . .

Less naïve members of the House would scorn such an analysis. To an Innocent, however, 'The average person in this House isn't really interested in politics.' Whipping is unimportant; nor is this group ambitious.

The Lords doesn't tick at a high rate. The young hereditary Peers are ideal House of Lords men, doing it not because they need to but because of generations of service. They're interested and disinterested, prepared to devote a chunk of their lives here. Then the ex-M.P.s, promoted warhorses from the Commons, they're taking their hair down. They're not ambitious. It's a comfortable home.

Innocents care affectionately for the House and, liking the people there, hope to 'listen to the arguments and make up our minds accordingly'. Still, the high incidence of, for example, well-off hereditary Peers who are faithful Conservatives suggests that the Innocents' diagnosis of voting behaviour is touchingly naïve. Voting tends to be more often an instinctive than a rational business.

But the Innocents too have a contribution to make. Not only do they often intervene on some small point about which they know (like Service conditions, traffic jams, detailed information about foreign countries), treating the Lords like a more ample correspondence page in *The Times*, they also form an attentive and harmonious background for those Peers who do provide impetus to push the House forward. As a wiser and more business-like Peer puts it, 'even *prima donna*s need an audience'.

The 'Adventurers'

The Adventurers are an obvious driving force, forthright about their own place in the House, many confessing surprise at finding themselves there. Of the sixteen who discussed their role at length two were Bishops, three hereditary Peers, and the rest, in a majority, Life Peers. A typical observation comes from a trade unionist:

It's an anomaly for me to be here. But there's muddled thinking in the trade union movement about these questions and in fact my peerage probably helps the Labour movement. I finally took it with the unanimous approval of my union.

An academic says:

I was shattered at first, said 'No' straightaway. I told the P.M. I had considerable commitments at home. He said 'I don't expect you to attend regularly; come whenever you feel you can make a contribution.' If it meant anything, it was to try and improve the general level of debate and perhaps help the party vote.

The late Lord Francis-Williams describes in his autobiography how Gaitskell induced him to accept a peerage 'as my own man . . . and we need more Socialists there and as the first Press Lord who didn't own a newspaper'.[16] (Innumerable autobiographies tell how reluctantly prospective Peers accepted the tantalizing offer. Lord Robbins, created in 1959, and Lord Lindsay of Birker, in 1945, provide interesting details.) A pleasing confession is that of Baroness Wootton, who found it 'hard to resist blitzing an all-male institution'.[17]

In justifying their acceptance of peerages, Adventurers talk of their role of the House in terms of *function*, 'a sort of ombudsmanship', 'a platform for the things you're interested in', 'pester them with Questions and in the end you can show them up'. This has historically been very much a function of the Lords, as a former Leader proudly reminds visitors, giving as examples the debates on pesticides, environmental pollution, and the structure of government, initiated by individual enterprise in the Lords long before they became sufficiently fashionable and urgent to discuss in the Commons.

Baroness Summerskill has stressed what a private member can do in the Lords in steering through legislation[18] and Lord Soper, untroubled by being called 'My Lord' ('I've been revered for forty years'), has said he can now 'attract attention to issues which would otherwise not get the notice they deserve . . . presenting them from a non-Conservative religious point of view . . .'[19]

As for the hereditary Peers, the three in this group feel the House is a place where 'you get small things done' and one of them, Lord Milford, says that his role as the only Communist Peer is to act as a single-handed ginger group: 'I speak purely as an individual—my party—wants this House abolished. But as it is, I skirmish.'

Adventurers are purposeful, with a variety of motives for their activism. The idea of a general 'public duty', for instance, is most

---

[16] Lord Francis-Williams, *Nothing So Strange* (1970), p. 330.
[17] B. Wootton, *A World I Never Made* (1967), pp. 267–77.
[18] E. Summerskill, *A Woman's World* (1967), chapter 19.
[19] In a broadcast on Yorkshire Television, 17 Oct. 1971.

significant for a hereditary Crossbencher, a self-confessed back-woodsman:

If one's born a Peer, one ought to do it . . . Where one's had most effect is where other positions you hold, in local government, trusteeships, nature conservancy, public foundations, have brought you into contact with Ministers.

This Peer explains how Adventurers focus on specific pieces of legislation, bombarding the House with Bills and harrying with Amendments. They seek out 'People with an identity of view, enlisting support and acting in *ad hoc* groups'. A reputation as an activist becomes self-fulfilling:

I suppose now my reputation is that I'm pro-murderers, pro-queers, pro-wildlife, that sort of thing. Annan wrote to me about his Bill because I supported him in two others. At the moment we've a strong move on foot to get regulations to control zoos and the like . . .

Another Peer says:

There are people I like—I'll go to them about raising the issue of controlling proprietary drugs. One's a Liberal, one a Conservative, but we have similar humanitarian sympathies. These were the two I got together on the Gypsies Bill . . .

And according to a Labour Life Peer:

There are trade union animals here. We helped to get 'In place of Strife' dropped. On the E.E.C. I'll handle the Peers, organize a Peers' meeting against joining the Common Market, and then carry the fight to the Floor.

This remark illustrates the Adventurers' nonchalance about party, for it was made when his own front bench were in office and in favour of joining the E.E.C. (Subsequent events enhanced its piquancy—and he was notably unsuccessful in organizing his colleagues to oppose entry, as the Peers voted 451 to 58 in favour of joining.)

All the Adventurers show a boisterous independence and all but two sit on the Labour or cross benches (one of whom was the Communist hereditary Peer). Even the Conservative hereditary Peer 'started as a Liberal, then a Conservative, left-wing Conservative, so I never bothered with party very much . . .' and he not only worked in cahoots with the Labour Leader to push through a Bill but has since embarrassed the 1970 Conservative Government by dividing and carrying Amendments to a Government Bill.[20]

A Labour Peer says:

> I've been carpeted when I voted against the Government on the Films Bill. A Whip came up to me and said 'There's quite a lot of resentment in the party because you keep voting against the Government.' I said 'Twice at the most' and he checked and had to apologize.

In their House of Lords' manners Adventurers are equally free-wheeling. For them 'the worst sort of Peer is a combination of the trivial and the pompous'. The most important thing is that 'in this House there is scope to be eccentric' and they talk about its value as a platform on which one needs to speak well and confidently: 'It has great value as a forum—but you mustn't tub-thump.' They feel that their influence might 'bounce back' to Ministers—and to the public, from whom they receive constant correspondence, and to the interest groups that keep in touch with them. However, one Peer is quick to emphasize 'we're not bribable, we have no constituencies and we only receive here our expenses to cover costs . . .'

Unlike the Apprentices, this group are more prompt to criticize the House and they share outsiders' opinions of its shortcomings. Scornful of mere tinkering with procedure, their approach is cavalier: 'The whole thing's an anachronism and reform would make it worse . . .' but 'since we've got it, we may as well make it work. It all helps, probably, like the continuous dripping that wears away stone.'

Thus the Adventurers see the Lords not as a forum for advancing a political programme but as an extension of a personal platform, an additional arena for promoting their own causes. In this courteous and dignified environment, peopled by members of a high average age and some tendency to somnolence, this group have a particular role as characters with lively bees in their bonnets. The Lords welcome idiosyncrasy and the Adventurers bring an enlivening impetus to the place. They make it still more attractive to the 'Peers of occasional excellence' or the directors of advisory bodies or of voluntary associations, who are in the 1960s and 1970s offered peerages to counter allegations that the House is staid and un-influential. Not least important is the fact that the Adventurers' stimulus is not principally associated with one party or another.

---

[20] Conservation of Seals Bill (HL); Wild Creatures and Forest Laws Bill (HL).

This allows the Lords to be all the more proud of them and to regard them as an excellent advertisement for their chamber.

The 'Legalists'

A more sober note is given by those Peers fittingly described as 'Legalists' (or by a former Leader as 'Proceduralists'). The term indicates that they are not necessarily lawyers or solicitors but that such Peers share an attitude of mind, careful and judicious. Only one in the sample is a Law Lord, sitting as a scantily camouflaged Conservative on the cross benches; two others sit on the Conservative and two on the Labour side.

These are Peers whose purpose is 'to get the thing right', to tidy up Bills, to give precise expositions of matters before the House. They delight in exquisite language and, though occasionally circumlocutory, their speeches are often barbed and always shrewd. A young hereditary Peer exemplifies their professional outlook:

> Comparatively few people here are in the thick of political advances and manœuvres. There are *vestiges* of old battles by people who've fought them as Commons members; we operate through hangovers . . . But Government legislation is our *positive* duty here. It's team work. On our own Bills, I've done it because people have asked me. Behind the scenes it's a matter of knowing roughly what's going on, who's involved. It's not a matter of inducements, it's part of the organism. This is a place to *work* . . . Legislation is a professional job. We're hard-working to see that the thing is right.

When he speaks of 'our own Bills' this Peer means Lords' Bills, not those of his own party. Legalists as a group tend to attach less importance to party affiliation. Each accepts his party loyalty as an unchangeable fact about himself, a background assumption, but rather than party animals they prefer to be 'a powerful nucleus, infecting the House with an independent approach, a political integrity'. The former M.P.s in this group are nostalgic for the Commons where, they say, power rightly lies, but they stress that the House of Lords 'is an ideal chamber for lawyers—dispassionate, considered, careful with intricate points. It has a steadying effect on the Commons.'

When asked to discuss the issues of the years between 1964 and 1970 the Legalists consider them utterly objectively as matters of constitutional and practical detail. They eagerly explain the precise intricacies of, for instance, the Stansted affair—where the Government were induced to follow the advice of a former Lord Chancellor who put the case for the Lords' opposition, speaking first as a lawyer and only incidentally for the Conservative Opposition.[21]

On the Seats Bill, too, and the Southern Rhodesia (United Nations Sanctions) Order, the Legalists patiently unravel the constitutional positions of the Lords and of the Government, seeking to advocate, on the basis of principle, actions which either side found dangerous on merely tactical grounds.

Indeed, for this group the ideal House of Lords member is not just a tactician but rather a man like themselves, 'restrained, considered, with an older, mature wisdom', 'active behind the scenes, on tricky points most remarkable . . .' Though not apolitical, the members of this group try always to find a balance of interests. They enjoy putting Bills through, taking up Committee points, and, especially on legal points, often recall cases they dealt with professionally or which came before the House years ago.

It has been argued that there would be far less need for this painstaking work of amendment to be done in the Lords if the staff of Parliamentary draftsmen were increased—an argument appealing to those responsible for Parliamentary time-tabling, who wish to expedite the passage of legislation through both Houses. But the draftsmen themselves have observed that the problems in fact stem from departments where policies are drawn up, presented in a rush to Parliament, and very often altered as a result of undertakings in the House. They are therefore glad of the careful scrutiny the Lords give to legislation. The Legalists in particular are temperamentally inclined to ensure that Bills are technically correct. At the slack times of the Session, too, the Lord Chancellor has introduced Bills to change the civil law or the structure of the judicial system and here this group can make an important contribution.

Specific work or exposition and revision are not the sole function of the Legalists. Their moderate attitude nicely counterbalances the enthusiasms of Adventurers and Politicians and, while they themselves are not unduly solemn (the occasional frivolous interventions of Lord Chorley and Lord Conesford are examples), they can intimidate other Peers. One elderly Peer declares that he is

[21] Viscount Dilhorne, a former Conservative Lord Chancellor, now sitting on the cross benches as a Law Lord, attended meetings of the Cabinet Committee considering this affair.

scared to sit next to a lawyer at lunch, and another describes them as having

a complete difference of attitude. For instance, we were talking about the sentences on the rioting Cambridge undergraduates. He thought this was right—skinheads would have been treated like that. I thought it was a bit harsh. But these are men of great honesty and integrity. For them, the law comes first.

This story illustrates a basic theme of this investigation: the odd isolation of individual members of the Lords. Certainly Peers can be grouped into categories but essentially they are private men, each bringing his own principles and eccentricities to bear on the collective body. Such individualism is particularly the case among those classified here as Adventurers and Legalists, whose personal quirks provide their most significant contribution to proceedings. 'Politicians', on the other hand, are the most 'public men'.

The 'Politicians'

These are the Lords with the most explicit image of the House as a Parliamentary workshop. The twenty-three appearing in the sample have strict loyalties to party—none is a Crossbencher. Thirteen are Conservative, eight Labour, and two Liberals. (This is a neat, accidental cross-section, reflecting the broad party balance in the Whole House.)

Nine are Life Peers and fourteen hereditary; there are two women, one Conservative and one Labour. It is interesting that all have held or still hold frontbench office, save for two hereditary Peers who have only recently succeeded and one former M.P. who prefers the freedom of the back benches. Evidence of their political proclivities is the fact that seven have been M.P.s and three of them candidates; it is also apparent in the reasons they give for attending the Lords:

I thought I'd take my seat when my father died—I got sort of hooked on it, caught up in things . . .

I *came* as a Labour supporter. I wouldn't have done it otherwise and, I've been a constant attender from the very beginning . . .

I've given myself a political identity I didn't have before . . .

. . . a very natural projection of what I did in the Commons. A lifeline to a drowning man when I got my peerage . . .

Got sucked in. Don't vastly enjoy it. Bloody hard work in Opposition.

Deeply involved in politics, always have been. My husband was in the Commons for all those years . . . I couldn't at my age start in the Commons, beetling about at the bottom of the tree . . . If I was twenty years younger I'd have had some office here, but if you've been married to a Cabinet Minister for years, to be a Junior Minister here would be being just a bottle-washer in the departments.

Politicians eagerly discuss the strategy and tactics their parties have adopted on various Bills, recalling work they themselves have done in steering legislation through or leading opposition. They are the most informative exponents of the mechanics of politics in the Lords, matters of whipping, party meetings, and so on. (From these accounts comes much of the material in chapter 4.) They give thorough accounts of the 'camps and cabals' in the deliberations on such questions as the Abortion Bill, the Tees Valley Water Bill, or the Murder (Abolition of the Death Penalty) Act. One Labour hereditary Peer is able to check off the names of Peers voting on the Seats Bill, the Commonwealth Immigrants Bill, and the Southern Rhodesia Order, pointing out how his colleagues have voted on various Amendments, how the party has been 'split right down the middle', which Peers are 'under the wing of each of our three Whips'.

Politicians in the Lords are as much students of form as their Commons' counterparts, sensitive to the faintest signals:

Did you notice X was sitting on the front bench today? He's not an *official* Whip . . .

They've brought old Y back to the front bench to make it look respectable . . .

I don't think Z is really happy with the Tories. He's thinking of coming over to us . . .

Should be an interesting afternoon today. If they're sensible they won't press the Amendment . . .

Such remarks are dropped in the Peers' Lobby and the corridors—and after the 1970 election tricked out with speculation: 'Things are really sharpening up. We may start calling snap Divisions, even dividing on Second Reading . . .'

This group tend to regret that Lords' reform has been dropped and they emphasize their desire for more Bills to have First Reading in the Lords, for new types of adjournment debate or Unstarred Question, better briefing for Frontbenchers, a niche in departments for Lords-in-Waiting. (Ministers of State, usually from the Commons, have always been given facilities in their departments and the 1970 Conservative Government was insistent on providing them for Lords-in-Waiting.) United as they are in their zeal for improvements, Politicians are fundamentally divided in their feelings about partisanship in the Lords. Some, especially former M.P.s, want a more professional House, closely resembling the Commons; others favour the absence of party and constituency constraints that allows them to speak frankly. All none the less welcome the influx of Life Peers and see them as introducing a better party balance and more bite (invariably called by Peers 'cut and thrust'). They imagine that this can restore prestige to a House insufficiently appreciated by the public and the Commons.

It is true that although a great many Peers despise the Commons as a hotbed of party faction (particularly the 'intellectuals' in the Lords), the Politicians have something of an inferiority complex, a waspish admiration for the other House. Perhaps it provokes them to keep things moving in the Lords, and stirs their political ambitions in their own sphere. Certainly it is this group that ensures that the Lords act as an effective legislative chamber, that Peers are organized and cajoled to attend, speak, and vote. It is the Politicians who see to it that Government business is smoothed through and that the Opposition is tenacious. Lord Shepherd is an excellent example of such a Politician, a hereditary Peer who rescued the Labour rump in the Lords from the Opposition doldrums of the 1950s, throwing himself into the task of organizing teams and rotas to harry the Government on Bills (such as the London Government Bill in 1963). Such enthusiasm has assisted in the striking development of party machinery on all sides of the House. Despite their inherent majority, even the Conservatives have become very professional about whipping (particularly Lord Denham in 1972, Captain of the Yeomen of the Guard), out of instinctive self-protection.

Thus the Politicians pull together an assembly that might otherwise disperse its energies in unco-ordinated directions. Undoubtedly an understanding of their influence is central to appreciating exactly why and how the Lords behaved as they did in the period from 1964 to 1970.

The 'Elder Statesmen'

With the bursting of a Politician's chrysalis an Elder Statesman emerges, to move discreetly from the front bench to a seat at the end of the chamber furthest from the Throne. Of the twenty Peers in this group, six have spent more than twenty years in the Lords, eight between ten and twenty years, and only six less than ten. And of the six more recent members, all have spent decades in political activity, whether as M.P.s, as party workers, or married to prominent politicians whose work they have shared. Long political service has given them a philosophical approach, deepened by age. Ten of the group are in their seventies and eighties, six aged between sixty and seventy, and the other four, in their middle fifties, have reached what one of them calls 'the cynical wisdom of the mature'.

Though all have held Government or party office (and in the case of the two Crossbenchers, are recognized as unofficial mentors of their benches), all but three now sit only intermittently on the front bench. From their less conspicuous seats below the gangway the Elder Statesmen rise to support party Leaders on a procedural point, recommend a business arrangement, advise, warn, and admonish. They are a real group, 'not uninfluential' (a senior Clerk's meiosis), particularly in the Conservative Party. Not only do they stimulate or check the enthusiasms of younger colleagues but their shrewdness will be respected when it comes to giving a lead on controversial policy, pronouncing in favour of liberalizing laws relating to divorce, abortion, or the death penalty, or voicing their qualms on the Stansted or Southern Rhodesia Order. (But they are sufficiently subtle practitioners of the counsellor's art to know when to do so publicly and when by a quiet word in the right quarter.)

This group show a curious blend of the non-partisan and the suddenly fanatically political. For instance, theirs are the most informative remarks on the working of the 'usual channels' and on the mellow co-operation underlying Lords' proceedings, a spirit they try to instil in younger members. But when they have determined to take a stand—on the Seats Bill, for instance, or Rhodesia—they believe in sticking to it. Take the distinguished Peer who on the Southern Rhodesia (United Nations Sanctions) Order was 'a notable leader of the rebels. But after that initial outburst, he subsequently contented himself with making speeches and letting things go through.'

Having made their point, such Peers emphasize the importance of behaving with restraint, citing the War Damages Bill, the London Government Bill, the Land Commission Bill, the Iron and Steel Bill, as cases where it has been necessary for the Government to behave 'sensibly'. The time and dignity of the House, they feel, is saved by eliminating unnecessary party rancour. In everyday affairs the preservation of the influence of the House and its members is worth the sacrifice of party prestige. They show, like another influential group in the Lords, its servants, an instinctive affection for their House and a sensitivity to ridicule from the outside world. Such loyalty is not a characteristic of newer members who are less blind to the self-congratulatory complacency to be found in the Lords and who are more astringent in their criticisms.

Elder Statesmen, on the other hand, speak of the co-operation, respect, and friendliness of the Lords but regret that the introduction of so many new Peers makes it difficult to know everybody, not to mention the problems of fitting everyone on to the Speaker's list and finding days for everyone's Motions. They are particularly struck by the decline in courtesy, as speeches become longer and more acerbic, and are distressed by the way in which the good manners formerly prevailing inside and outside the chamber have deteriorated as members become 'more professional'. Such remarks are always forthcoming from the old and they are typical of this distinct group. (But other Peers and officials also make this point.)

Their comments about themselves are modest:

I do small things about ex-prisoners . . .

I keep an eye on lifeboatmen's widows, go and visit them . . .

My old union know they don't have to write to me. I've belonged for fifty years and I'll help them if I can . . .

They discern in the Lords an unobtrusiveness, whether in their colleagues' readiness to assist the old and deaf, or the unpushing behaviour of their ideal House of Lords man, frowning on 'those who try and make speeches about "I, I" all the time—who try and get themselves into the papers; it's so silly.' Such Peers, though loyal to party, tend to put principle and service first. As one of the Life Peeresses says:

I'm essentially an old-fashioned Socialist, not a party politician like some of the other women . . . I do try to believe in the *basic* philosophy of Socialism—the system should be changed, but here we are trying to make it *work*!

The other Life Peeress says:

I get lots of ideas here, new approaches to old problems. I write them down and then I go to different people, here or in my office . . . I come here because I believe if you undertake to do a thing you do it . . .

A former M.P.

was utterly astounded to find I could do useful work and more useful than I was doing in the Commons . . . My God, was I ever a part of that down there—and did I take pleasure in it?

After forty years of wanting 'to kick the whole place over', another who came reluctantly to the Lords found 'It was another twenty years of life to come here . . . I came to scoff and stayed to praise . . .'[22] Unlike Politicians, the Elder Statesmen do not want to see sharper party divisions (the son of a pioneering pre-1918 Socialist speaks bemusedly of 'these so-called left-wingers; I never know what it means'), and a Conservative hereditary Peer sums up the general view: 'We can't make party divisions clearer-cut while the House is composed as it is. No point in having a Second Chamber as a complete replica of the Commons, a rubber-stamp.'

A Labour Peer refers to a speech on Africa by a Conservative Frontbencher:

a very able political speech, entirely unhelpful and pretty cynical. Able from the Parliamentary point of view and he put himself in with his own Backbenchers, but I'm sure he doesn't feel that way. I'm about to write to him now and I'll get a reasonable response and co-operation.

They prefer the roundabout way, less provocative and ostentatious but more constructive (especially for older campaigners needing to preserve their strength).

While the Politician seeks to promote his party's or even his own fortunes in his dealings outside the House, the Elder Statesman is primarily a publicist for the Whole House. One smiles at 'being the sort of patron saint of the village I took my title from . . .' Another 'acts as a sort of bazaar-opener really. This House needs all the P.R. it can get.' Within the House these Peers smooth acerbities, encourage new recruits, and urge that tried conventions and standards of behaviour be maintained. They provide continuity in the Lords, and symbolize the spacious sense of time that permeates

[22] It is a pity that Life Peers are generally created at such a late age that they cannot give long and vigorous service in the Lords.

the House in contrast to the Commons' rushed and ephemeral frenzy. Like the Officers and Officials of the House, with their familiarity with precedents of political decorum, with the personalities, and even geography, of the House, they reassure its individual members, drawing Peers together, and conserving an 'appropriate' Lords' style of behaviour.

This brief classification shows how there are always groups of temperamentally sympathetic Peers to which an individual can attach himself, while retaining his individuality and finding his own style and role in the House. Some of these groups exhibit the characteristics sketched above. The fact that they cut across party lines helps the Lords to tolerate the strains of their peculiar situation. Though the years of the Labour Administration presented the Upper House with special political problems they were helped by the fact that party is not the only matrix within which the Lords conduct their affairs. Other principles and loyalties frequently dictate the handling and outcome of their deliberations.

But what do the Peers deliberate about, or do they, in W. S. Gilbert's phrase, do nothing in particular and do it very well? Chapter 2 investigates their activities.

2

LORDS' BUSINESS

IN 1964 the Lords remained both a deliberative body and a legislative chamber in the fullest sense. As a deliberating assembly they provide 'a forum for full and free debate on matters of public interest' and 'for the scrutiny of the activities of the executive by means of Motions and Questions'.[1] In their legislative capacity Peers can initiate as much of their own legislation as they are able or inclined to do, through Public Bills and Private Members' Bills. (The Lords also scrutinize private legislation. Private Bills are discussed in a separate section of this chapter.) Moreover, as the Second Chamber of Parliament, the Lords are obliged to consider all legislation that has passed through the complementary Lower House.

Although the Lords' strength perhaps lies more in their deliberative role where they exercise influence over the longer term, it is as legislators dealing with Public Bills, Private Members' Bills, and subordinate legislation that they face more immediate political problems. It is in this sphere that they are concerned with the actions of the executive, presented before Parliament, and here is displayed the Lords' dilemma of appearing either a redundant rubber-stamp or an obstacle ripe for abolition. This chapter describes the difficulties the Peers found during the years of Labour Government in exercising their rightful powers, but powers that often encroach upon territory that the Commons have come to consider their own strict preserve.

In other ways, too, life had become more complicated for the 'New Look House of Lords' after 1964. The principles on which time was allocated and by which proceedings were ordered were inappropriate to a House where the average attendance was now higher and the proportion of purely legislative business heavier than in the years of the 1950s. These special difficulties are described below. Particular items of business, taken from the years 1964-70,

---

[1] Cmnd. 3799, para. 8.

are given to illustrate the sort of work with which the House was engaged in a period that is peculiarly self-contained. (For a picture of the House before 1963 Professor Bromhead's book is indispensable.)[2]

(When Labour came to power the Lords enjoyed, as they still do, considerable latitude for hampering the executive by directly delaying the passage of Bills and rejecting subordinate legislation.) What is more, customs of organizing business in the Upper House also allow individual Peers ample scope for frustrating and harassing the Government. In significant ways the Lords' freedom is greater than that of the Commons where since the mid nineteenth century the Government have assumed complete control of the Parliamentary time-table. By putting down for 'tomorrow' more business than the Commons can possibly deal with, the Government ensure that only the device of the adjournment Motion allows M.P.s to interrupt business and, despite the innovations of the 1966 Parliament, Backbenchers are still effectively suppressed by procedural rules devised in the 1880s to subdue minority groups like the Irish Members. Careful whipping has put still another hurdle in the way of Private Members' Bills.

But even today (1974) it is different in the Lords. There is no effective Speaker with power to enforce procedural rules. These are anyhow mainly indicative, and precedents are frequently conflicting.[3] All business down for a particular day is certain to be discussed on that day (if last-minute alterations are made, Peers are unhappy) and backbench Peers know that every Amendment will be discussed and every Question answered. Any Peer may add his name to the list of speakers and, with only the notional leave of the House, any Peer may introduce and discuss a Private Member's Bill. Consideration of Bills is open-ended for there is no guillotine and no selection of Amendments, and—unlike the Commons where Bills are generally sent to Standing Committee—in the Lords all stages are taken by the Whole House so that each Peer can make his personal contribution. (A new system for taking stages of some non-contentious Bills in Committee 'upstairs' is described below.)[4]

[2] P. G. Bromhead, *The House of Lords and Contemporary Politics, 1911-57* (1958).

[3] The Standing Orders governing the order and manner in which business is taken are to be found in the *Companion*. Recent developments and their historical background are described in the Clerks' own journal, the *Table*. (See the *Table* (1967) for a useful article by R. W. Perceval.) The Tenth Report of the Procedure Committee discusses recent recommendations. [4] See pp. 54-5.

In the Commons, also, the Leader of the House with his Chief Whip will usually collaborate with the Opposition Chief Whip on matters of time-tabling but in the Lords this must always be the case, for there is no alternative to co-operation between individual Peers and parties if the place is to work at all. Ironically, therefore, although Peers are not elected representatives they seem to have more freedom than members sitting by popular vote to fulfil what they believe to be their legislative duty.

Between 1964 and 1970, however, the Lords faced pressure from three directions: a large number of new Peers were unaccustomed to the traditions of the House and this also egged on older members to intemperate behaviour; there was a heavy programme of legislation, much of it contentious and some of it urgent; and the party balance in each House required the Lords to practise self-restraint. In this risky period they had to adapt their conventions of business in order to perform their Parliamentary and party roles successfully, while trying to keep the privileges of freedom and flexibility that the Commons had lost long ago. To understand how they coped with this, it is convenient to start by examining the Lords as legislators, beginning with their work on Public Bills and with the disputed question of their usefulness as a revising Chamber.

A. *Public Bills*

By 1964 the catalytic effects of the 1958 Peerage Act meant that two hundred or so Peers were ready to treat legislation with a new professionalism. Coupled with the fact that the incoming Labour Government presented Parliament with a heavy programme of detailed enactments, this made the Lords' role more arduous. As the Peers became more closely involved in legislative affairs, so their powers became more controversial.

The Workload

Peers complained that their work had increased and hours had grown later and longer but this was not in fact the case.[5] The number of sitting days actually increased very little, with an average of 110 sitting days per Session between 1964 and 1970 compared with 108 in the corresponding years a decade earlier.

The average length of sitting days did not increase very much— and even a 25 per cent increase only meant an additional hour—for

[5] See Tables 5-7, appendix.

it was four hours in 1957–60 and five hours in 1967–70. Nor is there any significant indication that late sittings had increased, as they varied according to the number of contentious Bills, or Bills guillotined in the Commons.

The percentage of Monday sittings actually dropped; from 60 per cent of sitting days in the years 1965–8 to 30 per cent in the Session 1968–69 and 25 per cent in the Session 1969–70. Indeed, since Mondays were so often free of business it was proposed in August 1971 that the House meet regularly on Mondays for short or topical debates (the Clerk of the Parliaments estimated that an average Monday sitting would cost an additional £1,972 for Peers' expenses, Hansard, etc.). But the House shied away from the suggestion that every Monday be set aside as a matter of course, with especial inconvenience to Peers residing far from London. The proposal was abandoned.

In the 1964–70 period, therefore, the vastly increased attendance was not matched by a similar heavy increase in hours. The Chief Whip, Lord Beswick, did not encourage Monday sittings or long hours, and perhaps an assembly imposes, instinctively, an upper limit on the length of its discussions. Also Labour's frontbench spokesmen were perhaps more confident than they had been in their previous period in Office, between 1945 and 1951, and dealt more firmly and succinctly with Amendments in their replies to Backbenchers.[6]

But Peers did become accustomed to ending the day at 8 p.m. to 9 p.m. rather than the 6 p.m. to 7 p.m. of the 1950s and certainly they *believed* that their work had become heavier. It is very difficult to give a general explanation for this except to suggest that Peers felt somewhat weighed down by the technical complexities of Government legislation, in which many new recruits to the House of Lords were particularly eager to participate. Undoubtedly the proportion of time that the Lords devoted to Government activity increased. Even one aspect of this, Public Bills introduced in the Lords, quite apart from those coming up from the Commons, increased from an average of nineteen per Session between 1952 and 1962 to twenty-nine in the years 1963–70.[7] These figures concern Bills introduced in the Lords as first House. Where it is a question of Bills coming up from the Commons, the amount of

---

[6] The *Table* (1963) discusses the increase in sitting hours between 1920 and 1964.
[7] See Table 8, appendix.

time spent on them by the Lords still depends on both technical and political considerations—how controversial the Bills are, how popular the Government, and how large its majority. But where the Lords is acting as second House, the time required to deal with a Bill is also determined by the treatment it has received in the Commons, and how thoroughly it has been considered there. It is important to remember that in the twentieth-century House of Commons, though the Opposition are at a disadvantage as far as numbers of supporters are concerned, being always in a minority, they can nevertheless make life difficult for the Government by exploiting the rigours of the Parliamentary time-table. The Government are then forced to produce Motions (the guillotine is one such device) to expedite business and end discussion. This then throws more work on to the Lords. The Government in the Commons do not necessarily curb discussion there as a matter of course. A balance must be struck so that there is full scope for the adequate consideration of legislation and for party polemic, while pushing business through as fast as possible. To achieve this, the Commons' business managers (the Lord President and his Chief Whip and the Opposition Chief Whip and his Deputy, working through the Chief Whip's Private Secretary) attempt to agree 'through the usual channels' on time-tabling. But on occasion, and particularly where controversial Bills like the Transport Bill are concerned, this is impossible. Moreover, when the Government do resort to time-tabling Motions, and Motions to cut discussion short, these are themselves debatable, so that yet more time is lost for considering the actual substance of the legislation. Even when the usual channels do achieve co-operation in the Commons, discussion is often skimped in Committee upstairs and on the Floor of the House, leaving a great deal of amending work to the Lords. Here, in the Upper House, the balance has to be struck again, for although the Peers might wish to scrutinize legislation thoroughly they too are bound by the constraints of the Sessional time-table and the Government's desire to get laws on to the Statute Book. As in the Commons there is scope for the Opposition to obstruct business by exploiting all opportunities for amendment and debate—and indeed five determined Peers can effectively frustrate the Government. Unlike the Commons, however, the operation of the usual channels is far more open and explicit.

The reason is that a majority of the Peers realize that this sort of co-operation must exist in order to make the Lords work at all. The very absence of such procedural controls as closure or the guillotine, of a Speaker to select Amendments and choose speakers, gives the Peers such wide scope for obstruction that self-restraint is the only way to ensure that their work-load does not become intolerable. Thus the informal co-operation between the party Leaders in the Lords serves a dual purpose. Their House is deterred from pro-tracting discussion to such a degree that Commons' sensitivities are disturbed; and the Peers themselves are prevented from swamp-ing themselves with business. Were they to become overwhelmed, the Lords would either have to settle for a five-day/five-night week or fundamentally to alter their character by introducing the sort of Standing Orders adopted in the Commons in the 1880s. And by the end of Session, Peers are tired and eager to get away.

Between 1964 and 1970, inter-party co-operation continued to work satisfactorily in the Lords and not just at the level of the Leadership. Backbench Conservative Peers were also self-restrained (no doubt comforted by their secure majority and well aware that the Labour Government would have no truck with a recalcitrant Upper House). Labour were allowed considerable latitude (the 'Shepherd's Pie' of accelerated legislation, discussed below, is a good example). But further problems of business management depend less for solution on the Lords' goodwill than on the Com-mons' good sense, and this is not always forthcoming. The question of the initial introduction of Bills into Parliament is another area where the Lords' constitutional position *vis-à-vis* the Commons brings difficulties for the Lords' time-table.

Uneven Distribution

Since the 1670s the Lords have tacitly accepted that the right of granting supplies to the Crown lies with the Commons alone (with the precedents regarding 'tacking' dating from an Order of 1702). The 1911 and 1947 Parliament Acts reinforced the principle that all Bills of this sort, together with Public Bills involving changes in rates or taxes, should originate in the Commons.[8] The Commons' Procedure Committee considered in 1970-71 how these con-

[8] The *Table* (1951) explains these conventions and some exceptional cases. See Epilogue for the most recent development.

ventions prevent a more even distribution of Bills between the two Houses, and since their evidence was drawn from the most recent period, 1964–70, it is relevant to introduce it here.

In their submission, Lord Jellicoe and Lord Shackleton gave sixteen examples of Bills that might well have had their first introduction in the Lords (with at least two more containing only a few Clauses concerning finance).[9] They explained that when a Bill dealing with financial matters reaches the Lords, Peers avoid infringing Commons' privilege either by omitting the financial provisions on Third Reading or by adding a sub-section purporting to nullify the Bill's financial implications, these Amendments being either restored or omitted when the Bill returns to Committee in the Commons. But, as the Leaders emphasized, even with the use of such procedural devices it is difficult to persuade Ministers to introduce non-controversial Bills in the Lords first. The choice of House depends to some extent on a Minister's desire for prestige. 'Ministers like to see their own babies learn to walk in the Commons', as Lord Jellicoe said.

Although the Commons' Procedure Committee reiterated the suggestion of the White Paper on Lords' Reform that a more even distribution of Public Bills between Lords and Commons would benefit both Houses, still most Bills beginning in the Upper House tend to be legal Bills (the Lord Chancellor's territory), Amending Bills, Independence Bills, and Board of Trade type of Bills (Weights and Measures, Trade Descriptions, etc.). Thus distribution is vastly unbalanced. In the Session 1966–67, for example, excluding Bills of aid and supplies, Consolidation Bills, and Bills of first-class importance and controversy, all of which are inevitably introduced in the Commons first, of the remaining seventy-three Bills introduced, fifty-four began in the Commons and only nineteen in the Lords.[10]

As a result there has been constant complaint that at the beginning of a Session there is a dearth of activity in the Lords while at the end Peers are hard pressed for time. In a Resolution of 1670 and in the evidence to the 1970–71 Commons' Procedure Committee, the Lords have made their distress known.[11] Their assertions

---

[9] Select Committee on Procedure (HC), Second Report, 1970–71. Memorandum, pp. 212–13.

[10] HC Procedure Committee, Second Report, Appendix, para. 26.

[11] Their problems were depicted in a *Punch* cartoon on 24 July 1907.

are substantiated by statistics from two typical Sessions, set out below:

Distribution of Business: General and Legislative

Session	Period	General	Legislative
1967–68			
beginning	15 days	$52\frac{1}{4}$ hrs.*	$17\frac{1}{4}$ hrs.
	(31 Oct.–30 Nov.)		
end	24 days	$17\frac{1}{4}$ hrs.	$122\frac{3}{4}$ hrs.
1968–69			
beginning	14 days	$55\frac{1}{4}$ hrs.*	$13\frac{1}{4}$ hrs.
	(3 Oct.–28 Nov.)		
end	29 days	16 hrs.	$85\frac{3}{4}$ hrs.

* Including, of course, $20\frac{1}{4}$ and $15\frac{1}{4}$ hrs. on the Queen's Speech, etc.

Source: Second Report of the Procedure Committee (HC), 1970–71, p. 213.

The contrast revealed in the last column between the amount of legislation the Lords are obliged to handle at the beginning and the end of a Session shows how heavy their workload becomes as legislation emerges from the House of Commons' kitchen. Peers frequently express their anxiety that they will be obliged to sit after the Commons has gone into Recess. While this tends to happen in the middle of a Session, at Christmas, Easter, and Whitsuntide, it is less likely than Peers fear at the end of a Session because Lords' Amendments still have to be dealt with by the Commons, who are reluctant to come back for this purpose.

It has been suggested that Bills might be carried over between Sessions so that the Lords can consider at the beginning of a Session business brought over from the previous one, thus flattening out the legislative bulge. This is absolutely opposed by Commons' business managers who value the end-of-Session deadline as a tactical means of shoving business through. It is also a fact that Bills do not come from departments fully prepared and in smooth progression but spasmodically, in sudden rushes and dribs and drabs. In allocating them between the Houses the exigencies of the Commons' timetable will necessarily receive more consideration than the wishes of the less rigorous Lords. It seems that only an alteration of composition, with more Ministers sitting in the Upper House, will allow more Bills to originate there. Peers understand this situation but none the less they resent cavalier treatment from the Commons or any implication that they are being taken for granted.

It is not surprising, for example, that they are exceptionally sensitive to requests from the Government for accelerated legislation. The next section discusses thóse cases that did arise.

Expediting Legislation

This procedure was used on five occasions, for the 1965 Southern Rhodesia Bill, the 1966 and 1967 Prices and Incomes Bills, the 1968 Commonwealth Immigrants Bill, and the 1968 Customs (Import Deposits) Bill.[12] In each case the Peers were sympathetic to the need for emergency legislation and allowed the Government to use procedural expedients (like the simultaneous introduction of identical Bills in both Houses). It is important, though, that such loopholes are sparingly used, and Peers began to feel put upon, blaming the energetic Lord Shepherd and grudgingly referring to the Shepherd's Pie of emergency legislation.

Alternative ways of expediting the legislative process were discussed in the White Paper on Lords' Reform. Some Bills, it suggested, do not need consideration in as many stages as present procedure requires, and proceedings in one House might be curtailed or, more promisingly, some form of joint procedure devised. Certain classes of Bills (Consolidation Bills, legal Bills, measures that are technical but less controversial) might suitably be introduced in one House and then given detailed examination in a Joint Committee. This suggestion recognized the importance of the Lords as a complementary chamber of Parliament but it inevitably inspired opposition. M.P.s considered that it gave the Lords an opportunity to encroach still further on their legislative territory and Peers saw that joint Committees would undermine their own status as a revising chamber.

On matters like the distribution of Bills between the Houses and their expeditious consideration through simultaneous or joint Committee Stages, Lords and Commons still have to reach agreement. With innovations concerning only their own chamber, the Peers are able to experiment. Business managers in the Commons

---

[12] The new Conservative Administration operated in a similar way, as in 1970 in the Bill to nationalize the Rolls-Royce Co. Ltd. and in the N. Ireland Bill (1972).

must always reckon with the obscurantist conservatism of other M.P.s (who suspect that all changes tend to benefit the Government front bench); in some respects the Lords are able to appeal to the good sense of the House and introduce or revive procedural devices with less fuss and bother. One example is that of taking some Bills 'upstairs' in Committee.

Committees 'Upstairs'

(All Public Bills usually have their Committee Stage in the Lords on the Floor of the House so that every Peer can take part and propose Amendments. In response to the pressure of legislation in 1968 the Lords tried the experiment of taking some Bills 'upstairs' for their Committee Stage, following a precedent of the early 1900s.) The success of the experiment was endorsed by the House in April 1969 when the House accepted a Report of its own Select Committee on Procedure on this subject.

Such Committees upstairs are like miniature Committees of the Whole House, 'select' only in the sense that members are named. Unlike Commons' Standing Committees 'upstairs', there is no automatic Government majority and the twelve to fourteen Peers taking part are drawn with equal representation from all parties— Government, Opposition, Liberals, and Crossbenchers. Public Bills suited to this treatment are therefore the less politically controversial; the procedure was used for the 1968 Gaming Bill and the 1969 Development of Tourism Bill.[13]

The original hope of the Leader, Lord Shackleton, was that the Committee should consider the fully drafted Bills, but divide not in Committee but after debate on the Floor of the House, to which all contentious issues should be recommitted. (This has been dismissed by a senior Clerk as 'a cosy pipe-dream'.) The procedure that was eventually adopted does show the remarkable adaptability of the Lords. Any Peer, whether or not a member of the Committee, may attend proceedings, and propose and speak to Amendments. This compares interestingly with the Commons where M.P.s do not enjoy this privilege even when Bills are reported from Standing Committee to the Floor of the Commons. There, all Amendments have to be submitted to the Speaker for 'provisional' selection and although he will customarily select Amendments noted with favour

[13] Precedents are described in *Parliamentary Affairs* (winter 1971-2). The Lords have since used Committees upstairs for the 1970 Highways Bill and the 1971 Civil Aviation Bill.

by the Government, or those given inadequate discussion in Committee or some proposed by the Opposition or by Backbenchers, his selection will necessarily be arbitrary. The Lords' procedure is therefore an unusual departure from normal practice and preserves the right of every Peer to offer and speak to Amendments, whether in the Committee of the Whole House or in the microcosm of Committee upstairs. Only the members of the Committee may vote on Amendments but Divisions by no means follow strict party lines, as the Divisions on the 1968 Gaming Bill demonstrate.

The disadvantages of the device are two. There is some anxiety lest the House should sacrifice the agreeable feature of finding the odd expert impulsively intervening in debate. More seriously, the new procedure may mean that consideration of Bills becomes even more time-consuming because a fourth wheel of Committee upstairs has been inserted between Second Reading and recommitment to the Committee of the Whole House. A less complicated solution might be to omit Report Stage altogether or to amalgamate recommitment and Report Stage, allowing Peers who have spoken to Amendments in Standing Committee to vote upon them when the Bill returns to the House.

For the most part, however, Public Bills are discussed by the Whole House and the growth of this work in the later 1960s called for considerable self-discipline so that business did not become insuperable. It also provoked familiar argument about the role of the Lords as a revising chamber.

The Revising Function

Apart from the financial provisions of Bills, where amendment by the Lords would infringe Commons' privilege,[14] the Upper House fully complements the Lower House in every sphere of amending work—the legislative improvement of Bills, their deliberative elucidation, and the tactical exercises of opposition and defence.

Volume of Amending Work

The volume of business in each Session and the amount that the Government leave for the Lords vary widely. Lords' Amendments

[14] Occasionally, as in the case of the 1952 Transport Bill or the 1967 Land Commission Bill, such Sections reach the Lords without any previous discussion in the Commons. The Lords amend these Clauses and then pass an Amendment to nullify their own Amendments.

for which there has been insufficient time in the Commons can also vary from major Ministerial amending, where new provisions are inserted at a late stage, to minor drafting alterations in dates, or grammatical surgery) John Vincent has explained[15] how difficult this makes any attempt to measure the Lords' contribution as a revising chamber, but certainly in years when the Government have had a heavy legislative programme an impressively large number of Amendments have been made in the Lords. The Sessions of 1946–47 and, more relevant here, 1966–67 are good examples. In 1946–47 the Lords made 1,027 Amendments (of which 974 were accepted) to a total of 23 Bills; in 1966–67 they made 978 Amendments (of which 930 were accepted) to a total of 39 Bills. A fuller picture of the amending activities of Lords and Commons since the war is given in Table 9 (see appendix).

This table also shows that the percentage of Lords' Amendments rejected by the Commons has remained fairly small in postwar years, varying only between four and six per cent. (A glance at the Division Lists reveals that where the Commons have subsequently rejected Lords' Amendments, these are in a substantial number of cases Amendments passed in the Lords by Peers dividing on strict party lines in Committee and Report Stages—so these are apparently cases of opposition on politically partisan lines.) (The one case between 1964 and 1970 where the Lords insisted on their own Amendment after the Commons had rejected it occurred on the 1969 Seats Bill and is treated in a later chapter.)

In terms of time, the typical Session 1967–68 shows that the Lords spent about 511 hours on Government Bills (out of 802·5 hours) and even in the untypical Session 1968–69, when the Industrial Relations Bill and the Lords' Reform Bill were dropped, the Peers spent 267 hours (out of 396·5 hours) on legislation. This is not simply because the Lords think that Bills reach them ill-considered and incomplete. It is also deliberate Government policy. (As Douglas Houghton explained to the Commons' Select Committee on Procedure: 'If there is not time . . . one relies on the House of Lords, sitting very long hours, to try to do the job that we fail to do.'[16] In the case of the 1967 Transport Bill, for instance, the Lords made 258 Amendments, of which 203 were accepted by the Government. It is naturally difficult to assess how much of this

---

[15] In an article in *Parliamentary Affairs* (1967–8).
[16] Select Committee on Procedure (HC), Second Report, 1970–71, paras. 773–6.

work is of a major or minor sort or how much Amendment is
inspired by the Government, by departments, and by M.P.s even
before a Bill reaches the Lords. Nor, on the other side of the coin,
can one gauge how many unsuccessful Lords' Amendments nevertheless add something to the eventual Act. But it is true that the
Government did rely on the Upper House to complete and to tidy
up many of the Bills that passed through the 1966 Parliament.

A great deal of amending work falls upon the front benches where
a departmental spokesman, generally not a Minister and sometimes
not even a junior Minister, takes on the task of steering the Bill
through the House. Backbench Peers may pursue lengthy arguments in Committee on a Bill like the 1970 Industrial Relations
Bill but, as in this case, it is often by the front benches that most
Amendments are tabled. (On the 1971 Industrial Relations Bill
intricate discussions in Committee were sustained throughout the
long nights not by the Backbenchers vociferously present in the
middle of the afternoon but by party stalwarts on the front benches.)

However, certain types of Bill will attract Amendments from
individual Peers with a specific or professional interest in the legislation and, like M.P.s, Peers receive representations from outside
groups. They will often acknowledge this in proposing Amendments—excellent examples can be found in the Animals Bill, the
Theft Bill, and the Countryside Bill.

The amount of amendment to a Bill depends on a number of
factors and, as well as the obvious ones like the thoroughness with
which it has been prepared beforehand within the department and
the time and care which it has received in the Commons, it is also
important to emphasize the part played by the idea of Government
or departmental *credit*. Sometimes it is possible for a Minister or
for the Cabinet to alter provisions or Clauses of a Bill not only
because suggested Amendments will improve it technically but also
because their own standing allows them to be magnanimous.

Lords' Amendments serve another purpose as well as that of
improving or altering legislation. On Bills where the Government's
intentions are unclear, the Lords' Committee Stage allows Peers
to propose Amendments of a 'probing' nature, drawing out undertakings from the Government as to how the Bill will operate in
practice and how the Courts, the civil service, and the public are
to understand its philosophy. Such Amendments are often withdrawn and do not therefore appear in a total of statistical successes

but even so they can contribute substantially to the way legislation is eventually applied. Some of the Labour Government's legislative proposals had been conceived in Opposition and were taken up when the party came to power with more enthusiasm than rigorous analysis. Despite the best efforts of the departments, Bills like the Land Commission Bill came to Parliament incomplete, inconsistent, and ambiguous, and here the Lords' deliberative function became important.

As in the Commons, revision and deliberation are not the only motives for Lords' amendment. It is also an Opposition weapon for obstructing and attacking the Government and, depending on the nature of the Bill and on political circumstances inside and outside the House, the Opposition in the Lords vary their technique. Sometimes they concentrate on pressing a few Amendments, sometimes they try a 'broad-brush' approach. They will try being quick and surprising the Government or they will speak laboriously on every Clause. They can be adamant or attempt to secure concessions in a friendly way. But the Lords always risk being accused of using their amending role to delay or frustrate the business of the Commons. The more they intervene, the more their 'interference' is resented by M.P.s. For this reason the Opposition front bench in the Lords generally find it more rewarding to emphasize the substantive purpose, not the tactical one, of their amending role. This, as a subsequent chapter makes clear, was their strategy at the time of the Seats Bill.

Within the constraints of what the Commons and departments allow, the Lords make a sizeable contribution to the consideration of legislation. If a reform of the Upper House allowed its members to be more resolute and drastic in their amending work, their legislative activities might be still more far-ranging. But where they are able to initiate legislation, in the form of Private Members' Bills, for example, the Lords do take advantage of their comparative freedom.

B. *Private Members' Bills*

(The private member in the Commons finds it very difficult to bring in a Bill, let alone get it enacted, but in the Lords it is the privilege of any Lord of Parliament to present a Bill without moving for leave to bring it in.)Unless the Bill substantially affects the Royal Prerogative or unless it is contemplated that First Reading be debated, no notice of intention needs to be given except to the Table. (The *Companion* describes the form of a Bill and the stages through which it must pass.)

Private Members' Bills are those introduced by a Peer other than a Government Frontbencher. In recent years the number proposed each year has dramatically increased, from an average of three a year between 1952 and 1962 to an average of eleven a year between 1962 and 1971.[17] And, whereas in the 1950s the Lords were fortunate if a single Bill of this sort survived all its stages in both Houses, since 1962 an average of three a year have been successful (with a low score of no Bills out of ten in 1967–68 to a high point of seven out of eight in 1963–64).

Moreover these figures take no account of Bills like the Sexual Offences Bill, Abortion Bill, or Conservation of Seals Bill that have been eventually taken up by the Commons after being first introduced in the Lords, nor of those like the Sunday Entertainments Bill which, though unsuccessful, have been pursued in the Lords and thus kept alive in the mind of Parliament and the public until the time is ripe for their acceptance.

The number of Lords' Private Members' Bills may seem small but, despite the absence of the sort of time-tabling and constituency restraints hampering M.P.s, Peers still face the hurdles of opposition in the House. In addition, Bills can always be interrupted at the end of a Session or by a General Election. (Lord Silkin's Ponies Bill and Lord Hurcomb's Protection of Birds Bill encountered these obstacles.) If a Bill has the support of the Government, who are willing to find time for its Commons' stages, it might survive the end-of-Session threat. For example, Baroness Birk introduced a Bill in May 1970 to amend the 1889 Indecent Advertisements Act and allow attention to be drawn to the risks of venereal disease without incurring prosecution. It seemed that the imminent General Election would force the loss of the Bill but the Government made time available and it passed into law.

Perhaps the most complicated story is that of the Earl of Cranbrook's Conservation of Seals Bill, which encountered every hazard. Despite the opposition of Government departments (the Home Office and the Ministry of Agriculture in particular) who would be obliged by the Bill's terms to provide an inspectorate, and of the salmon-fishing lobby amongst the Peers, Lord Cranbrook was

17 Table 10, appendix.

spurred on by his sympathizers on all sides and introduced his Bill into the Lords. The unpredictability of the legislative time-table meant that he had to try several times before sufficient time could be found to allow a debate—on the first occasion when there seemed to be a spare half-hour twelve Peers put their names on the speakers' list at the last moment and the Bill had to be postponed. The Bill was, however, helped on its way because the official frontbench spokesman, Lord Stonham, whose attitude was at best neutral and at worst discouraging, was ill and absent when the Bill was eventually debated. Instead, an ally of Lord Cranbrook's spoke to the Bill and advised the House to accept it. Eventually, after further postpone-ments, redrafting, and rejection by the Commons, the Bill ulti-mately reached the Lords as a Commons' Private Members' Bill and in May 1970, just before the Election, it was passed.

In the Commons, the Government might deliberately block a Private Member's Bill but in the Lords they only intervene to 'advise' the House. It is exceptional for a Frontbencher to speak in a private capacity on such a Bill and Lord Shackleton, who as Leader of the House emphatically discouraged this, can recall only one instance, when Lord Longford spoke in opposition to the Abortion Bill. It is the convention that a Frontbencher speaks to indicate the attitude of the Government, of neutrality, disapproval, or approval and, if the latter, often to promise assistance in drafting and in making time available for discussion in the Lords. (This happened, for example, with the Earl of Malmesbury's New Forest Bill, introduced with the Government's blessing in December 1969, and with Baroness Summerskill's Matrimonial Homes Bill of 1966, when the Lord Chancellor and Parliamentary draftsmen gave her their help.)

⎰ Bills may be thrown out by the Lords themselves.⎱ A reasoned Amendment can kill a Bill if the House supports an Amendment declining to give the Bill a further reading—this happened to Lord Windlesham's 1969 Lotteries (G.L.C.) Bill. Or the House can substitute for 'now' the Amendment that a Bill be read 'this day six months', as with Lord Raglan's 1969 Euthanasia Bill. By such devices, or through attracting Amendments utterly altering the nature of a Bill, the Peer is obliged to withdraw it. This happened, notoriously, to Lord Chorley when in 1968 and 1969 he attempted to bring in a Street Offences Bill to make 'kerb-crawling' illegal.

Sometimes a Peer will be discouraged even before First Reading, like the Earl of Balfour, who explained in June 1970 that he would reluctantly defer the introduction of his Strengthening of Marriage Bill to a more propitious moment (which has not yet arrived). Lord Willis at least got a Second Reading for his Copyright (Royalties on Records) Bill in January 1970 but, when not a single speaker supported it, he despondently withdrew the proposal.

However, if Peers and Government are sympathetic, a Private Member's Bill can survive prolonged vicissitudes. Although no Bill can get through if both Commons and Government are opposed to it, it is remarkable how the Lords have sometimes succeeded in shaming the Commons into accepting legislation unpalatable to M.P.s mindful of constituency opinion. During the middle 1960s, when informed 'progressive' public opinion and the law seemed somewhat out of step, it was in several notable cases the Peers who took and maintained a lead in pressing for legislative change in delicate areas of public and private morality. Two Bills provide good illustrations of proposals that the Commons found inopportune or distasteful and which were inappropriate matters for executive legislation. The Lords were able to try them out, as the views of enlightened opinion, and keep them alive. These notable examples were the Earl of Arran's Sexual Offences Bill[18] and Lord Silkin's Abortion Bill.[19]

Lord Arran's Motion was debated in May 1965 and a simple Bill introduced later that month was given a Second Reading by 94 votes to 37. In October 1965 the Bill was passed by 96 to 31 votes, and though it lapsed at the end of the Session the Peers' vote and the discussion it provoked indicated to M.P.s that there was a good case for persisting with the matter. Humphrey Berkeley introduced it as a Commons' Private Member's Bill but it was dropped again at the General Election. Undeterred, Lord Arran kept the issue before the public and introduced it again in the Lords in May 1966. It was passed in June but lost again in the Commons. Yet the fact that the Bill was obviously a runner induced the business managers in the Commons to encourage support there and the measure was reintroduced as a Commons' Private Member's Bill, the Sexual Offences (No. 2) Bill. As a result of Lord Arran's efforts, when it was reintroduced in the Lords in July 1967 it swiftly became law.

Lord Silkin's Abortion Bill, which had the additional hazard of

[18] *HL Debs.*, vols. 266 and 284 and *Encounter* (Mar. 1972).
[19] *HL Debs.*, vol. 284.

Roman Catholic objection, is a similar case of liberal kite-flying in the Lords, introducing legislation without identifying with the issue either the Government or M.P.s sensitive to constituency objections. Lord Silkin first brought in the Bill in November 1965 and an Amendment to delay it (that is, to kill it) was defeated by 70 votes to 8. At the end of the Report Stage in March 1966 it was clear that the Election would force the dropping of the Bill but Lord Silkin pledged himself to reintroduce it and brought in a fresh Bill in May 1966. When David Steel was successful in the Commons' Ballot for Private Members' Bills Lord Silkin did not proceed with his own, but the Commons' Medical Termination of Pregnancy (No. 2) Bill that finally received the Royal Assent incorporated features of his original Bill. This would not have been introduced at that particular time had not the Lords broached the issue and persisted with their campaign.[20]

Such use of Lords' Private Members' Bills as *ballons d'essai* to test public opinion has been an extremely interesting development in recent years, helpful to the Cabinet and to sympathetic M.P.s as well as clearly giving satisfaction to the Lords themselves. The House that in 1956 rejected Sydney Silverman's Bill to abolish the death penalty now enjoys credit for introducing legislation to reform laws like those affecting divorce, homosexuality, and abortion. Peers are gratified by their new liberal reputation as a sounding-board for controversial ideas and as representatives for oppressed minorities.

Nevertheless the Lords can do little on their own. It is not always the case that the Cabinet are on balance sympathetic to the purpose of Lords' Private Members' Bills and they are not always smoothed through that chamber. The scarcity of time in the Commons means that they can easily fall by the way, especially as the Government do not conventionally make time available for a Lords' Private Member's Bill even when it has passed through all its stages in the Upper House. All they undertake to do is to provide time for Lords' Amendments to Commons' Private Members' Bills. Moreover, the fact that an M.P. who has been successful, but in a low place, in

---

[20] The recent efforts to promote legislation removing discrimination on grounds of sex promise to have a similar history. After the Commons' Private Member's Bill was talked out of that House in Jan. 1972, Baroness Seear immediately introduced a similar Bill in the Lords to keep the issue alive, and a Select Committee of the Lords was established to take evidence. The Government were induced to promise that a Public Bill would be introduced in the 1973–74 Session.

the Commons' Ballot is none the less not allowed to take up a Lords' Private Member's Bill for its Commons' stages means that this device is not available to ease Lords' Bills through the Lower House.[21]

On the other hand, it is rare for M.P.s not to find a Peer to sponsor a Bill in its Lords' stages (though if a Bill were to lie on the Table for two weeks without finding a sponsor it would be dropped). The Clean Air Bill, for example, was taken through the Lords by Lord Raglan, the Caravan Sites Bill by Lord Wade, and the Divorce Bill by Lord Stow Hill. The Chronically Sick and Disabled Persons Bill was another for which the Commons had insufficient time, and at the very end of the 1966–70 Parliament it was passed quickly through the House in the hands of Lord Longford and four paraplegic Peers. While the Commons may not always accept Lords' Private Members' legislation, the converse is not the case. The only Commons' Private Member's Bill rejected by the Lords since 1945 has been the 1955–56 Homicide Bill, proposing the abolition of capital punishment. The compromise measure that the Government subsequently introduced as their own Bill was passed in 1957.

Thus in the field of Public and Private Members' Bills the Lords have a significant legislative role to play. But an equally important function is their work on subordinate legislation, a subject that requires a section to itself.

c. *Subordinate Legislation*

Since 1945 the amount of legislation delegated to departments has increased enormously. The Lords' powers in this respect were not curtailed by the 1911 or 1947 Parliament Acts and they still share with the Commons the right of veto or delay. Where affirmative resolution is required both Houses must give their approval before such Orders can be passed; where an Order becomes effective unless a Prayer for annulment is carried by either House (the negative resolution procedure), the Lords again enjoy the same rights as the Commons.

To be sure, M.P.s have found that in recent years there has been insufficient time to debate at least 50 per cent of such Prayers for annulment and, as the Second Report of the Commons' Procedure

---

[21] When David Steel's version of the Abortion Bill was considered in the Commons, it was starred to indicate that it would have priority and some Government time, without committing the Government to explicit change of the legislation.

Committee has suggested, the Government are therefore given excessive scope for bypassing Parliament. But (while the Lords' more flexible time-table allows them the opportunity to discuss Prayers, other constraints prevent them from vetoing delegated legislation.)This brake has become even more of a hindrance since the middle 1960s.

(Orders are known in the Lords as Special Orders; the *Companion* explains their variety and the procedures for considering them. (A short summary here is needed only to make it easier to understand why the Lords' position is so delicate.[22])

Affirmative Resolution

Orders or Instruments requiring affirmative resolution are referred to the Special Orders Committee, set up at the beginning of each Session. On the advice of the Chairman of Committees the Special Orders Committee divide these into two categories. The first covers Orders that but for the terms of the empowering Act would require enactment by a Public Bill.[23] An Order falling into this category will be considered by the Special Orders Committee, whose report includes a brief description of the Order. They state whether they feel it expedient to draw to the attention of the House any other matter within the Order (or the enactment under which it is made) and whether they have any doubt that it is *intra vires*.[24] However, the Committee's terms of reference are in fact extremely narrow because they are, with very few exceptions, permitted neither to vary the terms of an Order nor to report on its general merits or expediency, for these are matters of general policy debatable only on the Floor of the House. Thus, although no Order requiring affirmative resolution can be effected unless the Lords have reported to the House upon it, their powers respecting the first category are nevertheless considerably limited.

Hybrid Special Orders

However, the Chairman of Committees can advise that a Special Order be assigned to the other category, that of Orders that but for the provisions of the empowering Act would require enactment by a Private or Hybrid Bill. (Private Bills, dealing with legislation

---

[22] *Companion*, pp. 139–48.
[23] Private Bill Standing Order 216.
[24] A recent important case concerned the Swiss drug firm Hofman–La Roche (1973).

affecting particular individuals, are described below. Hybrid Bills are those affecting private and public interests together.)

In this second category, Hybrid Special Orders, the Lords' powers are wider than the Commons', for under the terms of the 1926 Statutory Instruments Act the Lords are able to hear petitions against Special Orders that are opposed. Petitions may be presented by any person who would be entitled to pray against a Bill containing the same provisions—this requirement allows petitions from private individuals but makes it difficult for protests to be lodged by groups or organizations. The problems of preservation societies or ramblers are a case in point.[25]

Another difficulty is that petitioning is slow and expensive. Petitioners are represented by Counsel or Agent although (as those to whom fees accrue are quick to emphasize) there are advantages in this quasi-judicial method. This difficulty has been alleviated to some extent by the recommendation in the Fourth Report of the Lords' Procedure Committee that the Special Orders Committee may also examine written representations from the parties concerned: the Petitioners and the Minister. When the recommendations were put before the House, Peers were reassured that the Committee would be most circumspect in considering *all* written representations before deciding whether a Select Committee should be appointed to hear oral evidence.[26]

Such a Select Committee is appointed if the Special Orders Committee reports that there ought to be further inquiry into the matter of a Hybrid Order. The Select Committee, of five Peers, then follows the procedure of a Committee on a Private Bill.

It is, however, the initial report from the Special Orders Committee itself that states whether the Order has been petitioned against and whether the petition discloses substantial grounds of complaint, whether these have been adequately investigated by a departmental inquiry, and whether there should be further inquiry by a Select Committee. As with the first class of Orders ('Public' Special Orders), the Select Committee cannot pronounce on the merits of a Hybrid Order but they can report on whether

[25] In Jan. 1972 on a Motion by Lord Molson, former Chairman of the Council for the Preservation of Rural England, the frontbench spokesman advised the House that the newly established Joint Select Committee on Delegated Legislation would examine the whole subject. *HL Debs.*, vol. 327, cols. 277–317.

[26] Fourth Report of the Procedure Committee, 1966–67.

it seems to raise important questions of policy or principle, departs from precedent, or seems to be *ultra vires*.

It is plain that where Hybrid Orders are concerned the Lords' privileges surpass those of the Commons and not unnaturally the Peers resist any efforts to curtail them. There have been attempts to do so. For example, Peers regarded with some suspicion the abbreviation of the time during which petitions could be heard. The Special Orders Committee is unable to report on an Order until petitioning time has expired, this being fourteen days after the date on which the Order is laid upon the Table. This gives a generous amount of time for any aggrieved party to make an objection. Peers are reluctant to cede any of this time, especially if the motives seem to be to allow the departmental machine to roll more quickly over the private citizen.

But there is another class of '28-day Orders', those that are already in force when they are laid and which will expire unless both Houses approve them within twenty-eight days.[27] The pressure of Parliamentary business means that such an Order might sometimes lapse before the Lords have time to consider it. This seemed likely in the case of the 1966 Solus Petrol Order and, after considerable argument, on that occasion the House took the opportunity to resolve that the petitioning time for such 28-day Orders might be abbreviated. The 28-day period may be shortened to ten days (and then extended to fourteen if the Chairman of Committees gives special leave).

This description relates to Orders, Public and Hybrid, requiring affirmative resolution. Where the negative procedure is concerned, in Prayers for annulment, the Lords' practice is especially interesting because it shows how the peculiarity of their composition and status as the Second Chamber effectively limits their statutory powers.

Negative Resolutions

Although the Lords have greater opportunity to debate such Prayers they can always be accused of encroaching on the preserve of the elected Government. Unless Orders requiring annulment are debated they automatically come into force, and lack of time in the Commons means that the only way in which their provisions

---

[27] The Southern Rhodesia (United Nations Sanctions) Order 1968 was one of these. It was already in force when the Lords rejected it.

can be discussed in Parliament at all is for the Lords to consider them. But if the Lords carry a Prayer they immediately defeat the Order in question and thus veto Government legislation—a situation the Lords wish to avoid. So it has come about that the Lords debate Motions for annulment and then withdraw them or, if the House divides, hope that the annulment resolution will be defeated.

Between April 1950 and December 1971 twenty-two Resolutions for annulment have been debated and all but four withdrawn by the Mover. As Lord Silkin said, in withdrawing his Motion for annulment of the Matrimonial Causes Rules 1968, the last occasion when the House successfully divided to defeat a Statutory Instrument was in 1911, and, he added, 'I should hate to create a precedent'.[28]

Although the Lords do not use the powers of veto they possess, nevertheless their debates on Orders have some effect. For example, in the 1964–70 period there were a number of Orders making local government boundary changes, and Peers were generally ready to raise objections in the House by means of a resolution for annulment. The 1965 Northampton Order, the 1966 Exeter Order, the 1966 Plymouth Order, the 1967 Sheffield Order, and the 1968 Derby Order were such cases.

The Torbay Order, in 1966, was a good example of the scope and limits of the Lords' influence. This created a new borough by amalgamating the borough of Torquay, Paignton R.D.C., and other R.D.C. areas, and the Minister himself doubted the wisdom of the change. Local M.P.s and councillors made strong representations against it and the Peers felt they had good grounds for asking the Government to delay. In the Lords the Opposition alleged that the amalgamation would produce not a mere boundary readjustment but a major change of local government in the county.

In reply the Government discussed not the principles but the technicalities of the Order and the threatened constitutional repercussions from a clash between the Houses if the Order were rejected. However, there was no Division on the reasoned Amendment and, after debate, Lord Kennet withdraw the Order. The Minister was consulted and the matter was investigated afresh. When the Government reintroduced the Order the following February, the Opposition took the Leader's advice that 'this was not the right moment to divide the House'. The Lords had imposed a short

---

[28] *HL Debs.*, vol. 290, col. 1455.

period of delay and obliged the department to re-examine the proposals but although it was said that the Government had been made to look 'very foolish and silly', the Lords had little alternative but to accept the Order.

Another difficulty that Peers encounter in protesting against local government boundary changes, on grounds of inadequate consultation and inquiry, is that, whatever their personal associations with the area, they may appear to be trespassing on the constituency role of M.P.s (even though M.P.s have less chance to raise such Prayers in their own House). Viscount Amory and those Peers supporting him attracted this criticism in the case of the 1966 Exeter Order.[29] But these discussions in the Lords are not altogether fruitless and in the lifetime of the 1964-66 Labour Government they certainly had some part in persuading the Ministry of Housing and Local Government to establish a Royal Commission on Local Government and embark on wholesale rather than piecemeal reform.

(The constitutional delicacy of the Lords' position stems from the fact that by carrying a Prayer against an Order they do not simply delay it but veto it altogether.)The Government are then obliged either to drop the order or to re-lay it. This problem was epitomized on two occasions between 1964 and 1970. One concerned the Government's plan to build a third London airport at Stansted in Essex. Even in the very early days of the first months of 1967 the Leader and Deputy Leader of the Lords indicated to the Government that the Upper House would not stomach the Order to proceed with the project. This was one factor in the complicated sequence of events that led to the reappraisal and ultimate abandonment of this particular enterprise.

The other episode was that of the Southern Rhodesia (United Nations Sanctions) Order described in chapter 5. Indeed, on that occasion, the Leader of the House suggested, to the Opposition Leader's evident dismay, that the Government might be unable to re-lay the Order in the identical form of the original. The Lords' misdemeanour in forcing the Government to drop legislation already in force would thereby seem even more severe. This was actually the only case where the Lords did reject an Order and, as chapter 5 shows, the consequences were serious.

At a time of increasing executive power the Lords are reluctant

[29] *HL Debs.*, vol. 274, col. 521.

to lose their right to dispose of subordinate legislation. But their powers are somewhat hollow. In the discussions on Lords' reform, it was suggested that some procedure might be devised whereby the Lords could disagree with an Order that could then be re-laid and passed by the Commons, to be carried formally by the Lords.[30] Alternatively it was suggested that joint examination by a Committee of both Houses would be a sensible and economical way for Parliament to discuss affirmative resolutions and Prayers. One result of the increasing disquiet that has been expressed since the middle 1960s is that the whole subject of delegated legislation has been referred to a joint Select Committee, under the chairmanship of Lord Brooke of Cumnor. There, since February 1972, the question has been under review.

This exhausts the various forms of public legislation; private legislation is the next area to be considered.

D. *Private Bills*

Private Bills originate outside Parliament, on a petition of a private individual or specific organization to be given rights in law. Parliament's duty is to see that the interests of other individuals are not adversely affected. In the eighteenth century this was the way in which most legislation came before Parliament (the stream of Enclosure Acts was passed in this way)[31] and the importance of private legislation in the past is reflected in the fact that Lords' Standing Orders relating to Private Bills were codified long before those relating to Public Bills. In the 1964–70 period the Private Bills considered in the Lords ranged from a petition from Berkshire County Council for statutory powers to borrow and lend money, to petitions from the Church to develop a burial ground, and the request of a commercial company to build a marina at Brighton.

The *Companion* describes how the Examiners for Private Bills in each House scrutinize Private Bills, to ensure that proper procedures have been followed, and it sets out the guiding principles governing their allocation between the Houses.[32] All Bills must eventually pass through both Lords and Commons. They must be

---

[30] Lord Carrington implied that the Conservatives were using this tactic on the Southern Rhodesia Order.

[31] Of the 12,736 Statutes enacted between 1700 and 1800, about three-quarters were Local or Personal Bills.   [32] *Companion*, pp. 149–61.

deposited by 27 November and on 18 December the Examiners begin their scrutiny.

In the Lords, after a formal First Reading, the Chairman of Committees takes responsibility for subsequent stages of unopposed Private Bills. These are then referred to an Unopposed Bill Committee and the work of seeing the Parliamentary Agents and those witnesses representing the Promoters is customarily done by the Lord Chairman and his Counsel. (Representatives of the Government Departments reporting on the Bill, and such Peers as think fit, will also attend.)

Opposed Private Bills

If notice is given to oppose the Second Reading, the Lord Chairman will not move for the Promoters, who must then find another Peer to act for them. Earl Waldegrave did this, for example, in moving the Bristol Corporation Bill, against which eight petitions had been received. Opposed Private Bills must then be committed to a Select Committee of five Peers named for the occasion by the Committee of Selection.[33] All members of the Committee have then to attend all its proceedings and no other Lord is able to take part. (If one member is prevented from attending, the Committee may sit with only four members, subject to consent of all parties.)

Those Peers—like Lord Champion, Lord Royle, and Lord Strang—who make a habit of sitting such Committees exercise their duties with a great feeling of responsibility, and the Lords regret the fact that the public are ignorant of the man-hours they devote to the scrutiny of private legislation. It is sometimes privately suggested that the Lords are more assiduous than the Commons' Private Bill Office in their attention to these Bills.

At any time between Second Reading and Committee Stage, but usually on Second Reading, Peers may move Instructions to the Select Committee. Instructions can be permissive or mandatory but the most usual type are cautionary, ensuring that the Committee consider circumstances or objections that the parties appearing before them or the departmental reports might not have raised. For example, on the Tees Valley and Cleveland Water Bill proposing a reservoir at Cow Green, Lord Molson moved an Instruction asking that the Committee give special consideration to the scientific

[33] In the case of the Calderdale Water Bill this was increased to eight to ensure full attendance over a long period.

and amenity value of the site, and that they look at other ways of supplying water in this area. On Third Reading, the Chairman of the Select Committee, Lord Grenfell, reported that they had deliberated for nineteen days and visited the site on a tour of inspection in accordance with the Instruction.

The Bristol Corporation Bill provides another good case of the results of such an examination. At Third Reading, in February 1971, when the Select Committee recommended that the Bill be allowed to proceed, Lord Grenfell described the evidence they had heard and their visit to Bristol Docks. Their Special Report recommended the retention of the Floating Harbour and suggestions for doing this had been worked out with the Promoters. Peers who had been doubtful on Second Reading were happy to accept the Report.

The disadvantages of the Private Bill procedure is that it is cumbrous and expensive and, though the fees of agents and lawyers are doubtless deservedly earned, there is anxiety about the costs incurred by Petitioners against private legislation. An active group of such Peers as Lord Inglewood and Lord Molson have persistently drawn attention to the difficulties of those petitioning against Water Orders, for instance. During this period a large number of these were undertaken by Private Bills. The matter has eventually been resolved by the decision to embody all Water Orders in Acts, allowing for the public inquiry procedure into a Ministerial decision, and avoiding a lengthy and expensive investigation by each House.

A further drawback has been that in recent years Peers have felt it unwise to question the details of a Private Bill too deeply on Second Reading, until the Committee have had a chance to investigate and report. On Third Reading, however, the House has been dissuaded from querying the report of the Committee, which at this juncture is better qualified than the superficially informed House to decide the issue.

Nevertheless, in this sphere the Lords' work is useful and thorough and when in 1967 the Clerk of the Parliaments was asked what functions he would give a reformed House he immediately suggested that they deal with all Private Bills. The White Paper on Reform proposed that joint Lords'/Commons' Committees on Private Bills should again be considered but the arguments against this are two. It is said that Petitioners will be put at a disadvantage without the opportunity of a second hearing in either House, for in the House first hearing the Bill the Petitioners can discover the Promoters' case and the Government's attitude and prepare their objections accordingly for the hearing in the other House. The interval between hearings also allows time for bargaining between the parties. In 1974, therefore, these proposals are still in abeyance.[34]

E. *Starred questions*

Peers share with M.P.s the right of access to Ministers, with their letters going straight to the highest level of a department. Where public questioning is concerned, a Peer has a far better chance than an M.P. of raising a Question on the Floor of the House. In the Lords all Questions are taken and all answered by frontbench spokesmen, whether they are put down by a Peer's private enterprise, in concert with his party, or planted with the connivance of the Government.

Parliamentary Questions are utterly different in the two Houses. Questions in the Lords are addressed to the Government and not to a particular Minister. In any case there is not always an officially appointed spokesman for every department, and Frontbenchers will arrange to cover different subjects. Peers only rarely object that their Questions are being answered by an inappropriate spokesman but the fact that the Frontbencher who replies is frequently only a stooge for the real Ministerial target in the Commons means that very often Questions lose some of their directness and are less frequently used to pillory an individual.

By definition, Starred Questions are used for information only, and their wording and subject-matter are ultimately for the Whole House to decide. Questions casting reflection on the Sovereign and Royal Family, or relating to matters *sub judice*, or phrased offensively, are regarded as inadmissible. The House also dislikes 'constituency' Questions, which are better left to M.P.s. If a Question offends, the House can ask the Questioner to rephrase it or refuse him leave to put it. (Backbench Peers have as much authority as Frontbenchers to do this—Lord Saltoun silenced Lord Boothby on one memorable occasion.)

Peers claim that their House is sensible but discreet, and there is evidence for this. For instance, Peers tactfully decided not to pursue Lord Glendevon's Question in July 1969 on the sale of the

---

[34] Lord Molson raised the matter again in a Motion on 25 Jan. 1972.

Duccio painting,[35] and, with equal delicacy, silenced the Earl of Arran when in April 1969 he attempted to ask about a male contraceptive pill.[36] On the other hand, Lord Milford's Question on Cambodia in May 1970 was queried as embodying concealed propaganda but none the less given a hearing.[37]

Starred Questions first appeared in the Lords in 1919 and at first there was a strong resistance towards adopting a device so suspiciously reminiscent of Commons' practices. Innumerable Procedure Reports were produced and only in 1940 did Starred Questions become a regular feature of business. They have priority on the Order Paper but, unlike the Commons, their number is limited. Peers are rationed; from 1954 to 1959 the allowance was three a day, from 1959 the House permitted itself four a day. Whereas the Commons by no means exhaust the list of Questions down for reply each afternoon, the Lords are sure to discuss every one. Though no Peer may ask more than two on any one day, unlimited supplementaries are allowed from all Peers and this means that occasionally a small debate develops. While the Commons may race through some thirty-five Questions in an hour, the Lords may take twenty minutes to deal with their four.

Peers are troubled about the length of Questions and Supplementaries. In 1970 Lord Denham asked that expressions of courtesy be less effusive and time-consuming[38] and in July 1968 Lord Mancroft asked that questions 'involving numerous, complicated or divergent matters' could be prompted to appear as Unstarred Questions or Questions for Written Answer.[39] But the House has been unwilling to trespass on members' rights—for instance a Question in March 1967 from the Earl of Dundee, on the pound unit and decimal currency, led to eight columns of debate and provoked twenty-two interventions.[40]

The number of Starred Questions asked per sitting day has, on average, increased steadily over the years, and markedly so since 1964. Despite their initial resistance, Peers have taken to Starred Questions as a jealously guarded and enjoyable means of publicity, knowing that their Questions will be taken on a named day, before a House that at the beginning of the afternoon is likely to be full.

[35] *HL Debs.*, vols. 303–4 (bound as one volume), cols. 249–52; vol. 310, cols. 710–13.
[36] *HL Debs.*, vol. 301, cols. 436–7. [37] *HL Debs.*, vol. 310, col. 220.
[38] *HL Debs.*, vol. 308, cols. 805–6. [39] *HL Debs.*, vol. 295, cols. 302–3.
[40] *HL Debs.*, vol. 280, cols. 1320–7.

The daily average has crept close to the ration of four Questions (there are often four put down for a named day with one withdrawn at the last minute, which brings down the average). There is evidence, too, that pressure tends to build up before each Recess, particularly the Summer Recess, when all the available slots are taken. In the autumn of 1970 there was heavy pressure on Starred Questions and all places were taken for a month in advance. This was partly after the long Summer Recess and partly because of the pre-empting of twenty-five places by two Peers. (Some of these twenty-five Questions were subsequently shared out amongst other Peers.)

Suspicion that a few Peers have been abusing their privilege and 'hogging' the Order Paper has caused the Procedure Committee to examine this and related matters in a series of Reports. The offenders (chiefly Lord Brockway and the Earl of Kinnoull) have been asked to restrain themselves. The Tenth Report of the Lords' Procedure Committee has since suggested that there be no general increase in the number allowed each day, nor a limitation on the right of Peers to ask up to two each, though they stress that abuse of this right will quickly make a new system necessary.

Ministers also have to ensure that their replies are short, so discouraging lengthy or argumentative supplementaries. It helps to make the ration of four a day sufficient if Questions of local interest are normally covered by means of Written Answer. On the urging of Leaders from all sides of the House, these have increased fourfold, from an average of one a week in 1968 to one a day in 1971.

The Tenth Report has also considered the suggestion of an experimental 'topical Question' with two stars, as an extra Starred Question which could not be put down more than three days in advance. This would be subject to the rules governing Private Notice Questions—that is, concerning a subject of urgent national interest, within the Government's competence to answer. The Peer himself, with the advice of the Table, would decide whether his Question fell within the definition, and the ultimate decision would as usual lie with the House. The suggestion has been shelved but it is favoured by Peers (like Lord Shepherd, the Deputy Leader) who incline to a more Commons-like Upper House.

Peers use Starred Questions to inquire about the progress of legislation, push for new policy, harry the Government, or take up urgent developments in foreign affairs. The House can be persistent when an issue catches its imagination—favourites of the 1966–70 Parliament were decimal currency, the two-tier postal service, and the anti-Stansted campaign. Individual Peers ask recurrent Questions, on consumer safety, or the establishment of the Sports Council, pressing until they are successful. There are oddities, like the Earl of Harrowby's suggestion in a Question for Written Answer that inland rockets be used for food transportation, and ombudsman-like Questions on the problems of minority groups, the rights of individuals, and local matters of amenity and conservation.

Putting a Question sometimes leads to action and also allows Peers to let off steam. Civil servants vary in the attention they pay to Lords' Questions, depending on personal and political circumstances. Some Departments, particularly 'technocratic' Ministries like Transport or Technology,[41] occasionally scorn the Lords but others, like Agriculture or the Foreign Office, will take as much trouble, if not more, over Lords' Questions as for Commons'.

There are good Questions and bad, and sometimes departments can be tested and Frontbenchers made to look foolish. But they are less a method of blooding Ministers than Commons' Questions, and a larger proportion of Starred Questions in the Lords' are not party-political in intention. Though less valuable than Commons' Questions for testing Ministers' surefootedness, Lords' Questions are none the less an important means of extracting information. Persistent pushing, too, can sometimes lead to action.

F. *Private Notice Questions and Ministerial Statements*

A more immediate method of questioning frontbench spokesmen is by Private Notice Question or comment on a Ministerial Statement, the essential difference between the two being that the Question openly requests information while the Statement volunteers it. The *Companion* describes the procedure for submitting a Private Notice Question 'on a matter of urgency'. A Peer must send it, in writing, to the Leader of the House by twelve noon on the day on which he proposes to put it. Thus it is in the first instance the Leader, and his Private Secretary, who decide whether the Question falls within the definition of urgency. Ultimately the decision rests with the Whole House.

[41] Now the Departments of the Environment and of Trade and Industry.

Peers rarely challenge the Leader's ruling but their rights were upheld in a dispute on a Question from Lord Teynham on 16 February 1966, when he asked about the Secretary of State for Defence visiting the United States. The Government declined to answer. This provoked objections from Viscount Dilhorne and Lord Saltoun, and the Leader of the House, Lord Longford, was obliged to clarify the matter. On the following day he agreed that the decision lay ultimately with the House rather than the Leader. But he added that adequate notice should be given to the Leader that the Questioner proposed to challenge him in the House if the Question were refused and that it should be made perfectly clear to the House that an appeal was being made against the Leader's views.[42]

Backbenchers usually accept the decisions of the Leader's Office, especially when Leaders and their Private Secretaries are firm and clearly divorce their rulings from political considerations. According to the Leader's Office, 90 per cent of Private Notice Questions suggested by Backbenchers between 1964 and 1970 were refused by the Leader. The rarity of backbench challenge suggests that on the whole they are satisfied. The number of Private Notice Questions has diminished from seventeen or eighteen a year in the early 1960s to eleven or twelve by the end of the decade and, as Leaders, both Lord Longford and Lord Shackleton have applied the definition of 'urgent' very rigidly.

There is good reason for discouraging the Private Notice Question. Not only is it Government policy to give more information by Questions for Written Answer but there is some feeling in the Lords that it is hard on frontbench spokesmen to have to reply on urgent or contentious matters for which they have no direct departmental responsibility. Such replies are more fittingly made in the Commons. If the Question is to be raised at all in the Lords, it is better to deliver it as a Statement, inviting only dispassionate comment.

During the Labour Parliaments of 1964 and 1966 the sort of Questions which urgently troubled the Peers and were the occasion for close supplementary questioning included such issues as the confiscation of Sir Frederick Crawford's passport; Israeli air cargo; troubles in Londonderry; Anguilla; the Seamen's strike; foot-and-mouth disease. Looking over the complete list gives a misty view of the topical concerns of the times.

[42] *HL Debs.*, vol. 272, cols. 1045–1149.

There is only a negligible distinction between an 'inspired' Private Notice Question and a Ministerial Statement. Statements are even more of a bother to Frontbenchers than Private Notice Questions. In both Houses the Government have tried to prune the number of Statements; in the Lords in particular they cause an inconvenient interruption of business. If a Minister sits in the Lords, a Statement can be made after Starred Questions before major business begins, but if he is in the Commons and delivers the Statement, as he must, after 3.30 p.m., the Lords must wait until 'an appropriate moment after 3.30'. The length of the Commons' Statement and of the speech of whichever Peer happens to be on his feet may then mean that delivery is delayed until as late as 4 p.m. It has recently been suggested that Black Rod should examine the bush-telegraph system to try to synchronize Statements in Lords and Commons as far as possible. Sometimes it might also be appropriate to interrupt the speeches of Backbenchers in order to have a Statement for which the House is waiting.

While all Commons' Statements are repeated in the Lords, in recent Sessions some long and complicated Statements have been set out in Lords' Hansard, with the front bench only informing the House that this is being done. Since 1964 the number of Statements has gradually diminished, from the seventy-six of the Session 1964-65 to thirty-two in 1969-70. On occasion the Government spokesman in the Lords might say that a Statement will not be made there in the first instance but will be given in reply if a Private Notice Question is put requesting it. There is also the convention that if the Government in the Commons chooses to reply to a Private Notice Question from the Opposition front bench there, a similar Private Notice Question will be accepted in the Lords. Wherever a Commons' Statement is to be made the Whips will inform the Lords' Whips so that, if the Leader of the Opposition in the Lords wishes, it can be repeated there (perhaps by planted Private Notice Questions). Sometimes this bush-telegraph system breaks down, when the Lords' Whips do not know that at noon the Commons' Speaker has received a Private Notice Question, but on the whole the system works well. One source of difficulty, however, is that the Treasury has refused to allow certain types of financial Statement to be made in the Lords, on grounds of Commons' privilege. This is still a matter of dispute.

Statements might seem to offer members an opportunity to

criticize the Government's handling of policy, but conventionally only frontbench Peers have an established right of comment. Though all Peers may ask questions for clarification, Statements may not be made an occasion for immediate debate; on controversial matters there has nevertheless been a tendency for prolonged debate on supplementaries—Lord Chalfont's Statement on British peace efforts in Vietnam, in January 1968, was such a case. Lord Brockway and Lord Milford both wished to make lengthy interventions.[43]

This, as usual, remains a matter for 'the good sense of the House'. Ministers and Opposition Frontbenchers are frequently reminded of the need for brevity, and backbench Peers are asked to familiarize themselves with the terms of Standing Order 32 and, if necessary, to call offenders to order. But while Statements, to the disgust of Backbenchers, are very much a frontbench affair, if the House seems anxious to discuss a Statement urgently and in full, it is at this point that Backbenchers will request an immediate debate.

In the Commons, since 1967, debates on 'matters of urgency' can be held under Standing Order 9, which allows for a half-day debate if the Speaker so decides, to be held within three days of a matter arising. Ministers in the Commons feel that they should put their case to the Lower House first and there is no such arrangement in the Lords. There has been evidence of a desire for this (on the issue of the American presence in Cambodia, for example), but the flexibility of the Lords' daily and weekly time-table permits topical questions to be debated at short notice and no explicit alterations in Standing Orders are necessary. Moreover, the device of the Unstarred Question (discussed below) provides an excellent method of discussing topical issues at greater length than Statements of Starred Questions allow.

Since Unstarred Questions are a type of Motion, it is best to describe first of all the various categories of Motion used in the Lords, dealing with this unusual feature last of all.

G. *Motions*

There are three different types of Motion available to Peers: Motions for Resolution, Motions to 'take note', and Motions for Papers.

[43] *HL Debs.*, vol. 279, cols. 133-42.

Motions for Resolution

These are used in cases 'where a Lord wishes to obtain the support of the House for some positive action or expression of opinion, or to come to a definite decision . . .'[44] A Resolution, if passed, does not constitute the formal conclusion of the House on the matter. They are therefore often used by the Opposition for headcounting, as in a vote of censure, or to ask for action on some specific issue of policy. The Government will not use a Motion 'to resolve . . .' if they wish to avoid a Division explicitly showing the feelings of the House, as in the case of the debate on siting the Third London Airport at Stansted. If the Government do want a Division they will use such a Motion. The debate on Lords' reform was such an instance.

Motions to 'take note'

When a Minister wishes to put down a neutral Motion, so that the House can air a subject in debate without accepting a resolution in definite terms, he uses the formula 'That this House takes note . . .' This formula can be used by any Peer but it is particularly useful to Ministers because, unlike Backbenchers, they can neither withdraw a Motion nor 'move for papers'. (Papers would in any case be laid by a Minister's own department or the Government.) The device of the Motion to take note is used where Reports of Royal Commissions, Committees of Inquiry, or Green Papers are being discussed.

Motions for Papers

Demanding State papers historically afforded the Commons both the material on which to base their criticism of the executive and an opportunity to reassert the power of their House to act as the inquest of the nation. The Motion for Papers has survived in the Lords and its somewhat curious justification is described in the *Companion*. The practice of adding to the end of a notice giving a subject for debate the words 'and to move for Papers' is

to comply with the requirement that there must be a Question before the House and to give the Mover a right of reply. It is recognised, however, that such a motion should normally be withdrawn, since it is treated as a neutral motion and there is neither advantage nor significance in pressing it. The opinion of the House is expressed in the speeches made

[44] *Companion*, p. 72.

by its members rather than on a division. If a Peer wants the support of the House for some positive action or decision, his intention should be made plain in the form of a resolution.[45]

For example, the Earl of Arran wished to test the feeling of the House on the Wolfenden Report and on new legislation regarding homosexuality. Though he thought about making this a Motion for Resolution, he decided that it would be more sensible and discreet just to sound out opinion by means of a Motion for Papers. (He somewhat regretted this afterwards when Peers expressed their approval of reform, but nevertheless felt it inexpedient to draft a long Bill. For this he would need Home Office help and, during the months this would take, impetus would be lost.) On the Clerks' advice he therefore drafted a simple one-clause Bill and introduced it.

The House has always made good use of Motions for Papers (see Table 11 in appendix), which average between twenty and thirty a Session. Debates are distributed between the parties on a basis of half the time for the largest Opposition party, a quarter for the Liberals and Crossbenchers, and a quarter for the Government. In the 1960s these debates were channelled into Wednesday afternoons for, although Peers may by right initiate debates on any sitting day, Standing Orders give priority to legislation, Government or Private Members', on days other than Wednesdays.

This has tended to put 'Wednesday debates' on something of a pedestal but it has ensured a high rate of participation. Peers know that on that afternoon there is likely to be a debate of some special interest and it is also easier for many of them to come in the middle of the week. Those who suggest that Wednesday debates are somehow a concession made to Backbenchers and the other parties out of 'Government time' are in error; the notion is not strictly appropriate in the Lords. However, it is certainly the case that out of the main debates held in the House, Backbenchers initiate more than half of those held on a Wednesday, compared with a third on other days. The totals for three Sessions, 1967–70, bear this out (see Table 12, appendix).

The party Leaders take pains to see that opportunities to propose Motions are fairly distributed between individual Backbenchers, and Motions for Papers have by no means been discouraged.

[45] *Companion*, p. 72.

(Unlike the Commons, a Lord does not append the names of fellow Peers wishing to have a particular debate. When a Peer puts down a Motion for future discussion, it is his Motion. The House has testified, in a debate on 10 February 1972, to the fairness of the usual channels.) Motions for Papers have become an important and characteristic feature of the House, employing its resources of time and of qualified participants, both experts and generalists. Individual party Leaders who are interested in original ideas have also prompted discussion and when they have not been interested have left the arrangements to their Private Secretaries, who are.

General debates, like Lord Arran's on Wolfenden, can have considerable influence on policy. For instance, the weight of Lords' opinion on the British Museum Library, on the Report of the Roskill Commission (on the siting of the third London airport), on the revision of the laws concerning abortion, divorce, and gambling, certainly affected thinking in the Cabinet. It is difficult to judge how much effect came from the interventions of influential Peers speaking on their special subjects but, for example, there is good reason to believe that Lord Radcliffe's remarks on the D-notice affair worried the Prime Minister and his Cabinet.[46] In another case, speeches on economic policy by Lord Balogh, Lord Robbins, and Lord Cromer had evident repercussions.

Much depends on chance factors. The Press were naturally interested in the D-notice question, for example. Or the attention a department pays to a Lords' debate may vary according to the ability of the Minister to pass on his own observations after he has heard or read it. The fact that a frontbench spokesman does reply to a Motion for Papers and that another will speak at the end of the debate means that there is inevitably a captive frontbench audience to whom backbench Peers can express their feelings. While some speeches and some debates are perhaps superfluous, others can be important in their long-term influence on policy, if not in the short term. Senior civil servants in the former Ministry of Transport have said, for instance, that they gave significant attention to a series of debates on Fuel Resources, initiated by Lord Wynne-Jones, and others have referred to the authoritative group of Peers who speak

---

[46] Chapman Pincher, defence correspondent of the *Daily Express*, was held to have broken the 'D-notice' convention by which journalists do not reveal sensitive information. A Committee was asked to look into the episode but the Prime Minister was disinclined to accept its Report.

on ports and shipping. The best Lords' debates are possibly the non-polemical. Like a set of letters to *The Times* or articles in *Encounter*, speeches from distinguished Peers on such subjects as the Fulton Report on the Civil Service, the Duncan Report on Overseas Representation, the Redcliffe-Maud Report on Local Government, or the speeches on the White Paper 'In Place of Strife', develop important arguments and help shape opinion.

Debates of this kind have been so successful that by 1970 Peers wished to extend the practice and at the end of this period it was suggested that Mondays might also be used for the purpose. But, rather than asking the House to sit regularly on the first day of the week, in February 1972 the Lords began an experimental scheme to make better use of Wednesdays. On predetermined Wednesdays, two limited-time debates, of two and a half hours each, have been tried, with Peers putting down their topics in advance and balloting for time. There has been an enthusiastic response to the first year of this scheme (after some initial controversy over the procedure to be adopted for making the selection).[47]

To ease the pressure and to encourage the House to ventilate this sort of topic, the party Leaders have also promoted another device, the Unstarred Question, peculiar to the Lords and admirably suited to their requirements.

H. *Unstarred Questions*

The direct Question to Ministers was originally a technique of examination found only in the Lords and adopted by the Commons in the 1760s. But while the Commons eventually introduced the daily hour of Parliamentary Questions, the Lords limited Questions with priority to four Starred Questions a day, as this chapter described in an earlier section. Thus the Unstarred Questions, without priority, have continued to be discussed at the end of the day's business. They have therefore come to be defined by negative characteristics, as shorter than debates on Motions and taken late at night. But Unstarred Questions still resemble debates rather than any sort of Question in the Commons' sense—like so much of Lords' procedure they are a reminder of general Parliamentary practice before the 1880s, discarded by the Commons but embalmed in the Lords.

[47] *HL Debs.*, vol. 327, cols. 1270–1310.

Peers have been encouraged to put down Unstarred Questions as a means of raising topical matters and to amplify Starred Questions that have provoked discussion. Since 1964, too, they have been used as a less solemn substitute for shorter Motions for Papers of specific or general interest. From a dozen or so a year in the 1960s their number has grown steadily to some forty or so a Session (see Table 13, appendix).

There has been a fair balance (fortuitously so) between the parties in the number of Unstarred Questions asked. It is important to remember that with a minority Government, as Labour was in the Lords between 1964 and 1970, they provide a useful way for Peers to discuss critical or contentious matters, and for the Minister to reply, without the necessity for either a Division or a full-dress Motion for Papers.

It has been usual for the Minister replying on behalf of the Government to speak at the end of the debate after intervention from all parts of the House, for as long as Peers wish. The *Companion* states that the Lord asking the Question has no right of reply, because he moves no Motion, but this convention has frequently caused dispute. Some Lords argue that the Government cannot claim the inherent right to the last word and, moreover, that some Peers will not wish to speak until they have heard the Minister and discerned what Government policy is. On the other hand, the Government might be at a disadvantage if the Minister, having sat down, cannot then reply to make further points without the leave of the House. Anyhow this makes for untidy debate. The most notorious occasions of this controversy were in March 1969, when a number of Peers rose to speak on Peers' voting rights in a reformed House, and in November 1969 when Lord Chorley attempted to intervene 'in the ordinary way of discussion' on a Question concerning a dismissed police constable. In the first case the Leader conceded that 'it can be done, but it is very unusual'; in the second, Lord Chorley was unsuccessful.[48] Thus precedents are conflicting. In 1969 the Sub-Committee on Observances and Customary Behaviour set up by the Procedure Committee declared that though

---

[48] Lord Chorley had challenged this, successfully, on an earlier occasion in June 1966. Lord Alexander of Hillsborough also used to make a regular practice of lying in wait and then commenting on the Government's reply when he was Leader of the Opposition. In June 1967, Earl St. Aldwyn, then Opposition Chief Whip, called this tactic 'very nearly normal procedure' but after June 1970, as Government Chief Whip, he became more critical.

the decision should continue to be regulated by the House, it is undesirable for Peers to speak further, save by the cunning device of claiming to question the Minister 'before he sits down'.[49]

The Lords do feel that some issues require more than the brief treatment that a Starred Question allows. During this period, such subjects included the details of brucellosis testing, Spanish–Gibraltar relations, aid to Malta, the E.E.C. Two kite-flying Questions that led to action were Lord Royle's on tattooing and Lord Raglan's on British Standard Time. Peers are also prone to use the Unstarred Question to discuss miscarriages of justice and the problems of newly independent territories.

The major drawback of this device has been that, as Motions take precedence over Unstarred Questions, these tend to come late at night and are often poorly publicized and badly attended. To alleviate this, the Procedure Committee recommended in April 1968 that unless there are special circumstances, it is undesirable for a second Unstarred Question to be taken after eight o'clock. If Peers put down Questions on days when business appears to be light and subsequently pressure of business increases, they should be prepared to postpone them to a later date (subject also to the convenience of the House and of other Peers who may wish to speak).

The Unstarred Question is thus another of the ancient devices which the Peers adapted to new purposes. During this period they made use on an unprecedented scale of the various types of procedure catalogued in this chapter, and the complications that resulted inspired the Procedure Committee and Sub-Committees to devise several innovations and to clarify old conventions. This was one symptom of the reawakening of the House of Lords between 1964 and 1970.

It is not surprising that the Peers complained that hours seemed longer and traditional procedures ineffective. This was partly a sign of boredom with detailed legislative business and it was fortunate that the Lords had their particular opportunities to put Motions for Papers and Unstarred Questions to leaven the tedium. There are those who aver that now Frontbenchers pre-empt time and that backbench opinion is bypassed by a cabal of the usual channels when the order and handling of business is arranged.

[49] In 1973 a new Standing Order was devised, stating that no Peer could rise a second time to introduce new matter after the Minister has finished.

They are partly giving voice to a generalized objection to authority (according to a former Leader) but their complaint also emphasizes the new assurance of Backbenchers and the importance of continuous communication between parties and benches in the Lords. It has even been suggested recently that a small committee of Backbenchers could advise the Leader and transmit 'worries and grievances'. But this could in no way supervise the daily running of the business of the House because as a practical matter, both in administrative and political terms, this must be run from the office of the Leader and the Chief Whip through the usual channels.

The tradition of the Upper House has been that the party Leaders and in particular the Leader of the House should always be available to everyone. A multiplicity of mechanisms, it is thought—however many illogicalities it permits—encourages harmonious relations. This chapter has described the sort of business that engages the Lords' attention, their legislative and deliberative functions. The next chapter shows how the usual channels are of supreme importance and certainly more overtly active than in the Commons, in arranging when business is taken and how it is managed.

3

THE CONDUCT OF BUSINESS

IN both Houses business is organized and Parliamentary time
allocated through 'customary processes of consultation' between
the offices of the party Leaders and their Chief Whips. In the
Commons frontbench co-operation is discreetly veiled and party-
political skirmishing attracts more attention than the efficient
manœuvres of 'the usual channels'. The Lords are more open about
the accommodations that the parties habitually make. This co-
operation is justified on several grounds.

In the first place, the oddities of the party balance in the Upper
House give the Leaders an interest in working together, especially
when Labour is in power and the governing party is in a minority.
Secondly, as a former Conservative Leader put it, 'We have to stick
together as a Second Chamber and show forbearance and common
sense . . .'
Leaders of all parties in the Lords are mutually concerned to
help their House behave decorously towards the ever-watchful and
suspicious Commons. Thirdly, the Lords' own traditions of
a Speakerless House where every member has equal right and equal
authority means that 'The whole House is run by co-operation—
otherwise you'd never get anything passed. It's a unique chamber
in that it runs itself.' But the former Lord Chancellor who made this
remark went on to say, 'I'm appalled at the low standard of the
Commons. They don't do their stuff and they talk the most extra-
ordinary nonsense . . .', exemplifying the way in which Peers tend
to congratulate themselves on the absence of partisan friction in
their House, making a virtue out of habits that are strictly necessary.
To M.P.s who argue that the Lords' world is one of unhealthy
party cordiality, Peers reply that 'political bias' and party rancour in
the Commons is often only a time-wasting, carefully rehearsed performance. Lord Erroll and Hale said from the Conservative front
bench at the end of the Committee Stage of the Iron and Steel Bill:

I hope that those who have followed the long-drawn-out and somewhat sanctimonious proceedings in the Committee stage in another place will not think that, because our proceedings are perhaps calmer, we do not get as much out of the Government . . . Indeed, we are often more successful than they . . .[1]

Only a lengthy examination of individual Bills would substantiate or refute this assertion, and this study does not pretend to be an exhaustive comparative analysis of the work of the two Houses in recent years. But it is not only possible to look at the machinery with which the Lords seek to achieve these ends; it is also useful to consider what features of the Upper House persuade its members that methods of co-operation and consultation are more appropriate for the conduct of business when, after all, it is more usual to think of partisan loyalties and philosophies as the driving force in political affairs. Here, however, customary processes of mutual accommodation are practised at the highest level. Certainly brief descriptions of the roles of the Leader and Chief Whip in the Lords are essential to an understanding of the workings of the usual channels.

The Office of Leader

The Leader in his Governmental role is a member of the Cabinet, appointed by the Prime Minister, with responsibility for the conduct of Government business in the Lords. Sometimes he combines this with another Ministerial post—Lord Shackleton, for example, was also Lord Privy Seal and Minister responsible for the Civil Service Department. In this sense, the Leader is very much the central figure on the Government front bench.

This supports his second role as the guide and representative of his party, the chief spokesman of its frontbench team. In the Labour party the Leader, Deputy Leader, and Chief Whip in the Lords are elected by Labour Peers (just as Labour M.P.s elect the party Leadership in the Commons).

As well as his Government and party responsibilities, the Leader has a third role as avuncular adviser to the House on matters of procedure and orderly behaviour. As the *Companion* emphasizes, this does not give him formal authority or any of the powers of an effective Speaker. Still, though the maintenance of order is the responsibility of the House as a whole and therefore of every Peer present, 'nevertheless the Leader frequently acts as the voice of

[1] *HL Debs.*, vol. 280, col. 1077.

the House in this respect'. On formal occasions, such as Motions of thanks, sympathy, or congratulation, it is for the Leader to express the sense of the House, supported by seconding speeches from the other party Leaders. This chapter will also show how the Leader looks to his fellow Leaders for assistance in smoothing the business of the House, in the more technical sphere of time-tabling as well as in preserving standards of customary behaviour. Irrespective of party, the Leader and his Private Office will assist and advise every Peer.

The Government Chief Whip

It has become the practice for much of the everyday management of business to be undertaken by the Government Chief Whip as the Leader's other tasks, especially when he has departmental responsibilities, have grown more onerous. The Government Chief Whip's duties are, in similar fashion, threefold.

As a member of the Government he is responsible for planning the work of the House, which means both the short-term arrangement of business and speakers' lists so that appropriate spokesmen and interested Peers can be present, and also the long-term organization of the Sessional time-table, including efforts to secure as much legislation as possible for introduction in the Lords as first House. It is important that he arrange matters in conjunction with the Lord President and Chief Whip in the Commons so that the Lords' particular talents can be used to full advantage (with early debates on White and Green Papers, Royal Commission Reports, and so on) as well as planning business to fit in with the Government's over-all legislative time-table.

Business management often involves political considerations and, like his fellow Chiefs and their Commons' counterparts, the Government Chief Whip in the Lords also has a significant party role. It is his duty to ensure that Backbenchers on his own side are fully informed of projected business and advised when their presence to speak and vote is especially welcome. With the Leader, he seeks out party members to explain decisions and policy important to the party and to listen to those with particular enthusiasms or qualms. Chapter 4 looks more closely at this aspect of his work.

In the third place, the Chief Whip is as much the servant of the Whole House as the Leader, seeing that time for debate is allocated fairly and that speakers' lists, especially for general debates, show no favouritism in the placing of individual speakers. As a former Chief Whip said musingly about his duties:

> ... there's a tendency to use us as a channel of communication for the complaints and proposals of all Backbenchers. I sweeten them by being nice, chatty, or nasty if people show bad taste. But here, when you're dealing with voluntary, unpaid people, no sanctions over any of them, you can't lay down the law. Just appeal to their good sense and good taste. Then there are the nuts and bolts of general living. If people have inadequate room for doing their work, or want better ventilation, they come to me ...

The Private Secretary to the Leader

The interests of the Government, the party, and the Whole House form a web at whose centre is the Private Secretary to the Leader, who also serves as the Secretary to the Chief Whip. As a member of the Parliament Office, he has the sensitivity to the feelings of the House and a clerkly detachment that equip him to advise the Leader and Chief Whip on questions of management and procedure, especially when political and procedural considerations seem to conflict or when his two masters differ in their interpretation of what is prudent. The Private Secretary is the link between backbench and frontbench Peers, between the Leader and Chief Whip of the Government party and their Backbenchers, and between the Leaders of all parties.

This last duty requires him to keep the Leader of the Opposition in the Lords, the Leader of the Liberal Party, and to some degree the activists in the crossbench organization fully informed of the business programme, of changes, Amendments tabled, and so forth. Since arranging how and when business is taken cannot be done without some consultation with Leaders of other parties in the House, the 'usual channels' are not just a method of informing and communicating but, to a considerable degree, of devising a programme as well. Though in the last resort it is for the Government to decide how time is allocated, bargaining between the party Leaders takes place on all but the most bitter issues—and such co-operation especially prevails in the Lords. Moreover, as this chapter shows, co-operation and concession are not limited to the *organization* of business, for very often bargains about the *substance* of legislation become inextricably intertwined with discussions about the way it is to be handled.

This brief outline illustrates why the Leader's Office has to be accessible to all Peers at all times and how necessary it is for the Private Secretary to be in close touch, personally, by letter and telephone, with Leaders of the other parties and with other Private Secretaries, as well as having instant access to his own master. It is important to stress that frontbench Peers are in close informal communication every day, in the corridors, dining-room, and bars of the House, and that the offices of the Leaders of the three main parties in the Lords are next door to each other on the West Front Corridor. A word before or after a Committee meeting, a quick telephone call or a message between Private Secretaries or a Clerk, a calculated indiscretion (best left for politicians rather than Officers of the House), can be as useful as an official meeting, a memorandum, or a brief. Where party Leaders and their Chief Whips are exceptionally sympathetic, on a personal level, such informal relations are still more significant.

But even in the Lords there are issues of irreconcilable political difference. The amount of top-level discussion on the strategies of piloting business through varies with a Bill's controversiality and importance, and magnanimity from Government or Opposition can depend on the credit they possess in the country and in Parliament. To explain how the usual channels work and why they are occasionally befouled it is helpful to trace the formal route by which legislation passes through the Lords.

A. *Taking Government Legislation Through*

The detailed policy of any Government Bill presented in the Lords or Commons will have been worked out in the departments and Cabinet Committees and blessed at some stage by the full Cabinet. In Cabinet the Lord Chancellor and Leader of the Lords, and other Cabinet Ministers drawn from the Upper House, provide a link with the Lords, though the weight their views carry varies with the nature and circumstances of the Bill.

It is at the point when a Bill reaches Legislation Committee that matters of time-tabling are broadly settled. Here the Lords are also represented by the Chief Whip. He and the Leader make their bid for a Bill to be introduced in the Lords as first House. The Government will consider in which Session and which weeks they hope to take a Bill, but its several provisions are not normally discussed here. This Committee will, however, act as a longstop if inter-departmental squabbles arise and if Ministers maintain that a Bill has been inadequately worked out in other Cabinet Committees it can be referred back for further detailed argument. The Legislation Committee also takes a view on Private Members' Bills, especially any which have been taken up by M.P.s with the encouragement of the Government.

In this idealized model, when a Bill reaches the Lords (generally following, not preceding, Commons' stages), the department running it turn their attention to briefing their spokesmen in the Upper House. Sometimes, of course, a frontbench spokesman will be a Minister or Minister of State with specific responsibilities in the department but more often he is a junior Minister or Lord-in-Waiting without direct involvement.

The department will brief the Lords' spokesman or spokesmen at meetings before their speeches, ideally on the morning before a Bill is taken, though the customary scramble of legislative procedures often means that for many minor Bills briefing takes place at the last minute. A spokesman is given his instructions, told how accommodating he can be in Committee Stage, what undertakings and concessions he can make, and where he must stand firm. If in doubt, he has the officials to send notes from the Box in the chamber.

Where a Lords' spokesman is not himself a Minister or is not taking through his own Bill, Lords' debates in Committee often take on an opaque appearance, because a junior Minister or spokesman with no direct responsibility for departmental policy cannot make promises committing the Government or a Minister. He can undertake to refer matters to his Hon. friend, but where particular Amendments are concerned his inability to make pledges means that proceedings become even more courteous, muted, and oblique —or, alternatively, that the Opposition occasionally over-emphasize their criticism of specific points so that no urgency is lost in transmitting them to the Minister.

While a tricky Bill is going through, the front bench may wish to take a broader view of its progress, and the Minister, or Leader of the Lords, or Lord Chancellor, or Chief Whip may join the officials and the Lords' spokesman to discuss this. As a matter of routine the Lords' spokesman is in touch with his Chief Whip on the strategic aspects of handling a Bill, conferring with the Leader if issues become delicate. If the Cabinet are worried about progress, they may discuss a Bill together and the Leaders of the Commons and

Lords can consider what strategies and modifications may be necessary to get it through. (On the Evictions Bill, for example, there was some anxiety about Peers' reactions to Clauses concerning agricultural workers' tenancies.)

Such questions may be discussed in Cabinet but more usually a Minister will have a quick chat with the Leader of the Lords in the useful 'five minutes before or after Cabinet' if he is anxious about progress. This informal contact, needless to say, together with the continual conversations between Private Secretaries, gives an opportunity to settle fiddly details rather than important matters of policy or tactics. These are more appropriately worked out in Cabinet Committees.

The Opposition

The Opposition have to take a line on Government legislation passing through the Lords but the interest of the Shadow Cabinet as a whole varies with the character of a Bill. The Leader of the Opposition in the Lords and his Chief Whip are members of the Shadow Cabinet and will join in the early discussion of the Opposition attitude to Government Bills, but to some extent there is a feeling that the front bench in each House will manage as best it can. On important issues, of course, like the Transport Bill, industrial relations legislation, or the Southern Rhodesia (United Nations Sanctions) Order, there will be more extensive discussion in the Shadow Cabinet of the mood of the backbench Peers, the scope of opposition in the Lords, and the risks involved. When in Opposition, the Labour Peers also elect a backbench representative to the Shadow Cabinet and he will attempt to transmit opinion back and forth.

As a Government Bill passes through its stages in the Lords the Opposition may be led either by the Leader of the Opposition himself, by his Deputy, by the Chief Whip, or another established frontbench Peer. This is sometimes a former Minister well acquainted from his Commons' days with a particular policy area. And he can undertake the entire responsibility for handling the Opposition. Lord Brooke of Cumnor's work on the Land Commission Bill or Lord Drumalbyn's on the Trade Descriptions Bill are examples of this. In such cases the spokesman consults the Opposition Leader or Chief Whip on immediate problems but the Leaders are glad to leave specific tactics on Amendments to the Frontbencher concerned. With no department to give assistance such work, thoroughly done, can be demanding.

It is principally on matters of time-tabling that Government and Opposition will co-operate. In the Commons much of this organization of business is undertaken by negotiation between the Leaders and Chief Whips of either side but, obviously, one of the Opposition's few weapons is to be as obstructive as possible. In the Lords, co-operation is inevitable, given the uncomfortable position of a minority Government, a majority Opposition, or, if the Conservatives are in power, a Government with an embarrassingly large majority. 'Fair play' is important. There are times, as the key example of the Southern Rhodesia (United Nations Sanctions) Order will show, when such co-operation is impossible. At the other extreme, on an occasion like the passage of the 1968 Commonwealth Immigrants Bill when delay would exacerbate the situation, Government and Opposition Leaders work together to get legislation through (some say with unhealthy speed, others with impressive competence).

Future Business

Though the other party Leaders are consulted and informed it is in the Government Whips' Office that the provisional Future Business Paper and the Order Paper are prepared. The provisional paper consists of two parts, the first covering the forthcoming week, giving for each item of business detailed information about the Ministers in charge, other speakers, and estimates of the time that will be required. The second part sets out a tentative forecast of forthcoming business beyond the immediate weeks and does not contain lists of speakers or estimates of time. The whole document, prepared on Wednesday evening or Thursday morning, is cleared with the Chief Whip before lunch on Thursday, ready for the Ministers' meeting in the Leader's room and the party meetings held before the Thursday afternoon sitting.

Into the Order Paper the Private Secretary fits all stages of Government Bills and Special Orders and arranges dates and times for other discussions on, for example, Private Members' Bills, Wednesday debates, Church measures, and Consolidation Bills.

The Whip

The Whips Office prepares the Government whip, which is sent out from the *Commons'* Whips' Office on Friday to Peers on the Government side. A replica of this, the unlined whip with voting directions removed, is sent from the Lords' Whips' Office to a number of Peers with no party affiliation, particularly the members of the crossbench group. The Liberal Whips' Office in the Lords send out their own whip and the Opposition in the Lords circulate their supporters with a whip from the Commons' Whips' Office. While each party is therefore apparently responsible for its own whip, there can nevertheless be private discussions between the Chief Whips on their parties' attitude to particular Bills or Amendments, on points of difficulty or problematical Divisions though not, of course, on politically 'hot' affairs.

The significance that Peers attach to the whip when it reaches them is discussed in chapter 4; the point to emphasize here is that, as a part of routine administration, consultations and soundings between party Leaders in the Lords are very much the business of the usual channels.

B. *A Well-mannered Performance*

'Playing fair' covers far more than co-operating over the timing of business, and refraining from procedural tricks that might damage the relations between all parties in the Lords. On the substance of legislation, too, there is considerable horse-trading on Amendments and undertakings, practised far more openly in the Lords than in the Commons.

In the Lower House the party fight between a Government supplied with drafts and briefs by the departments and the Opposition creating its own 'civil service' remains very real. Although M.P.s and Ministers approach members of another party to make representations and suggest bargains they are far more discreet about such tactics.

Many Peers are ignorant of how the usual channels actually work, unless they have had frontbench experience, but Frontbenchers readily describe what one Minister calls: 'not agreement exactly—more the end-product of a process of negotiation that's gone on beforehand . . .'

They stress that it is 'reputable and sensible' to have conversations about Amendments and, indeed, refer to this background of consultation in their speeches on the Floor of the House. (In the

Committee Stage of the Docks and Harbours Bill, for example, Lord Champion spoke of the informal consultations between the Government and Lord Jellicoe and Viscount Simon and how, 'in the light of what they have said . . . we have looked at the whole matter afresh'.[2] During the later 1960s a majority of Backbenchers shared the frontbench attitude that to bridge differences of opinion is very often more valuable and economical than to enjoy party skirmishing for its own sake.[3]

When Peers compare the treatment of Bills in Committee Stage in either House they often assert that in the Lords there is less party polemic and more dispassionate analysis in considering legislation. But this does depend on the nature of the Bill, for in either House some Bills will provoke party point-scoring. Some Peers, too, seek to jolt the House into a keener awareness of party differences and though most Lords have passed the climacteric of political activity there are still a few who want to make their mark. Nevertheless Committees have their reputations and careers to make and find their legislative work a suitable context for doing so. The fact, too, that Commons' Standing Committees always include Government spokesmen directly responsible for the particular legislation being discussed gives proceedings an immediacy that Lords' Committee Stages often lack.

Though it can be said that the Lords sometimes 'get down to work without political distractions and personal considerations', this does not necessarily imply that their Committee Stages enjoy a more efficient use of time. True, M.P.s use Committee Stage for purposes of obstruction and delay but the Commons' rules of order and ultimately the guillotine motion can be invoked to keep discussion to the point. In the Lords, as chapter 2 described, Committees are generally of the Whole House and any Peer can put any Amendment and speak to it at unbounded length.

However, this gives Peers opportunities far greater than those open to M.P.s to propose Amendments from a personal rather than a strictly party point of view. (It also gives the Government scope for planting Amendments with backbench Peers, even on the Opposition side, as they did with a number on the Transport Bill.) Of course individual Peers can be a nuisance with favourite Amend-

---

[2] *HL Debs.*, vol. 267, col. 400.
[3] A Hansard Society study in 1966 showed that, of the 266 respondents, 79 per cent of Peers felt that attention in their House to party concerns was about right.

ments, but the Government are always polite and often conciliatory. And when Backbenchers are trying to be constructively helpful, Frontbenchers are patient. Lord Hughes's good-natured explanation to Lord Strathclyde on the 1968 Town and Country Planning (Scotland) Bill is typical:

> Perhaps some time, when the noble Lord and I have an hour to spare in the Library, we can sit down and compare the two plans. He will then find that by what he is now suggesting he is asking me to undertake an impossible task and, if I were to undertake it, he would be able to comment on it only in the sort of naval language he never uses in your Lordships' Chamber.[4]

Where Opposition Frontbenchers persist with Amendments to which a Government spokesman in the Lords cannot personally commit his department the exchange between Frontbenchers is often of a graciousness that the Commons would find somewhat out of place. The frankness of ministerial replies is shown by this extract from Lord Kennet's reassuring words to Lord Sandford on the 1968 Medicines Bill:

> I do not want to be procrustean about this, but simply because I feel we might be . . . going into too much detail, I would suggest to the noble Lord that Clause 66 can be amended in another place because it has been amended here. There is a peg for the Government to hang their Amendments on. He has friends there and, if between now and then I or officials from the Ministry of Health can be of any help to him in private conversation by which any improvement can be made by agreement on both sides, then we shall be happy to do so.[5]

There could hardly be a more explicit declaration that the Opposition Amendment in the Lords had given the Government a hook for their own concessions in the Commons, and that the Government were willing to strike a bargain. Such overt demonstrations of concession and conciliation perhaps feature, on occasion, in Commons' proceedings but they are certainly a basic element of the Lords' Parliamentary manners.

Moreover there are times when Peers from all parties unite in intransigent opposition to Government policy—this happened in the case of the British Museum Library and the D-notice affair and, as chapter 6 will show, the Seats Bill was another occasion when the House outfaced the Government front bench. Yet another instance concerned the siting of the third London Airport at Stansted, where

---

[4] *HL Debs.*, vol. 297, cols. 1332-3.   [5] *HL Debs.*, vol. 296, col. 399.

the Government were fully aware of the Lords' hostility after a debate in December 1967.

It is amusing to take a passing glance at the subsequent history of this affair. At Cabinet discussions early in 1968, Ministers agreed that it was highly likely that the Lords would reject an Order should it reach their House but, though the Government themselves wanted another inquiry, to do so by voluntary initiative would mean losing face. On the other hand, to appear to capitulate to an all-party defeat in the Lords might raise the bogy of the Peers' powers over statutory instruments and jeopardize the negotiations on Lords' reform. The Government found a face-saving solution in the change of Minister (from Douglas Jay to Anthony Crosland) in the department most centrally concerned. They then justified the reopening of the inquiry by citing the recommendations of a report of the Council on Tribunals. But the fact that the decision to hold another inquiry was announced on the very day of the Report's publication, when such a decision would never have been taken on the spur of the moment, coupled with the fact that, for weeks before, Cabinet Committee discussions had included Lords' representatives (and in particular Lord Dilhorne, spurred on by Lord Plowden and Lord Goodman), suggests that this was no snap decision. The possibility of Lords' opposition was undoubtedly significant in persuading the Government not to press on with the Order.

In this case in particular it was less difficult for Backbenchers to take a united stand, setting aside purely party considerations, because of the healthy influence of the Crossbenchers. This is such an important clue to understanding how the House works that at this point it is sensible to examine the groups in the Lords that blur party lines and make non-partisanship a respectable attitude to take. These are the Law Lords, the Bishops, and the Crossbenchers who are nominally, and in many cases actually, independent.

c. *Obscuring Party Lines*
The Crossbenchers

The crossbench phenomenon is paraded as the strongest pillar of non-partisanship in the Lords. The White Paper points to 'the evidence that they do not possess any sense of corporate identity or act in any way as an organised group and they resist any tendency . . . to be regarded as such'.[6]

---

[6] Cmnd. 3799, para. 14.

H

At an earlier point, this chapter mentioned that those who ask are sent the 'unlined whip' issued each week by the Whips' Office. This is also sent to the 125 crossbench Peers on Lord Strang's list. In addition they receive a notice of meetings of the crossbench group when topics for Wednesday Motions may be discussed and allocated, or visiting speakers invited. A Peer who wishes to belong to the group has to register his name; this degree of organization suggests that the Crossbenchers are more of a corporate group than the White Paper implies. But Lord Strang emphatically denies that he is in any sense a 'Leader'. The Private Office therefore choose to regard him as a 'co-ordinator' of the Crossbenchers, along with Baroness Swanborough (before her death in 1971), and the Earl of Shannon. While the exact status of the organizing co-ordinators is ambiguous, the Leader's Private Secretary finds it prudent to keep in touch with them in planning forthcoming business.

The figures in the White Paper show that, of the Whole House, one-third continue to call themselves Crossbenchers (Tables 3 and 4). At first glance this is a strikingly large proportion and suggests a significant amount of crossbench influence. But it is worth looking more closely at the composition of this group. In fact, very many of these Crossbenchers attend the House extremely rarely. They are in large degree the sort of Peers who fall into the category of non-attenders. Indeed, of the total number of Peers who do not attend, as many as nine-tenths are Crossbenchers, taking no party whip. The preponderant majority of these are hereditary Peers. On everyday occasions, therefore, their influence as a body (though not perhaps as individuals) is less remarkable than a superficial reading implies.

Though half the Peers taking no party whip never come to the House, that leaves half who do attend at least some of the time. These are mostly intermittent attenders, of whom about a third sit on the cross benches. Life Peers form the majority and again this is to be expected. These are often distinguished men and women with heavy professional or voluntary commitments outside the House, 'Peers of occasional excellence', those who disdain political party or feel it improper to take a party affiliation when they are unlikely to come to the House regularly.

Of the working House of regular attenders, about a sixth are Crossbenchers. Half are hereditary Peers and half Life Peers and the evidence from proceedings in Hansard and from the Division

Lists shows that as a group they do show an independent attitude in their speeches. They also tend to split fairly evenly when they vote. To that extent, the remarks in the White Paper are appropriate. As a corporate group their voting behaviour is not foreseeable and they do resist any implication that they will swing, as a body, to one side or another. As individuals, however, the Crossbenchers are more predictable.

Many regular attenders in the House, on front and back benches, maintain that they can estimate which way at least half the Crossbenchers will vote in a Division and the Whips are still more confident that they know pretty well where the basic loyalties of individual Crossbenchers lie and which are worth 'sounding out' on particular issues. Theories explaining why individuals refrain from taking a party whip range from the plausible to the bizarre— sensible explanations include the point that Lords Lieutenants by convention sit on the cross benches, or the feelings of former civil servants that they should retain their impartiality. One Peer, whose colleagues suggest that he sits on the cross benches 'out of Loyalty to his predecessor as Master of the College' is probably only enjoying a freedom from the party whip, a freedom that he deserves after long years of obedience to the party whip in the Commons.

Some former politicians become genuine Crossbenchers, Lord Boothby, for example. Viscount Dilhorne, the former Conservative Lord Chancellor, followed the obligatory practice of dropping his party affiliation on becoming a Law Lord (and, being of a teasing disposition, undoubtedly appreciates his liberty). It is also conventional for Peers holding Chairmanships of nationalized industries or Government Boards to sit on the cross benches, like Lord Hill, Lord Wigg, or Lord Aylestone, so that they might seem to be above party politics. In recent years, however, the Leaders of the House have tended to feel that this practice is unnecessary, 'contributing to the stuffy sexlessness of the House', for such Peers, if they have obvious party sympathies, can always refrain from speaking on their own industries. By taking a seat with their party they would avoid bringing the cross benches into disrepute by affecting non-partisan status. Still, these 'crypto-Crossbenchers', as some Peers wryly describe them, are influenced by motives that are admittedly less mysterious than those which persuade some Lord Mayors to leave their parties during their term of office.

Backbenchers as well as party Leaders see that the purpose of the cross benches is easily abused and they value the presence of an independent element.[7] Some individual Crossbenchers describe themselves as 'men of reason' and others, who may nevertheless vote regularly with one party or another, still feel that the very possibility of their fickleness provides a stimulus to the House and to the Whips, especially now that twentieth-century politics is largely dominated by the two major parties. Indeed, Peers clung staunchly to the principle of keeping independent members when reform proposals were debated in 1968. But, as the last chapter will recount, extreme opponents of reform were able to exploit the absurdities of a situation where issues might be determined by a non-elected group of 'political eunuchs', as Michael Foot described them, in direct contradiction to the elected, partisan members of the Commons.

Whether the public, the Commons, or the Press attach much importance to the crossbench phenomenon is questionable. But it is easy to see how this group fits into the House and even assists other Peers who do take a party affiliation on occasions when they feel moved to vote against their party. On such occasions the Crossbenchers help to crystallize opinion in the Whole House.

Certainly they exemplify several features that are particularly characteristic of the style of the Upper House. They are there, they assert, not for purely personal or political motives but for the purpose of service to the public and the House. Like the House as a whole, they intervene in affairs not as a matter of course but when they feel they can be properly useful or influential. And lastly, at a time when the Second Chamber must be wary of directly challenging the Lower House, and only undertake it with the excuse that such challenge is for reasons of senatorial wisdom rather than party interest, it is fortunate that the Lords contain a flourishing group that preserves a core of non-party detachment.

It is in this context, too, that those who wish to defend the presence of the Bishops can make a case. This group deserves a section to itself.

---

[7] In Dec. 1967 the Hansard Society asked Peers about their attitude to Lords' reform and in a straw poll 42 per cent wanted to retain 'an important element of Crossbenchers with a determining influence'—although 21 per cent did not and 37 per cent did not care.

The Bishops

The White Paper[8] sets out the role of the twenty-six Bishops (the Archbishops of Canterbury and York, the Bishops of London, Durham, and Winchester and the twenty-one most senior Bishops) who are entitled to attend the House. Diocesan duties make it difficult for them to come regularly but, as an article by Gavin Drewry has shown, a large proportion try to make use of their privilege and they participate in proceedings to a significant degree, with an impressive impact considering their small numbers.[9] They tend to come to the House in ones or twos and very often the task of giving a speech from the Bishops' Bench falls to that Prelate whose turn it is on the weekly rota for Prayers. Bishops will, however, flock to the House between speeches at Meetings of the General Synod in Westminster.

The duty of organizing the rota lies with the Archbishop of Canterbury's lay secretary, who as a civil servant knows the Whitehall ropes. With the help of officials of the House he will therefore draw the Bishops' attention to matters which may interest them from a diocesan, episcopal, or individual point of view. But there is no sort of summons to the Bishops' Bench as a whole though an additional consequence of the secretary's efforts may be to bring a couple of Bishops to the House for debates when Peers might welcome a 'moral' view.

Peers, including the Bishops themselves, stress that each Prelate is independent. As Drewry's article shows, they have not shrunk from disagreement on fundamental points, particularly on 'moral-clerical' issues rather than on political topics. Their differences, on clauses of the 1965–66 Abortion Bill, the 1966–67 Sunday Entertainment Bill, or the 1969 Divorce Reform Bill tended to be few but deep-rooted. Some close observers of the House have expressed surprise at the way in which the Bishops, especially the Archbishop of Canterbury, stood up during this period for views whose liberality would have astonished the Lords a decade ago.

Even when some overwhelmingly controversial issue has brought a number of Bishops to the House, there has never been in any sense a 'whip from Lambeth'. Although there may have been some discreet telephoning beforehand, it was certainly not in any party-political sense, for instance, that the Bishops acted when on the

---

[8] Cmnd. 3799, p. 24.   [9] *Parliamentary Affairs* (1971–2).

Southern Rhodesia Bill eighteen of them voted to impose sanctions. Nor was this the case (as the Bishop of Southwark, a Labour supporter, pointed out in his speech) when a number voted against the Government on the Seats Bill, or when five Bishops and the Archbishop of Canterbury voted against the Government on the 1968 Commonwealth Immigrants Bill.[10] So independent of party did the Bishops show themselves to be during this period (in contrast to their historic role, as the *Parliamentary Affairs* article shows) that a few Peers suggested that true Independents should take their seats in a row behind the Bishops' bench rather than on the cross benches.

As individual contributors too, the Bishops' part is interesting. Their legislative and deliberative contribution is far from limited to Church affairs. On issues affecting their diocese Bishops take a quasi-constituency interest; the Bishop of Chester on foot-and-mouth disease or the Chester Assay Office, the Bishop of Truro on the Torrey Canyon accident, the Bishop of Exeter on Dartmoor Prison, and the Bishop of Durham on unemployment and the North-East provide some of the many examples. (Indeed, in February 1971 the Bishop of Derby wrote a letter to *The Times* about the effects on his diocese of the collapse of the Rolls-Royce company, using the newspaper columns because, he said, he had no seat in the Lords from which to speak.) And like every other Peer, each Bishop can also contribute his own peculiar knowledge and experience, whether it is as specific as that of the Bishop of Norwich, a trained geologist and Antarctic explorer, or the Bishop of Blackburn, a member of the National Union of General and Municipal Workers, or as wide as that of the Bishop of Coventry, who was Bishop for the Forces, or the Bishop of Chester, president of the Pedestrians' Association.

The Bishops themselves question whether representatives of the Established Church, and only that Church, should continue to enjoy the privilege of sitting as Lords Spiritual and, if so, whether twenty-six is not too large a number.[11] The discussions on Lords' reform have not settled the matter but in the late 1960s and early 1970s, at least, it can be said confidently that, whatever the historical and sentimental reasons for their continued presence

---

[10] Compare the vote on the 1971 Commonwealth Immigrants Bill when the Archbishop of Canterbury and the Bishop of Coventry spoke against it and with three other Bishops voted both against the Second Reading and in favour of the Opposition Motion deploring its effects. *HL Debs.*, vol. 320, col. 989.

[11] See Report of the Archbishop's Commission on Church and State, p. 155.

there, from a practical point of view the Bishops played as valuable a role in Lords' proceedings as any of the recently created Life Peers.

The Law Lords

The other group sitting in the House on a basis other than purely hereditary right are the Law Lords, comprising the Lord Chancellor and serving Lords of Appeal in Ordinary (with a statutory maximum of eleven), former Lord Chancellors and retired Lords of Appeal, and other Peers, like the Lord Chief Justice or the Master of the Rolls, who held or had once had high judicial office. Their functions, as the White Paper indicated, are two: the judicial, arising from the Lords' position as the supreme appellate court of the United Kingdom, and the more general function as specialist members of the Upper House.

The judicial side of their work means that they are constant attenders, although often preoccupied outside the Chamber itself.[12] As Gavin Drewry's analysis of their attendance in 1958-67 shows, though they are 'by no means passive spectators on the legislative touchline . . . they could hardly be regarded as cheerleaders'.[13] However, their professional expertise can lead them to make significant interventions, especially on the technicalities of legislation concerning legal tradition and the prerogatives of the courts. The section in chapter 1 on the Legalists' contribution to proceedings illustrates their more general role. Moreover, the fact that many Law Lords have presided over Royal Commissions, Tribunals, and Courts of Inquiry and other official investigations gives them added authority in debate. The rest of the House respects the Law Lords' strong convention of political neutrality, both for its own sake and for the implication that it preserves some mysterious essence of non-partisanship that pervades the Lords as a whole.

Other Groups

Apart from their specific contributions to Lords' activity, Crossbenchers, Law Lords, and Bishops thus play an obvious role in smoothing out party-political divisions. But there are few other groups which seem to cut across party lines, and, unlike the Commons, the Lords have no numerous small splinter groups or Subject Committees of members interested in specific topics. (Peers can

---

[12] See also L. Blom-Cooper and G. Drewry, *Final Appeal* (1973).
[13] *Parliamentary Affairs* (1968-9).

always join Commons' groups, of their own party, but many feel
uncomfortable if not unwelcome.)

The Scottish Peers, however, have their own association and
when Scottish business—roads, education, agriculture, or industrial
development—is discussed they do seem to be a discernible group.
They have been especially vehement in demanding better facilities
at Turnhouse Airport. In this part of the country M.P.s are often
few and far between and local Peers take a paternal interest in their
neighbours' and tenants concerns.[14]

Peers who come from the North-East and South-West have
a certain sense of community and occasionally meet to discuss
debates about their regions but, like groups of Peers interested in
ports and shipping and 'Services' Peers, these are very much *ad
hoc* coalitions. Trade union Peers, mostly among the Labour party,
sometimes try to act as a ginger group, especially if they feel that
their M.P.s are not sufficiently assertive. As in the Commons, pro-
and anti-Common Marketeers also straddle party lines.

It is noteworthy that while the Lords often draw attention to the
distinctive contributions of lawyers and younger Peers, they less
frequently pick out women as a special group. This is despite the
fact that in July 1970 there were twenty Life Peeresses and eleven
Peeresses by succession receiving Writs, of whom nearly all attended
the House regularly, specializing in different subjects no less than
the men and taking their full share of frontbench burdens. Although
a few Peers can be heard attributing minor changes in offices or
occasional acerbities to temperamental fluctuations among the
women, or ungallantly confiding that many Peeresses have become
hardened by their long fight to establish themselves in politics or
the professions, these are striking exceptions. On controversial
questions, too, the Peeresses are ready to disregard a party line and
be outspoken. If women Peers are thought of at all as a separate
group, they appear to carry fewer passengers amongst their numbers than the men.[15]

[14] After 1963 the Scottish Peers no longer sent only sixteen representatives to the House
but two unwritten conventions that had operated since 1806 may have bolstered their
corporate spirit. In the first election after the Irish Union, Scottish representatives decided
that no son should be elected in the room of his father, in order to ensure a fair distribution
of seats between families over time, and that if any representative Peer failed to vote at the
election for all his fifteen nominated colleagues, at the succeeding election none of them
would vote for him. These conventions lapsed after 1945 and now live only in the memories
of the older Lords.

[15] Since 1971 the women Peers have played a significant part in debates on such matters

D. *A Semi-detached Existence*

Peers of long standing often reassure new members that they have joined 'the best club in Europe'—'in touch with affairs, no entry fee, no subscription . . .' to which Earl Attlee was once heard to reply dryly that, yes, he supposed it could be called a sort of semi-detached existence. To those unaccustomed to its ways, the House of Lords indeed seems detached, curiously cut off from the less gracious life of the Commons and of the outside world. It is to some degree, as this chapter has shown, aloof from the cruder edges of party politics. Its proceedings appear to be ordered by a mixture of ancient precedents and artful *ad hoc* devices, but, even in that mellow world, informal conventions of proper behaviour are respected and perpetuated. This responsibility falls upon all Peers and upon the Offices and Sessional Committees of the House.

The Parliament Office

The Clerks of the House advise Peers on precedent and on the appropriate application of Standing Orders but within the penumbra of strictly procedural advice they may also suggest to an individual member what course of action is in his own best interest. The specific duties of the Clerk of the Parliaments and the other Clerks are described in the *Companion*; here it is only necessary to mention that the Parliament Office is another important force in maintaining Lords' traditions. There were only fifteen Lords' Clerks in 1973, compared with forty-three in the Commons, and, although their offices have an elegance that Trollope would recognize, their tasks are far more onerous than in the nineteenth century. But communication is easier (even telepathic) amongst such a small group.

The Clerks' continuity of experience and depth of judgement often give them a different perspective on affairs. They undertake much of the detailed management of business and the task of spelling out Standing Orders to Peers who are muddled or lazy about such matters. Where larger issues are concerned, the Leader and his frontbench team seek Clerks' opinion on the wisdom of different procedural strategies or the problems of managing a restless House. The fact that some Clerks, notably the Leader's Private

as the Sex Discrimination Bill and the Amendments to the National Health Service Bill concerning free contraception. Women all over the world seem to be more vigorously self-conscious and the Peeresses are no exception. They are now a sizeable and established group in the Upper House, and this undoubtedly increases their self-awareness.

Secretary, can carry the confidences of the Leader of the Opposition and understand his difficulties as much as those of the Leader gives their discretionary and explanatory role added importance.

The Clerks serve the various departments of the Parliament Office: the Public Bill Office, the Private Bill Office, the Committee Office, the Judicial Office, the Journal Office, the Printed Paper Office, the Record Office, and the Accountant's Office. They also assist the Select and Sessional Committees of the House. Chapter 2 discussed the Select Committees (on Public Bills or Unopposed Private Bills, for instance); Sessional Committees are composed of Peers serving for a whole Session rather than for the consideration of a particular legislative issue.

The Lord Chairman of Committees, in consultation with the Whips, is traditionally responsible for selecting nominees and encouraging Peers to put their names forward for service. The House itself approves the composition of the Committees at the beginning of each Session. Peers are by no means dumbly acquiescent in the Motions put forward by the Leader and Lord Chairman. The Select Committee appointed to consider the televising of Lords' proceedings was reconstituted after protestations by the Marquess of Salisbury, who considered that the minority opposing the experiment were inadequately represented. Backbenchers intermittently complain that newer or younger Peers are disregarded in favour of well-entrenched familiar members. (In November 1971 the House approved long-hatched recommendations in the Procedure Committee's First Report that members of Sessional Committees should retire by rotation after three years' service, although after one Session has elapsed they can be reappointed. The Lord Chancellor, Lord Chairman, party Leaders and Whips, and the crossbench Co-ordinator are exempt from this convention.) It is part of the Lord Chairman's duties to see that a balance is kept between front and back bench, senior and junior, reactionary and progressive members, as well as between different parties in the House.

The Lord Chairman of Committees

In some respects the Lord Chairman's role is like that of a Speaker, for historically his responsibility has been to ensure fair play between the Government and other parties when the House is in Committee and he himself (or one of the panel of Deputy Chairmen) in the Chair. His office is salaried and he is appointed at the beginning of every Session, not as a member of the Government by the Crown by Commission. When making announcements about forthcoming administrative arrangements, the Lord Chairman speaks from the Government front bench, whatever his own political sympathies. Though his personal loyalties may be well known (as Lord Chairman throughout the 1964-70 Labour Government, the Earl of Listowel was an avowed Labour supporter) the Lord Chairman finds it prudent not to take part in strictly political controversy.[16]

As previous chapters have explained, the Lords customarily meet in a Committee of the Whole House and here the Lord Chairman will preside. He is also a member—and takes the Chair—of most of the sessional Committees, where some matters of procedure, privilege, and administration are considered by smaller bodies of delegated members. This is less cumbersome than their being considered by the Whole House deliberating together.

The Sessional Committees

Some of these need only be mentioned here—the Leave of Absence Committee, for example, and Committees set up to consider particular types of legislation, like Special Orders, Personal Bills, Private Bills, Consolidation Bills, or ecclesiastical matters. Appellate and Appeal Committees belong more suitably to a study of the judicial functions of the House. The Committee of Selection rarely meets, and in practice the Lord Chairman carries out its functions of choosing and proposing Peers to serve on Select Committees (on Opposed and Personal Bills, for instance).[17]

The Privileges Committee also meets infrequently, for the Lords seem loath to fuss about questions of their privilege, of claims to peerage and to precedence. In recent years it has met only to deal with arrangements for the Introduction of Scottish Peers after passage of the 1963 Peerage Act and to hear the Petition of the Irish Peers. Where issues of privilege are concerned the Commons show more jealousy than the Lords.

The two Committees which deserve closer examination are the Procedure and Offices Committees, because it is their members

[16] The Lord Chairman also sits on the Woolsack at the beginning of the afternoon if the Lord Chancellor is engaged on judicial business. Peers like the Lord Chancellor to be present in person if there is an Introduction.

[17] Sessional Committees and their membership are fully described in the *Companion*, pp. 175-9 and in the First Report of the 1972 Procedure Committee.

who in the first instance act as the guardians and innovators of custom. Their Reports to Whole House recommend what adaptations there should be in the manner of conducting business and of everyday behaviour.

The Procedure Committee

This consists of thirty-two Peers, including the Lord Chancellor, the three Leaders, three Chief Whips, and the crossbench Co-ordinator, with the Lord Chairman in the chair. They consider whether changes in procedure are advisable and, if so, how Standing Orders shall be altered. If, for example, there is argument in the chamber on some procedural point (a Peer trying to speak after the Question has been put, perhaps, or rising after the Minister's reply to an Unstarred Question), the House will often devise some suitable compromise and then refer the matter to the Committee. On longer-term questions, they will have a series of meetings before preparing a Report to the Whole House. Here the ingenuity and attitudes of the Clerk serving the Committee and its sub-groups can be of fundamental importance. Indeed, in recent years energetic Leaders and Clerks and inquisitive Backbenchers questioning old assumptions have tended to refer far more frequently to the Committee. A flood of reports has appeared. Between 1919 and 1940 there had been only two reports, each of a single page. In the period 1964-70 this Committee produced twenty-five reports, covering ninety-nine pages and, in addition, setting out a great deal of useful evidence. (In the first two months of 1972 there had already been two more.)

The need to find new procedures for a more active House (and one that was particularly introspective at the time when Lords' reform was so much in the air) and to spell out traditions and precedents for recently appointed Peers has prompted a number of innovations. These have ranged from the manner of conducting Divisions to the complete rewriting of Standing Orders. The House is generally, though sometimes cautiously, ready to accept the Committee's recommendations.

Conventions of Debate. Only with the acquiescence of the Whole House, however, can such reform be put into practice and in considering how the Lords regulate their own proceedings it is necessary to remember that everything is done only 'with the Leave of the House'. In some cases, where to grant Leave might deny to any Peer the opportunity to speak or to object, to which he is always entitled, the consent of the House to grant Leave has to be unanimous and the objection of a single Peer can withhold it. In other cases, where the convenience of the House is concerned, Leave can be granted by a majority. While Peers may be unaware of the refined application of these terms they nevertheless attach great importance to the concept, beginning speeches with: 'My Lords, with the permission of the House . . .', 'If noble Lords will give me leave to intervene for a second time . . .', 'May I remind noble Lords . . .' Peers address each other, not a Speaker, and restrain their colleagues with cries of 'Question', deflecting speeches into an interrogative form, or 'Order', sometimes silencing an offender altogether.

Long Speeches. Loquacity is a common complaint in legislative assemblies and in the Lords, where every Peer by custom has an equal right to speak, without fear of closure or a guillotine, the problem is compounded as attendance continues to rise. It is for the Whole House to express their impatience and in the last resort a Peer can move 'that the noble Lord be no longer heard'. The device was last used in May 1960 but it is generally avoided for as the Motion is itself debatable its use only prolongs discussion.

Some Peers are persistent offenders and on average Frontbenchers and Peers introducing debates take twenty-five minutes and Backbenchers fifteen. The Procedure Committee have discarded suggestions for mechanical warnings, cards, or mandatory time-limits and have recommended experiments with large clocks to show a speaker how long he is taking.[18] Just as the Commons' Speaker can usefully interrupt M.P.s, the Lords' Chief Whip will more gently remind the Lords of the numbers wishing to speak, if his own interventions to announce arrangements for dinner or for taking business give him the opportunity. When they are reminded of their loquacious tendencies, as in Lord Egremont's Motion that speeches should be shorter,[19] Peers will be brief, but all too often individuals are convinced that their own speeches give proof that a long good speech is better than a bad short one.

---

[18] The clocks have now been installed but they harmonize so discreetly with the panelling that they are difficult to see and easy to ignore. [19] *HL Debs.*, vol. 268, col. 110.

It is considered 'alien to the custom of the House' that speeches should be read but, as in the eighteenth-century Commons where extempore speeches were also expected, the Lords interpret this requirement generously. What does disturb them is any tendency for Peers to intervene and then leave the chamber without awaiting a reply or hearing other speakers. It is customary for any Lord taking part in a debate to remain for as much of it as possible and to give his reasons and apologies if he is called away to another engagement.

The Batting Order. The latter convention is important because it is particularly easy for Peers to just come in and out to deliver their own speeches, since for each debate a speakers' list sets out the batting order with approximate estimates of time. Though it is explicitly declared that the list 'is for guidance only and may be varied', Peers have firmly accepted the principle that queue-jumpers should be reprimanded. Although speakers can swap places (but should explain such mutual arrangements to the House), any participant who has not put his name down beforehand should take his place at the end of the list. Having a list does solve some problems for while all Lords are entitled to contribute there is no Speaker to select and identify participants and no established hierarchy giving precedence, for example, to Privy Councillors or senior members. But other difficulties have arisen since the list was introduced in 1961, not the least of these being sensitivity about the batting order. It has been alleged from time to time that prominent members—party Leaders, a leading Crossbencher, a Bishop—are generally placed at the beginning and 'lesser mortals' at the end. No Peer likes being put at the end or at tea-time and it has been suggested that those to whom the Whips have obligations also have priority. There have been suggestions for an advisory committee to draw up the list, even for a law of the jungle or a ballot but as such expedients would invite lobbying or unseemly scrambling, the system has remained as it is.

In some cases, such as a direct political confrontation between the parties, the Whips do play a predominant part in ordering and balancing speakers; where general debates are concerned, the Mover of the Motion may ask to be consulted. The Leader's Private Secretary acts as conflator, trying to place better speakers throughout a debate with an attempt at a crescendo towards the end, but the ultimate responsibility for the list rests with the Leader himself. He is the representative of the Whole House and Peers can complain to him rather than through official or party channels. At any rate, backbench and frontbench Peers are all agreed that the Commons' system of catching the Speaker's eye is far worse than their own arrangements.

Declaration of Interest. It is customary for Peers to disclose any personal interest they may have in something that is the subject of debate—regulations about launderettes, for instance, or the merits of water-purifying equipment. Similarly, where an outside body, such as the Country Landowners' Association, has indicated its agreement with the view expressed by a Peer, he may mention this but he is not supposed to speak on behalf of such an interest.

In a situation where the House is discussing legislation where a Peer may himself be a party or an advocate who would benefit by some fee or pecuniary reward, it is considered undesirable that he should take part in discussion. (On the War Damage Bill, for example, Lord Shawcross omitted to refer to his interest in Shell, one of the companies involved in Burmah Oil, and this was felt to be an abuse of the trust of the House.) This convention was made explicit after a Peer opposed in the 1950s an Order where one of the parties had retained him as solicitor.

Statutory Disqualification. Some Peers are disqualified from speaking by the terms of their profession or appointment, a condition that has struck some, like Lord Napier and Ettrick, as a deprivation of their constitutional rights and a breach of their Writ. The civil servants' guide to behaviour, *Estacode*, does not permit Lord Napier to engage in political discussion, a rule that also affected Viscount Hood, who took no part in debates for thirty-nine years until he left the Foreign Office.[20] (This Treasury rule originated at the time of the Amritsar massacre when Viscount Cross, a lowly clerk in the Treasury, broke long-standing convention and insisted on voting.) It is interesting that when the Army regulations were drawn up the

[20] Various compromise drafts of a new paragraph in *Estacode* have been tried and discarded. Eventually, in June 1973, Lord Jellicoe managed to have the whole paragraph dropped altogether, in his dual capacity as Minister for the Civil Service Department and Leader of the House of Lords. Civil servants who are Peers are now obliged only to exercise a general caution in entering any political controversy.

authorities were more respectful of Parliamentary rights. Army officers in the Upper House are permitted to engage in debate.

Peers employed by public boards or nationalized industries are not thereby debarred from speaking in the House but if their views differ widely from those of the Board in question it is thought undesirable for them to participate in discussions of its affairs. Chairmen of boards like the B.B.C. or the N.C.B. will certainly not speak in debates relating to their board. This follows guidance set out in the Addison Rules, originally given by Viscount Addison, Leader of the House in 1951, after consultation and agreement between the parties. As the duty of replying to questions affecting a particular board, or public boards in general, rests with Ministers only and should not devolve upon Lords who also happen to be members of boards, it is clearly advisable for them to keep silent. They thus avoid the risk of usurping Ministers' functions and of disclosing information which might allow the House to exert a measure of Parliamentary supervision over matters of management.[21]

This guidance is ambiguous where Chairmen of Royal Commissions are concerned but it is generally considered proper for them to speak in defence of their Reports. The Earl of Halsbury's speech on the decimalization of the currency and Lord Redcliffe-Maud's exposition of his Commission's thinking on the reform of local government are two examples.

Improper Subjects. To avoid anything that may bring the two Houses into conflict or allow debate in the Lords to become a mere continuation of a Commons' debate, Peers do not quote directly from speeches made in the Lower House unless they are Ministerial speeches relating to Government policy. Nor will they mention by name or identity for purposes of criticism private members of the Commons.[22]

The Lords are hurt when the Commons fail to reciprocate these courtesies. In July 1968, for instance, Lord Leatherland regretted an M.P.'s description of the Lords as 'lethargic'. Peers were especially resentful because, in Lord Carrington's words, 'the

---

[21] Lord Melchett did speak in the 1971 E.E.C. debate on the implications of entry for the Steel industry (of which he was Chairman) but this breach of convention attracted no public attention.

[22] *HL Debs.*, vol. 293, col. 1119.

Commons debated all their measures at their convenience, and we sit through the rest of the summer debating them here'.

Extra care, too, is needed in the Lords' relations with the Press. (As a Peer and a journalist, the Earl of Arran committed a double offence in writing an *Evening News* article on Tory backwoodsmen.) While less swift than the Commons to lay complaints of contempt before the Privileges Committee, Peers do not hesitate to express their displeasure at unfair newspaper articles. A discussion in *The Times* in June 1968 concerning memoranda to the House from the Co-operative Insurance Society is a case in point.[23] Feeling that the Press are quick to mock their proceedings the House carefully avoids 'off-colour' questions or remarks imputing undesirable motives to others. Interventions from other Peers quickly silence those who raise 'unsuitable' subjects. In the D-notice affair, for instance, Lord Chalfont warned against acrimonious discussions of personalities. Lord Longford once deplored Lord Wells-Pestell's observations on the financial interests of the Rhodesia lobby and Lord Glendevon was advised not to press questions on the sale of the Duccio painting by auction.[24]

Style. The point of the Lords, its members are anxious to empha-size, is that Peers speak on what they know about, not on every possible occasion (as, they assert, M.P.s are wont to do to please their constituencies). Speeches must be relevant and, according to one critical Crossbencher, Peers should not lecture the House nor seem to speak 'for their own prestige'. In fact, a typical mannerism of the House is for a speaker to disdain any pretensions to special knowledge and then to reveal by modest argument that he is actually superbly equipped to illuminate the matter under discussion. The speeches of Lord Bourne on Burma, for example, or Lord Gore-Booth on the Duncan Report exemplify such quiet authority.

New Peers, however distinguished their careers, sometimes say that as amateurs they feel intimidated by the experts that the Lords produce on almost any subject, but eventually most Peers discover some field in which they can contribute. The House is tolerant to maiden speakers, expecting them only to avoid long or controversial remarks. Some new Peers in the 1960s, particularly ex-M.P.s,

[23] *HL Debs.*, vol. 284, col. 767.
[24] *HL Debs.*, vol. 271, col. 244; vol. 304, col. 249.

require gentle restraint rather than hearty encouragement, for they are occasionally over-eager to unravel matters of policy in which they have themselves been involved and are enchanted by a chamber in which there are no curbs on eloquence.

Former M.P.s also tend to feel that their Commons' training has equipped them to launch unfledged into debates in the Lords but the style of speaking in the Upper House requires some apprenticeship. Pointed remarks are veiled in diplomatic words; as Lord Champion says: 'In the Lords we use the best plush.' Proceedings do not decline into a deathly consensus, because sometimes provocative speeches are made, but asperity of speech is explicitly discouraged. The Clerk may be asked to read Standing Order 29 should 'heat be engendered in debate'. Occasionally Peers clash— Lord Gifford ruffled some older members at first—or infrequent attenders will come and make a fiery speech to arouse what they describe as 'a row of extinct volcanoes'. But in general the House is very tolerant of even the most unusual views (Lord Macleod of Fuinary on pacificism, Lord Milford on Vietnam) and if objections are voiced, other Peers will always intervene to smooth over the situation.

The style of debate, with carefully constructed speeches of a rational kind, diffident observation, intricate compliments, lengthy apologies and explanations, certainly tends to lack what many Peers describe, somewhat wistfully, as 'the cut and thrust' of the Commons. Vague though they may be about what constitutes 'cut and thrust', many do feel that their debates lack verve and excitement, and younger Peers and ex-M.P.s[25] in particular find this frustrating. But, as one hereditary Peer, a rueful 43, remarked, as time passes and the age-gap narrows, one becomes more tolerant.

Only by gradual acclimatization can Peers become used to such subtle courtesies and it is important that all Peers be encouraged to remind each other of these traditions, intervening in proceedings if necessary. The Leader of the House is heavily armed with precedent but even his arguments may be contradicted by the more ancient or better-informed. Moreover, in his dual role as Leader of the House and of his party, he tries to avoid asserting himself as

---

[25] The newly ennobled Sidney Herbert, for example, found speaking to the Lords 'like addressing sheeted tombstones by moonlight'. (C. Woodham-Smith, *Florence Nightingale 1820–1910* (1950), p. 358.)

primus inter pares. Accordingly, other party Leaders and Whips, the Lord Chancellor, the Lord Chairman, the crossbench Co-ordinator, and other elder statesmen in the House intervene in support, to prevent the Leader's over-exposure. Backbenchers too are exhorted to see that order is kept, preserving the unique self-regulating decorum of which they are so proud.[26]

An 'Enclave par excellence'.[27] The physical arrangements of the chamber encourage friendly exchange rather than hostile debate. The cross benches mean that discussion is not automatically polarized between opposite ranks of benches. Peers wander in and out of the chamber all the time (even crossing over for a whispered explanation with a colleague elsewhere in the House), flocking in to hear an eminent maiden speaker, an acknowledged wit or expert, or a respected elder statesman when word gets about that he is on his feet. (As individual Peers rise, announcements are made on a loudspeaker system installed throughout the Palace. Closed-circuit television is now being introduced.)

While the Peers seem to enter and leave the chamber casually, nodding to acquaintances and opening their mail, proceedings have a sense of dignity and ceremonial importance, enhanced by their surroundings of stained glass and gilded wood, brass rails and thick blue carpets, buttoned red-leather benches and statues of kings and ancestors (like debating in a Gothic cathedral, one Bishop observed).

Because people do not have to come to the House or stay when their business is done, it is perhaps easier for Peers to tolerate each other's company and in the early 1960s, when there was still plenty of space in the Library, bars, and dining-rooms, no one was forced to mingle for long with those of a different social or professional group and there was little intrusion on individual privacy. The substantial increase in attendance has somewhat upset this cosy world and the Offices Committee have recommended arrangements for improving accommodation and amenities. Nevertheless the

---

[26] According to the Tenth Report: 'Within the terms of our Standing Orders, we have great flexibility in our procedure, and we are therefore able to conduct our business expeditiously, politely and sensibly. We are not troubled by points of order, nor by the exploitation of time-wasting procedural devices which are often to be observed in other legislative assemblies.'

[27] A quotation from Lord Snow's novel *Last Things* (1970), in which the narrator takes his seat as a Life Peer.

Lords remains more of a physically comfortable haven than the Commons.

The Offices Committee and Black Rod

The responsibility for all the domestic arrangements of the House, for accommodation, staffing, and estimates, rests with the fifty-four members of the Offices Committee and its five Sub-Committees (on Administration, Estimates, the Library, the Refreshment Department, and Works of Art). The Gentleman Usher of the Black Rod (who is also the Sergeant-at-Arms) and his deputy, the Yeoman Usher, are the officials who carry out on behalf of this Committee the control of services and accommodation in the Lords' part of the Palace. As Keeper of the Doors, Black Rod supervises the admission of strangers during sittings. (In 1970 there were 45,295 visitors to the Strangers' Gallery.) He is also responsible for maintaining efficient but discreet precautions against disorder and disturbance and his duties have increased considerably since the late 1960s when security precautions for the Palace of Westminster were improved.

The House of Lords runs smoothly and politely (even the catering services make a profit, unlike those of the Commons) and Peers sometimes become tediously self-congratulatory when they speak of its warmth and cordiality. One politically sharp Front-bencher wondered if the lack of bitterness meant: 'we're hypocrites? No, I don't think so—we're not really the political half of Parliament so we can be low-key.'

Certainly a common regard for the conventional decorum of the House owes much to the high average age (over 65) of its members and to the fact that they enjoy much common experience—speeches frequently include references to shared schooldays, war service, political careers. There is no hesitation in offering not only formal condolences or tributes but even birthday greetings, welcomes after illness, and so forth.

An important feature of the Peers' own dining-room is the common lunch table,[28] encouraging Peers to mix at random for a short period of the day, and providing astute Leaders of the House with an opportunity for general soundings.

Peers stress that there is 'a genuine equality here. No distinction

---

[28] As well as the square crumpets that are unique to the Lords.

between what sort of Peer you are', and this applies to party and age and sex as much as to rank in the peerage. Curious though their establishment may seem to the outside world, the Lords themselves suggest that the overworked description of the House as 'the best club in the world' is indeed true:

A good library, all the books and newspapers you could want . . .

Intelligent and congenial people to talk to . . . and the best restaurant in London . . .

A nice club for women . . .

I feel I'm *liked* . . .

All nice chaps here . . . [Lord Montgomery of Alamein].

A good deal of club whiggery, but a clergymen's club, with a feeling of basic identity . . .

A terribly kind place. Old Stansgate said it was corruptingly *nice* . . .

Very agreeable. Everyone is here to help you, as the Doorkeepers said when I first came . . .

In this comfortable atmosphere it is not surprising that the Lords manage to restrain their more violent passions. To some observers, however, it appears that such a harmonious enclave is a mere anachronistic luxury, an expensive irrelevance in the legislative system. Before this question can be broached and the Lords' role at the present can be properly treated, it is necessary to describe the other, more partisan side of the Lords, for it would be inaccurate to suggest that party divisions are wholly absent. This is the theme of chapter 4.

4

PARTY POLITICS

SELF-CONTROLLED though they were, the Peers sniffed an under-current of political tension in the autumn air of October 1964. They were not, as in 1909, spoiling for a fight. The mood was more like that of 1945, an awareness that at all costs any clash between Lords and Commons must be on carefully chosen ground. The party Leaders, in particular, were interested in presenting their chamber as a useful working adjunct to the Commons rather than a perverse obstructionist Upper House and this desire was especially strong at a time when thoughts of reform were in the wind. The Conservative front bench did not relish the prospect of large regular majorities of blindly loyal backwoodsmen defeating the Government and bringing the House and the Tory party into disrepute. The Labour front bench, for their part, wished to tackle a heavy legislative programme as expeditiously and unprovocatively as possible.

But if Conservative and Labour Peers were to join battle, they could in 1964 look forward to an even contest. Chapter 1 showed how the 1958 Life Peerages Act and subsequent creations had levelled the party balance among the working House. For the first time Labour Peers could rejoice in numbers sufficiently augmented to enjoy the business of governing and the Conservatives could at last oppose the Government without feeling that they were bullying weaklings. Even the Crossbenchers and Liberals, with an optimism typical of third and fourth parties, hoped for a role where they would no longer just redress an imbalance but might actually on occasion decide an outcome.

The available evidence shows that the gap between Labour and Conservative had become narrow where regular attenders were concerned. Though the tables[1] quoted in chapter 1 do not refer to the beginning of the period but to the 1967-68 Session, roughly in the middle, they are the best estimate of party commitment that

[1] Tables 3 and 4. See appendix.

can be obtained. Normally the party Whips would not disclose the
names and numbers of those on their lists but these statistics were
prepared as a background to discussions on Lords' reform, when
all party Leaders were as anxious to be as accurate and co-operative
as possible. Nor are works of reference any guide. In such sources
as the *Parliamentary Companion* almost half the Peers are shown
with no party affiliation, in keeping with the fact that Backbenchers
are free agents with a freehold seat in Parliament. The White Paper
statistics reflect this, showing that of the Whole House of 1,062
Peers fully 554 received no party whip.

But not surprisingly the proportion of 'non-affiliated' Peers drops
in the categories of those attending regularly. Of the working House
of 291 Peers, all but 52 took a party whip and acknowledged some
party commitment. It is interesting to speculate why so large a proportion of the working House do describe themselves as belonging
to one of the three major political parties, when taking a whip is
not essential in the Lords and a Peer's freehold seems to be one of
its chief advantages. But as the figures are relevant to a study of
political tension only if 'taking the whip' implies more than a predi-
lection for sitting on one side of the House rather than another, first
one should explore what significance is attached to this purely
voluntary party affiliation.

A. *Accepting the Whip*

Chapter 3 described the preparation in the Whips' Office of the
notice of forthcoming business and the way in which the Whips for
each party circulate their supporters, after underlining certain items.
All parties send the whip to any Peer requesting it (Labour Peers
have to be subscribers to their local party). It is possible that new
Peers will not make up their minds for some time and ask for the
crossbench 'non-whip' until they settle for one of the three major
parties. Even the non-whip does not arrive automatically and the
Co-ordinator has to be informed. When a Peer decides to take
a whip, he finds space on the appropriate benches and asks his Chief
Whip if he may receive the weekly notice. None of this is as intimi-
dating a business as it sounds. Though the initiative is left to the
individual, in fact the various party Leaders are interested to know
what choice a new Peer will make and they, or their colleagues, will
jolly him along.

Occasionally a Peer resigns the whip but floor-crossing happens very rarely. It occurs only when a Peer has spoken or voted so constantly in contradiction to the general line of his front bench that it seems suitable to suggest that he may be happier outside the party or with another.[2] Though Peers remark on it when a colleague votes once or twice with the other side, this is tolerated good-humouredly and even respected as a manifestation of healthy independence, unless of course the issue is a crucial one. Only in very unusual circumstances does a Peer lose the whip at the Leader's deliberate request. (This has happened only once during the twenty-five years before 1971, when apparently the Conservative Chief Whip felt that a Peer's conduct in the Division Lobbies and his personal behaviour in the precincts of the House were embarrassing to the party.) There are no sanctions for disregarding the whip, save a reputation for unreliability, and, according to some, difficulty in securing a good place on the speakers' list.

Former M.P.s habitually express surprise at the looseness of the Lords' whip. No one seems to object very strongly if they fail to support their party on an everyday occasion and the Chief Whip receives apologies for absence with grateful astonishment. Those who have scruples about voting against the party can abstain or stay away, and in the Lords there is no need for a system of 'pairing'.

In fact there is among all parties some shyness about talking about whips at all. This is partly associated with the confusion about whether or not the Lords should be organized on explicit party lines like the Commons. Peers reiterate as part of the catechism of the autonomous Backbencher that Lords' whips advise and warn but do not coerce. They emphasize that the weekly notice is a whip in the sense of the routine weekly whip in the nineteenth-century House of Commons—an announcement of forthcoming business, not an order to attend, and still less to behave in a required fashion.

As on the Commons' whip, however, particular items are underlined. A single underlining for the Lords signifies that 'your attention is particularly drawn to this'; two lines that 'there is likely to be a Division on this subject and your presence will be appreciated'; three lines are very rare in the Lords and used only when a Division

---

[2] Some examples in the last fifteen years are: Lord Arran (Con. to Lib.); Lord Greenway (Con. to Cb., i.e. Crossbencher); Lord Macpherson of Drumochter (Cb. to Con.); Lord Ogmore (Lab. to Lib.); Lord Lucas of Chilworth (Lab. to Cb.); Lord Nunburnholme (Lib. to Cb.); Lord Terrington (Lib. to Cb.); Lord Kilbracken (Lib. to Lab.).

is expected to be important or very close and the party Leaders wish to make as full a showing as possible. The Labour whip on the Southern Rhodesia (United Nations Sanctions) Order was one example.[3]

While Frontbenchers loyally follow these recommendations (on which their salaries and office, or hope of it, sometimes depend), as far as Backbenchers are concerned the whip is more of an expression of hope than an instruction. The Whips have none of the sanctions that can be applied to recalcitrant M.P.s. Their only appeal can be to the individual Peer's reluctance to behave contrary to his own deep-seated party loyalties or to the expectations of his social group. Such loyalties can be strong, particularly in the case of former M.P.s, however much they ponderously disavow any vestigial strings tweaked by the Prime Minister through whom they received their peerages. And even among those who do not openly declare their party affiliation some can be expected to have strong inclinations to one party or another. (These would be former Commons' candidates, for instance, or trade union leaders, wives and husbands of the politically prominent, or those who have worked or still work for local or national party organizations. A surprising number of Peers are local councillors.)

So although the Whips lack sanctions, accepting the party whip none the less implies some loss of the complete independence that is the peculiar privilege of every Peer. Yet in return for surrendering part of his autonomy to the judgement of his colleagues in the party and the institution, a Peer's decision to take the whip seems to bring few advantages. What obvious reasons are there for doing so?

B. *Party Organization*

At the simplest level, it enables Backbenchers to feel they know what is going on. If they request the party notice or the non-whip they both know what is important to their party and feel themselves important to their party Leaders. It is pleasant to be part of a group, to be asked to attend and support it, even if one has no intention of doing so. Moreover, belonging to a party makes it more easy for a Peer to obtain a suitable time for a Wednesday debate or an Unstarred Question than if he is a freelance operator.

[3] It is said that the Conservatives' first three-line whip in the Lords was on the Opposition motion censuring the policy of resuming arms sales to South Africa during the debate on the Address in July 1970. The 1911 Parliament Act, some say, had a four-line whip.

It also tells him when party meetings are held and what opportunities Backbenchers have to meet the front bench and, as a group, to hear their Leaders put forward their own suggestions and discuss the party line. But whether or not Peers belong to groups from conscious, rational purpose or from some atavistic inclination does not matter here—party groups conveniently exist and deserve closer examination.

The Independent Unionist Peers

In the mid nineteenth century the balance between Liberals and Conservatives in the Lords was broadly equal and it was the Liberal split in 1886 that brought the landowning classes to the Conservative side and gave the Tories their large majority. The Liberal peers of the 1906 Parliament were a tiny rump of the old aristocrats and some auxiliary new creations. So great was the preponderance of Conservatives among the regular attenders that in the 1920s a group of these Conservatives and Unionists formally established the association of Independent and Unionist Peers (I.U.P.). This was a deliberate gesture to show that backbench Conservatives would display an independently reasoned party line in their consideration of issues. They feared that the security of a massive majority would otherwise make the front bench insufficiently responsive to backbench opinion and, while emphasizing their loyalty to the Government, they determined that their support would not be uncritical.

Theoretically at least, this distinct separation between front and back bench persists at the present time. While the Conservative Leader in the Lords and his Chief Whip are appointed by the party Leader in the Commons, the President and Chairman of the I.U.P. are elected by backbench Peers. They call themselves 'the Lords' equivalent of the 1922 Committee', with formal relations between backbench and frontbench Peers corresponding to those of Conservative M.P.s and their front bench. A Backbencher is always the I.U.P. Chairman and, while Frontbenchers are invited to meetings, they are not expected to attend as a matter of course.

Membership (in 1970) was put at 80–120 Peers, who make a small subscription to cover clerical expenses. At 2.15 p.m. on Thursdays, about 30–60 meet to discuss forthcoming business, the distribution of time and topics between members, possible subjects for debate. Little of their affairs is discussed openly. Members do not talk about its membership, officers, or committees and during 1964–70 the identity of the Chairman, though well known, was not broadcast. Even the Leader and the Chief Whip professed to be unsure whether Lord Conesford led the I.U.P. and there was some surprise among its members when in 1971 the names of his successor, Lord Brooke of Cumnor, and of the President, the Earl of Selkirk, were announced in *The Times*.

However, the public announcement only reflected the reality, for in fact the erosion of the Conservatives' massive majority in the Lords has simultaneously nibbled away at the independence of the I.U.P. Backbenchers still claim to form their attitude to policy independently and Frontbenchers still support the I.U.P.'s claim to be a separate body whose views cannot be predicted or dictatorially shaped by the party Leaders in the Lords. But the very fact that the guest speakers who address the group on particular topics are Frontbenchers, invited to explain the official line and outline the approach that Peers might most profitably take, suggests that the division is more formal than real. Occasionally, of course, I.U.P. meetings usefully stress the depth of backbench feeling on specific issues—the case of Southern Rhodesia is a good example—but, again, a firm Conservative Leader like Lord Carrington could often win round backbench Peers to support Shadow Cabinet tactics. Alternatively, the Leader can use his own interpretation of the mood of the I.U.P. to convince the Tory Leaders in the Commons that his strategy for the Lords is the right one.

The Peers' influence on the Commons vastly declined after the passing of the 1832 Reform Bill and 1872 Ballot Act and, more to the point, the waning of their economic power and social authority also undermined their influence on the Lower House. Until the early 1900s, however, leading Peers of both Liberal and Conservative parties worked in close alliance with Commons' Leaders, although their suggestions for formal committees of co-operation were frequently rejected. And, while their influence on the selection and support of M.P.s had, by the 1900s, given way to less direct forms of patronage, the anticipated reactions of the Upper House still significantly influenced the initiatives of the Lower. Members of both Houses were also frequently reminded of that other reserve of Tory support, the army of backwoodsmen who rarely attended the House, but, if induced to do so, could be expected to vote Conservative.

Things had changed by 1964. Conservative Peers select two

members of the Party's Advisory Committee on Policy and one member of the Advisory Committee on Party Finance but, under the arrangement adopted after 1965, only M.P.s may vote in the election of the new party Leader. However, one would expect that a successful candidate would require the support of influential Tory Peers and it is fair to say that in matters of party Leadership, direction, and policy, individual Peers by openly or discreetly making their opinions known can carry weight in party counsels. Not only Frontbenchers like Lord Carrington or Lord Jellicoe but those now on the back benches who have formerly played a part in party organization and finance, and perhaps still do so, can occasionally influence the thinking of the party in the Commons by a word in the appropriate quarter. (The late Marquess of Salisbury was a forceful example.) So although the Disraelian world of country-weekend mingling has been superseded by networks of more professional contacts, there is still some cross-fertilization between party Leaders in Lords and Commons on specific issues or occasions.

But where backbench Conservative Peers and M.P.s are concerned, formal and informal collaboration is still more ephemeral, not least because Tories in Lords and Commons are less likely to enjoy similar tastes and backgrounds than Peers and M.P.s in the Labour Party. There is also a cultivated aloofness between Peers and M.P.s in the Conservative Party, as if M.P.s find their assured support in the Upper House more of an embarrassment than an asset, while Peers sympathetically keep a tactful distance. The I.U.P. Chairman or his representative attends meetings of the 1922 Committee, for example, and any interested Peer can ask to go along, but no Peer presumes to speak. Even at meetings of other backbench groups in the Commons, like the Home Affairs group, where Peers taking the Conservative whip can attend and do so when issues are controversial, it is said that by convention they do not speak but only 'hover'.

A member of the 1922 Committee comes to I.U.P. meetings but Tory M.P.s generally disdain them. It is apparently considered improper for M.P.s to approach I.U.P. members systematically for support on issues or amendments—one prominent backbench Conservative M.P. has described how he was refused a list of I.U.P. members by the Lords' Whips' Office when he sought to organize opposition on some clauses of the Race Relations and Abortion

Bills. This is, of course, also in keeping with the principle that Peers' attitudes might be explored individually but not *en masse*.

Relations between Peers and M.P.s are perhaps more distant among the Conservatives than in other parties. Certainly, the other distinction, between backbench and frontbench Tory Peers, is unique, even if nowadays it is more formal than real. The Labour and Liberal party organizations make no such distinction and indeed their smaller numbers mean that such a contrivance has never been necessary. For the Labour Peers, particularly, organizational strategy lies in the opposite direction.

The Labour Group

In the early days immediately after the Second World War and before the passage of the 1958 Peerage Act, there were very few Labour Peers and it was essential to organize the activities of this small, close-knit body. Backbenchers and Frontbenchers met together and arranged the division of work in proposing, amending, and opposing legislation, trying to ensure that there would always be a good showing in the House. Each Session the Labour Lords elected their own Leader, Deputy Leader, and Chief Whip (together with a Peer to represent them on the Parliamentary Committee of the P.L.P.) when the party was in Opposition. This was still the case in 1970.

Of the ninety-five Peers taking the Labour whip, about thirty-five can be expected to turn up at the weekly party meeting (also held at 2.15 p.m. on Thursdays), with an assiduous core of about twenty. Many more appear when an issue is crucial. The party Leader presides at the meeting, or the Chief Whip as his representative, and a Whip is always present. There must be an atmosphere of formality, for some Labour Peers who remember the early postwar camaraderie speak regretfully of present arrangements. They murmur about a new headmasterly attitude shown by the Leadership to Backbenchers (even less palatable when the party is in Opposition) and grumble that whereas the chairs were once placed in a friendly circle they are now ranged in rows for a lecture.

For their part, the Leaders notice a greater degree of independence among their followers as the number of Labour Peers grows. In an attempt to encourage democratic spontaneity, some backbench Labour Peers have tried to establish small working groups on such subjects as education, home affairs, industrial relations, films, agriculture, and the E.E.C. hoping that a committed group meeting regularly can stimulate the rest of the party meeting and even provoke the front bench. Such groups are important (for both parties) in the Commons but in the Lords it is difficult to sustain Sub-Committees of this sort. Individual Peers with ties of their own to voluntary or professional associations tend to regard personal briefing as more important and more influential than briefing on a party basis. Moreover, when an issue like immigration or transport policy requires united action from Labour Peers, general support from a wide range of people is needed rather than an assault from a small specialized guerrilla group.

Where Labour Peers' influence on the party in the Commons is concerned, it is stronger at the top, as in the Tory case. Only M.P.s elect the party Leader but when Labour is in office the Lords have in their own Leader a member of the Cabinet whom they have themselves elected. In Opposition, the Peers' four elected representatives (Leader and, as his alternative, the Deputy Leader, Chief Whip, and Backbencher) are members of the Shadow Cabinet, by virtue of their membership of the Parliamentary Committee.

The representative Backbencher elected by fellow Labour Peers is also a member of the Liaison Committee, which exists to maintain good relations between P.L.P. members and preoccupied Front-benchers. During the 1964–70 Administration, Lord Champion had the duty of representing the Labour Peers and watching their interests at meetings of the Liaison Committee. He has explained that at these discussions he was able to advise on matters that were not solely Lords' matters, especially if the advice arose out of his previous Commons' experience.

At ordinary meetings of the P.L.P., however, his standing was exactly the same as that of any Labour Peer who takes the Labour whip and is therefore entitled to attend. All Peers have a right to vote on matters of policy affecting the P.L.P. as a whole, but on the application of policy to the Commons Peers are not entitled to vote, just as M.P.s would not be able to vote if the P.L.P. discussed the application of policy to the Lords. An interesting illustration of this rule occurred in January 1967, when some members of the P.L.P. wished to exclude the Peers' vote on the question of German support costs (policy), and of the extent to which party discipline should be enforced when the matter was voted on in Parliament (its application). The party Chairman, Emanuel Shinwell, maintained that the question was wholly one of policy and its application in the Lower House, and that accordingly Peers should take no part in the decision. Though generally accepted, the Chairman's ruling was defensible because, as in many cases, policy and its application were closely intertwined.[4]

Many Labour Peers do attend meetings of the P.L.P., dropping in more regularly than Conservative Peers do at 1922 Committee meetings. Since Labour Peers have no separate organization of their own in the Lords on I.U.P. lines, and since former Labour M.P.s are more accustomed to nostalgically visiting the Commons' Library, dining-rooms, and so on, this contrast is not unexpected. Labour Peers can also attend meetings of any party group (but as only sponsored trade union M.P.s attend the trade union group, Peers are also by definition excluded).

The Liberal Party Meeting

Here formal and informal liaison between Front- and Back-benchers, Lords and Commons, is even more crucial, for the number of Liberal Peers has long exceeded that of Liberal M.P.s. Some uneasiness is bound to arise in a paradoxical situation where the Liberals' most effective strength lies in the non-elected House. It comes, moreover, from a group of Peers of whom the majority are not even former M.P.s but have inherited their seats. Of the thirty-seven Peers taking the Liberal whip in 1967–68 and attending at all, as many as twenty-five were hereditary Peers and in every category of attendance Liberal Peers by succession outnumber those by creation.

Even if these hereditary Peers derive their Liberal sympathies from traditional connections, with Nonconformist or temperance associations, for example, they are no less dedicated party supporters. And whether by succession or creation, Liberal Peers show an enthusiasm for party policy and the concomitant legislative

---

[4] Though it is outside the scope of this period and *sui generis*, another interesting example is that of the P.L.P. vote on the Parliamentary Committee's recommendation that the party oppose a Government Motion on 28 Oct. 1971, supporting E.E.C. entry. At the party meeting on 19 Oct., Peers were permitted to vote on Michael Foot's Amendment as this was a matter of policy, but when the Amendment was rejected and the question of the application of the resolution was considered—i.e. on whether there should be a free vote in the Commons—only M.P.s were entitled to vote. Labour Peers took their own vote on the question of the vote in the Lords, choosing a free vote, unlike M.P.s who agreed to submit to a three-line whip.

responsibilities that compares well with that of their Commons
colleagues. Some Liberal Peers suspect that they are not really
supported by M.P.s—one Peer observed:

> Liberal M.P.s tend to regard us as being wayward. Jo Grimond was
> very anti-Peer. When I first joined very few of us went to the party
> meeting . . . but as soon as we got the first Liberal Life Peers, Wade and
> Byers, there was a more real basis for integrating business and tidying
> up liaison altogether.

At the Peers' own meeting on Thursdays there are usually seven
or eight members present, never more than a dozen, and those are
the regular attenders doing most of the work of the House. Lord
Byers takes the Chair. But there are also meetings on Wednesday
evenings at 5.30 p.m., held jointly with the Liberal M.P.s and party
officials such as the Press Officer, the Chairman of the London
Liberals, and the secretary to the Liberal Whips.

On their own ground, certainly, Liberal Peers work extremely
hard. They use the Lords as a platform for many of the party's
distinctive policy suggestions, making a specific contribution of
their own both to general debates and to the details of legislation,
mastering complicated Amendments and the intricacies of Bills.
As the group of regular attenders is far smaller than that of the Conservative and Labour parties (19, compared with 125 and 95),
although it is a high proportion of all Peers taking the Liberal whip,
this means that a large burden of work is shared among a minute
band of assiduous supporters. As in the early days of the Labour
group, this gives them a feeling of closeness and co-operation.

The Liberals do not take a full share in legislative business from
inclination only but by custom too. As earlier chapters have made
clear, the House of Lords is unlike the Commons in having no
single official Opposition. Though the smallest party, the Liberals
participate by right in discussions and consultation as much as the
representatives of the two larger parties. They are in theory as much
a part of the usual channels. Encouraged by an effective Chief Whip
and sympathetic officials in the Leader's Private Office, they enjoy
in terms of numbers far more than their proportional share of time
for debate and opportunities for discussing Motions, and they are
customarily allotted a quarter of the time of the House. Backbench
Liberal Peers and their frontbench spokesmen are represented on
all Sessional Committees of the House and when a delegation from

the Lords is asked to give evidence on some procedural question, Lord Byers or some other Liberal colleague enjoys the same privilege as Lord Shackleton and Lord Jellicoe.

In obtaining places on Sessional Committees and in debate, or having opportunities for access and discussion, Backbenchers thus see some advantage in belonging to a party organization. In return, despite the lack of any sanctions but those of conscience and convention, Peers are expected to support their party in speech and vote. A familiar test of party loyalty and cohesion is to analyse Divisions, assessing over a period of time the extent of cross-voting on issues controlled by the Whips. But where the Lords are concerned this is not an easy matter.

c. *Cross-voting*

To begin with, there are very few Divisions in the Lords. The average number per year, for example, for 1945–51 was eighteen, for 1951–64 fifty-two, and for 1964–70 forty. Between Sessions there is great variation, from a maximum of seventy-two to a minimum of sixteen in the 1964–70 period alone. The number depends less on the length of the Session than on the amount of contentious legislation with which the Lords is dealing. 1962–63, the year of the London Government Bill, is a good case. There were 158 Divisions in that Session. More recently, 1970–71 saw 196 Divisions, many being on the Industrial Relations Bill.

Since any party in the Lords can divide as often as Peers wish, the more controversial the legislative programme the higher the number of Divisions. Moreover, the activist House of the last decade has seemed more inclined to press matters to a vote, particularly in the Committee Stages of Bills. Still, the convention that the House only very rarely divides on Second Readings continues to operate, so that this analysis must mostly look to behaviour on Committee and on Report.

Despite the small number of Lords' Divisions, it is not practicable here to analyse every one over even a single Session. However, a fair picture of party cohesion can be acquired by first looking at typical Divisions on Government business, to see to what extent there is cross-voting between parties, and then, by comparing these patterns with Peers' behaviour on Private Members' legislation, to assess whether 'free votes' and 'whipped votes' differ at all.

K

Two- and Three-line Whips

Table 14 sets out only a very small selection of Divisions on two- and three-line whips, drawn from only three Sessions, 1965–68. But they are a fair selection, as a fuller examination of the Division Lists kept in the Public Bill Office would show. Detailed tables prepared for the Inter-party Conference on Reform show corresponding trends.

Several points stand out immediately. Liberals are quite accustomed to splitting their vote, and, as complete tables would show, during this period they did so on a majority of issues. Nor do the cross benches vote solidly with Government or Opposition on specific issues but split into Contents and Not-contents with a fairly even balance over Sessions taken as a whole.

But perhaps the most interesting feature is the lack of cross-voting by Conservative and Labour Peers. Where there were Conservative defections to the Government they were usually very small, and the records of Conservatives voting with the Government generally showed a blank. Those cases, like the West Midlands Order and the Milk Order where as many as twenty-five and twenty-one Tories voted with the Government, were not so much matters of party ideology as of sensitivity about certain types of delegated legislation, always a touchy subject. Other occasions where the Division Lists show that there are sizeable Conservative defections were, for example, on the Parliamentary Commissioner Bill in February 1967, the Criminal Justice Bill in June 1967, the Decimal Currency Bill Committee Stage in June 1967, and, notably, the Rhodesia Motion in December 1966. These, however, were episodes where all parties, in Commons as well as Lords, expressed considerable uncertainty as to what policy was appropriate, or else they were cases where Conservative Leaders could not restrain backbench Peers—the outstanding exceptions proving the rule that emerges from the comparative lack of Tory cross-voting.

On the Labour side, too, defections were significantly few. The absence of entries for Labour Peers voting with the Opposition shows that they voted very little with the Conservatives. The Milk Order again and two other cases of technical Amendments in the Committee Stages of the Trade Descriptions and Leasehold Amendment Bills are the most obvious examples in the 1965–68 records. The full Division Lists for 1966–67 show that in that Session the only other really striking instances of cross-voting by

Labour were on the Sheffield Order (four defections), Decimal Currency again (two defections), and the Parliamentary Commissioner Bill (three).

It is somewhat less surprising to find so little cross-voting by Labour Peers. As a self-consciously minority party in Government) they were accustomed to rally Backbenchers, bring them to the House, and encourage them to support the party. Even when pressure goes no further than giving the guidance of a two- or three-line whip, backbench Peers refrained from cross-voting out of instinctive loyalty. They were encouraged by the example of their front bench—on the Economic Policy debate in January 1968, for instance, there were fifteen Frontbenchers among the 87 Labour Peers voting Not-content. Certainly the lists of participants in Divisions recorded in Hansard show that from 1964 to 1970 the Labour Peers who voted were a hard core of the same assiduous members, whereas the Conservative lists tended to be more varied. Not only had Labour a smaller pool of members on which to draw but those who voted so diligently were almost a frontbench 'payroll' vote, staunchly backing the Government against the Opposition's sniping in Committee Stage.

It is also interesting to see from the Division Lists that on Bills where the Lords' Amendments were subsequently rejected by the Commons there had been numerous Divisions on Committee and Report Stages in the Lords. These were Divisions that had been pressed by the Conservative Opposition, with voting following party lines very closely. In other words, the points that Tory Peers felt sufficiently important to press to a Division were also points that mattered enough to the Government for them to overturn on reconsideration in the Commons.

Close study of the Division Lists emphasizes two further important points. First, there were some Bills where very strict party voting on Committee Stage Amendments would be expected, like the 1968 Transport Bill or the 1970 Merchant Shipping Bill—where Government Peers stoutly opposed Conservative modifications eroding these measures. In fact, on many of these Amendments there was cross-voting by members of all parties. The explanation stems largely from the privilege of any Peer to propose an Amendment that can draw in its support an unholy alliance, united on interest other than party. On the Transport Bill, for instance, right-wing Peers concerned about special conditions in the Highlands sometimes allied with left-wing Peers speaking on behalf of transport workers. In the case of the Merchant Shipping Bill, alliances were contrived across party lines when seamen's rights interlocked with complicated legal points.

The second factor that mere scrutiny of Division Lists does not reveal is the incidence of abstentions. Rather than explicitly disregarding the guidance of the front bench by voting with the other side, Peers often prefer to abstain, either by not voting or by staying away from the House. Only a comparison of the attendance figures for a particular sitting day (though again these cover a whole day and not any specific hour) with records of Divisions on that day might suggest the degree to which Peers choose to abstain altogether. Such estimates would be highly speculative. But, particularly where Labour is concerned, this is an important way for individual Lords to signify their disapproval. (And, as the story of the Rhodesia Sanctions vote will demonstrate, Conservatives also used this form of tacit dissent.)

With these reservations, then, records of Divisions do show altogether that both Labour and Conservative Peers vote on neat party lines on most issues when there is a two- or three-line whip. This phenomenon does not imply that they avoid cross-voting out of obedience to the Whips or from fear of repercussions. Indeed, it is impossible to disentangle the motives inspiring Peers to vote as they do. All that can be sensibly said is that Peers vote with their party from a mixture of habit and principle, following the example of Leaders they respect, and drifting into the Division Lobby with colleagues on neighbouring benches, as much as keeping to any independently reasoned party line.

There are important exceptions when Peers do not vote according to the recommendations of their front benches. One example in particular deserves description—the 1968 Commonwealth Immigrants Bill. Conservative and Labour Frontbenchers had agreed that this was a measure where party divisions and personal principles had to be overruled by considerations of urgency and practicality. Lord Brockway, however, proposed an Amendment deferring the Bill 'this day six months' and obtained substantial support in the House. As the table below shows, the Liberals voted unanimously in favour of the Amendment, along with three Bishops. Between Labour and Conservative there was no strict party distribution and they show as much division as the Crossbenchers.

Division No. 2 Commonwealth Immigrants Bill 1968
Lord Brockway's Amendment—29 February 1968

	Con.	Lab.	Lib.	Cb.	Bps.	Total
Content	21	19	19	23	3	85
Not-content	54	44	..	11	..	109

(The full table, among private papers prepared to show the implications of a reformed House, indicates that the Amendment would have received a majority had Peers over 72 years old been excluded, and that many such elderly Peers would have been Conservatives or Crossbenchers.)

Admittedly this occasion was unusual in that many felt that a Labour Government was acting in a right-wing fashion so that, whether Conservative or Labour, Peers were led to vote against their normal partisan inclinations. However, it does provide a striking contrast to the customary patterns of partisanship in Divisions on Government business.

But it is unusual in another way. While this was a policy matter it was also one where 'conscience' came into play and where, for some, private principles overrode other considerations. In this respect the Commonwealth Immigrants Bill resembles a certain type of Private Members' legislation, the sort of question which in the Commons would be allowed a free vote. If Peers do behave differently when a vote is free and not guided by a whip, Division figures will show a higher incidence of cross-voting. The next section examines this.

Free Votes: Private Members' Legislation

Unlike the Commons, the term 'free vote' does not connote for the Lords the unleashing of party shackles. The Lords in any case feel themselves more independent of the whips and this is especially true where legislation on moral, social, or humanitarian themes is being discussed. However, there is a clear difference in voting patterns of free votes and votes controlled by the whip in this period. Professor Bromhead has made this point for the earlier period 1911–56.)[5] The Division Lists on Private Members' legislation bear this out. (Table 15 gives some typical cases exemplifying the over-all pattern; see appendix.) The relative scarcity in the records of blank entries in both Pro and Anti columns for Peers of every

[5] Bromhead, *The House of Lords and Contemporary Politics, 1911–1957*, pp. 110–24.

party indicates how these groups do not keep as parties to one particular side on the majority of issues. Like the Crossbenchers, each party splits between Content and Not-content.

Taking the period as a whole, what is striking is the high degree of Conservative support for progressive measures. The statistics add weight to John Vincent's thesis that the House as a whole became more liberal after 1958.[6]

Although as a party Labour show almost as much cross-voting on this type of legislation as the Conservatives, they tend to favour the liberal view to an even greater degree. The Liberals show the greatest unity and indicate that as a party they are inclined to favour the progressive side. Crossbenchers nearly always split their vote and, taking whole Sessions, divide fairly evenly between progressive and reactionary. The Bishops, as Gavin Drewry's article explained,[7] divide on fundamental points of principle but on the whole they take the progressive line. And the statistics also exemplify the argument of his earlier article for they show that, while the Law Lords often abstain on such occasions, when they do vote the balance usually favours conservatism.[8]

The picture of voting patterns on Private Members' legislation is interesting because it bears out the earlier observations that, irrespective of party and composition, a substantially greater number of Peers tend to favour measures of a liberal and humanitarian complexion, compared with the House of the 1950s.

They also supported the suggestion that voting behaviour differs distinctly on free votes and votes guided by the whip. When a two- or three-line whip requests co-operation, Backbenchers do exhibit considerable party loyalty. It can be safely concluded that, for whatever reason, there is such a phenomenon as party-line voting in the Lords. It is therefore justifiable to speak of 'exceptions' and 'revolts'. Even party solidarity, however, brought problems for the frontbench Leaders, particularly on the Conservative side.

---

[6] See p. 19.   [7] See p. 101.   [8] See p. 103.

PART TWO

5

THE SOUTHERN RHODESIA
(UNITED NATIONS SANCTIONS)
ORDER 1968

THE party whip is no guarantee that backbench Peers will behave as their Frontbenchers wish; however, Labour Peers were more tractable than Conservatives. During our period, on the Labour side, instinctive party loyalty was reinforced by the awareness of their fragile strength in the Lords, of which the Leader did not hesitate to remind his Backbenchers if they were minded to rock the party boat.

Conservative Backbenchers were less predictable. The security of an assured majority made it easy to oppose Labour and for some Conservatives not to try to defeat the Government seemed cowardly. Tory Whips in the Lords were frequently obliged to restrain their followers, appealing to them not to injure the dignity of the party or damage the reputation of the House. While Earl St. Aldwyn, the Conservative Chief Whip, found it useful to have an ample reserve of supporters to call upon, the possibility that large numbers of Conservative Peers might misguidedly try to help the party by regularly voting down Government legislation was certainly embarrassing (especially if the loyalists should prove to be backwoodsmen).

If the Opposition had to win when Divisions were on partisan lines, it would be more seemly to win by only a small majority, avoiding any manifestation of 'St. Aldwyn's overkill'. It was quite clear that at some point Conservative Backbenchers must be allowed to let off steam by defeating the Government. However, it was not an easy matter to find an issue that could serve as a simple and suitable safety-valve. As the Conservatives would certainly lose credit on any question that could be interpreted as being one of Peers v. People, the occasion would have to be one where there was substantial public sympathy for the Opposition case. The Conservatives sought an issue where they could argue that the Government were acting unwisely and with undue haste and where their own motives would appear to be wholly constructive.

The Labour Administration had been in power for only a month when a group of Tory backbench Peers first discerned a shadowy opportunity to show their strength. This was on the question of the War Damage Bill (dealing with compensation for the Burmah Oil Company) in November 1964. The Liberal Party wished to divide the House, and with this additional support some Conservative Backbenchers pressed their front bench to insist on the Lords' Amendments to the Bill, which the Government were resisting.

But the front bench had a good case for recommending that their supporters exercise self-restraint on this occasion. In the first place, the original legislation of which the War Damage Bill was an extension had itself been passed by the preceding Conservative Administration so that it would be impolitic for the Opposition to argue that the measure was a bad one. And if they were to insist that the Labour Government's Bill was unsatisfactory while they had not ventured to put equally appropriate objections to the Conservative measure, this could revive the old charge that the Lords amiably acquiesced in legislation by Governments of the right but immediately leapt to attack Governments of the left.

Even without this extra complication the issue was not suitable ground on which to appeal to public sympathy. As the Marquess of Salisbury advised his colleagues, the Bill was too remote and complex to evoke much popular support and anyway it was too soon after the General Election for the Conservative resistance not to seem piqued and petty. The advice from this distinguished elder statesman, whom the older, more intractable Tory Backbenchers respected, assisted the Whips in their efforts to dampen backbench enthusiasm. Although various Clauses were pressed to a Division, moderation prevailed and the episode was not allowed to build up into a dramatic issue of partisan confrontation.

But it was impossible to curb Backbenchers indefinitely. During the first year or so of the Labour Government there was a strong spirit of fair play between the two main parties in the Lords and a feeling that Labour must be allowed a decent innings; no doubt the fact that despite Labour's slender majority of three in the Commons (until April 1966) they were determinedly and undisputedly governing persuaded some Conservative Peers to hold back. In the first few months, too, a sort of numbed passivity struck the Conservative benches. So accustomed to being the party of Government, they were deflated by their astonishing transformation into Opposition.

The Leaders of the two parties were equally statesmanlike and the usual channels worked to maintain a tone of circumspect co-operation. Nor were the Conservative front bench obliged to reject Government legislation outright to demonstrate their hostility to it. Far more prudent methods of opposition were available. Complaints were made that the Government were being dilatory in bringing matters to the attention of Parliament and the public, or on the other hand, that legislation was being rushed through with immoderate haste. Bills were denounced as ill-thought-out and doctrinaire and, without actually rejecting them wholesale, the Opposition proposed drastic alterations in their substance and implications when legislation reached Committee Stage. Simmered in Second Reading, they were 'roasted' in Committee.

Selective opposition often achieved much, as in the case of the 1966 Land Commission Bill. On other occasions the Government worried unnecessarily that the Lords would be recalcitrant. It is said that the 1968 Transport Bill was one such measure—in fact its passage through the Commons proved far more difficult than through the Lords. The doubts and uncertainties among members of the Cabinet who felt that to introduce such a massive Bill into the Commons, guillotining it there, was to give a hostage to fortune may have provoked their unwarranted anxiety about its fate in the Lords. In the event, the Upper House took all the time they needed in Committee Stage, showing hardly any rancour, and the Bill passed through Report Stage in two days with very little fuss.

Of course, such worries were to the advantage of the Opposition. They could be used to secure concessions that might placate Conservative backbench Peers. Astute bargaining behind the scenes could sometimes induce the Government to modify legislation at subsequent stages, in return for an Opposition undertaking to expedite proceedings. Nevertheless, while these were practical ways for the Conservatives to influence policy, they gave little tactical satisfaction to Backbenchers taking no direct part in such nice manœuvres. What Tory Backbenchers wanted was to threaten to reject legislation, even to carry out such a threat, and even if only *once*, to show the Labour Party that it could not always have its own way in the Lords. As the Labour Administration ground on, with a vastly increased Commons majority after 1966, impatient Conservative Backbenchers began to suggest that the Labour front bench in the Lords were using their minority status to exercise a moral blackmail, and that the time had come to take a stand.

The Vote against Sanctions

Their patience failed in the summer of 1968. A sizeable group of Conservative Backbenchers could no longer suppress their hostility to the Government, and refusing to be guided by their party Leaders, they seized on the issue of the Southern Rhodesia (United Nations Sanctions) Order to ventilate their opposition. This episode was to remain outstandingly fresh in the memories of Backbenchers and Frontbenchers alike for years to come and it was one where, as so often, the Lords' dilemma was exacerbated by the constitutional risks they were running.

The vote against sanctions was a case which, in the words of Lord Shackleton, the Leader of the House at that time, 'hung on curious chances'. It was the result of a fortuitous amalgam of personalities, timing, and procedural niceties that the issue developed as it did. But, to begin with, a brief background description is essential.

The Background to the Crisis

The Order agreeing to United Nations Sanctions against the rebel Rhodesian regime required the affirmative resolution of both Houses of Parliament.

The Commons first discussed and passed it on 17 June 1968. On that and the following day, it was debated in the Lords. The 'Rhodesia lobby', a small group of such Conservative Peers as Lord Salisbury, Lord Coleraine, and Lord Grimston, had felt for some time that sanctions were unwise, unnecessary, or both. In successive debates they had led the opposition to the Government's policy. On the other hand, some equally influential Conservative Peers (Lord Harlech, for instance) felt that the Government had given as fair a run as possible to the Rhodesian leader and that it was now important that sanctions should be continued and enforced.

In both Commons and Lords the Conservative leaders faced the possibility of a party split for, as accounts in the Press made clear, the Tory party was riven on several essential points. Not only was there argument on whether sanctions were wise or not and whether their imposition was likely to be effective or not but this was also an issue where the party was torn between loyalties to relatives, friends, and business and agricultural interests in Rhodesia on the one side, and hostility to a traitorous and racially discriminatory regime on the other. In the Lords there was still another problem; if the Tory Peers rejected the Order, the two Houses would come into conflict.

Lord Carrington was the Leader of the Conservative Party in the Lords and Lord Shackleton was the Leader of the House and of the Labour Peers. They were aware of each other's problems and each knew that in this situation the other party Leader and his Chief Whip had to be exceptionally careful of backbench feelings. While it was certain that the Labour Backbenchers would follow their Government's recommendations and vote for sanctions, the behaviour of the Conservative Peers was not predictable. For several days soundings were taken and speculation increased.

Up till now the Tory Peers had behaved with great self-restraint. Only a few weeks before the Sanctions debate they had taken their Leader's advice and refrained from rejecting the Solus Petroleum Order and now, according to Lord Carrington's subsequent justification, the time was ripe for the Conservative Peers to be allowed to let off steam. He had withheld them as long as he could. As Lord Salisbury described it later: 'The Leader kept telling us we had only one shot in our locker. We kept asking when we could use it and he told us repeatedly that this was an inappropriate time.'

Lord Salisbury was the most notable member of the backbench group who were becoming increasingly sceptical of the 'one-shot' argument. They argued that in fact the Government could ultimately override opposition from the Upper House by applying the provisions of the Parliament Act, reintroducing an Order, or relying on the Lords to concede gratefully if a measure they had rejected first time round were reintroduced a second time. This meant that, in practice, the Conservatives possessed any number of shots for use on different occasions—even if they were fired only as token blanks. Moreover, if Lord Carrington meant the metaphor to imply that the Opposition could only take a stand on a carefully selected issue where public opinion would support them, there was no reason why this could be done only once. The determined Tories felt not that the firing of shots but the metaphor itself had diminishing returns. Each time Lord Carrington urged it on them, it carried less weight.

At this time, too, the Government's stock in the country had fallen very low. They were losing Labour strongholds at by-elections and opinion polls made it clear that the electorate was dissatisfied with major aspects of the Government's policy. Labour M.P.s were restive and the mood was gloomy. Tory Peers also suggested that a case could be made for rejecting the Order, by alleging, as they ultimately did, that the Government had acted precipitately and that the issue should be more thoroughly debated in the U.N. and in Parliament.

However, this was not, as they asserted, a particularly appropriate issue on which to take up the attack. It was not a subject where strictly constitutional legislation was proposed, an area where the Lords have a traditional claim to impose a delay. Nor was there a majority in the country against sanctions to which they could refer to justify their action. The Commons had already approved the Order.

The whole question of the Lords' powers in relation to delegated legislation was anyway a delicate one. As chapter 2 explained, Orders, unlike Acts, are not secured by the provisions of the Parliament Act from sabotage by the Lords. Were the Peers to refuse to pass an affirmative resolution the only way for the Government to persist with their proposals would be by laying a new Order. The Order had been made as a matter of urgency after the agreement at the U.N. and it was already in force. Unless the Peers agreed, the original Order would expire after twenty-eight days. Though the Government could immediately lay a new Order, there was some doubt about the procedural intricacies this involved. This argument was to be used by the Government to suggest that rejection by the Lords might technically interfere with the Order and hinder the urgent application of sanctions. In any case, rejection would afford encouragement to the rebel regime.

The Constitutional Morton's Fork

The choice of this issue for the Peers' revolt was unfortunate for yet another reason. It was very badly timed because at this particular point the all-party talks on Lords' reform were progressing smoothly, and obstreperous action by the Peers would jeopardize negotiations between the parties. If antagonism between Lords and Commons were revived a carefully constructed agreement would be unlikely. This question soon came into the open.

On Saturday, 15 June, the weekend before the Lords were to discuss the Order, Roy Jenkins, the Chancellor of the Exchequer, implied in a major speech in Birmingham that the inter-party talks would be broken off if the Peers rejected the Order. His words were given splash treatment by the Press and the threat certainly voiced the thoughts of a good many Labour M.P.s who felt that soft dealings with the House of Lords had gone far enough. However, there was a touch of absurdity about the whole incident for it was not clear whether the Prime Minister had approved the speech. Some Ministers, coaxing the inter-party talks along, complained that the Chancellor's remarks would not only stiffen the Peers' resistance but could also lead to the sacrifice of a far-reaching constitutional reform on the altar of short-term partisan impatience.

The confusion on the Labour side became apparent when the Lords' debates began on 17 June. It was opened by Lord Gardiner, the Lord Chancellor, who was a supporter of reform and a member of the all-party Conference. He said that 'it would be most unfortunate if any action taken by any group on any side were to be such as to cause the end of these discussions . . .'[1]

But as the threat had been made and the Tory Peers could not fail to be aware of it, Lord Gardiner used it as a delicate hint that it would not be in the interests of the House to reject the Order before them. His advice was echoed by the other Government speakers and reinforced by Lord Byers's words from the Liberal benches. If the Tory Peers rejected the Order, he warned, they would be playing into the hands of the abolitionists and would 'revive all the old phobias about the House of Lords . . . and poison the climate of co-operation which has been established in the past year'. The Liberal Leader, Lord Wade, drew attention to the related point that, although Labour's standing in the country and morale in the party were at rock-bottom, rejection by a non-elected Upper House might not embarrass the Government but might be 'a godsend to the Labour party; it may be just what they are wanting to try to revive their somewhat lowered fortunes in the electoral field'.

The Government front bench used the continuation of negotiations on reform as a discreet bargaining-counter; the Opposition presented Labour's warnings as blackmailing threats to be con-

---

[1] *HL Debs.*, vol. 293, col. 342. It is from this debate that the subsequent quotations in this section are taken.

temptuously despised. Lord Jellicoe replied to the Lord Chancellor by saying that he had 'noted with interest, and some disdain, the minatory utterances of Ministers over the weekend . . .' and that though as a member of the inter-party Committee he would regret it if talks were abandoned, 'My Lords, we have our duty to do. The only right, the only honourable stance for us to take is to treat each issue as it comes before us strictly on its merits.'

It is significant that Lord Jellicoe's speech was firm and even-tempered rather than vehement and condemnatory. Though the Conservative Leaders had by now been obliged to accommodate their diehard Backbenchers, they were basically reluctant to use this particular occasion to assert the powers of the Lords and the strength of the Tory party. Quiet protest was therefore the note which the Conservative Leaders wished to strike.

In phrases of deliberately statesmanlike resignation, therefore, Lord Jellicoe and Lord Carrington spoke of the Lords' dilemma. In Lord Carrington's words:

> It would be unusual—more, it would be unprecedented, I believe, for your Lordships to reject this Order . . . yet it is equally clear that this House would be within its constitutional rights in so doing, and thus affording to public opinion, to the Government, and if you wish, to the Opposition as well, a period for reflection. After all, that is what a Second Chamber is for.

The safe Conservative argument was thus that the Lords were only exercising their constitutional role as a delaying Chamber, behaviour for which they could not be reproached. The reasoned delivery of the party Leaders contrasted strikingly with the passion of the diehards.

The Marquess of Salisbury described their case as the classic situation where the functions of a Second Chamber should be brought into operation, a case involving vitally important issues of policy on which the views of the British people were not yet known. But he let slip that the diehards' anxieties were not so much aroused by this specific issue as by their general objection to Labour's policy and tactics. Unwisely, he went on to say that 'The flashpoint happens to have been reached over Rhodesia, but if we give way over Rhodesia there is likely soon to be another exactly similar crisis on some other issue.'

This was more dangerous ground. It was indeed a crucial part of the Conservatives' argument that the dispute involved the general issue of the prerogatives of the Upper House and their constitutional rights to resist moral and political blackmail, from the Lower House and the Government, and to resist measures of which a majority of Peers disapproved. Such an argument appealed particularly to Tory backbench diehards. But when it was so plain that the Conservatives were acting from party-political motives, an attempt to justify their behaviour as a demonstration of honourable public service and constitutional rectitude could easily seem like sanctimonious hypocrisy.

It was therefore extremely astute of Lord Carrington, the Conservative Leader, to tie this general argument firmly to the particular argument that it was his conviction that 'the Government's policy on Rhodesia is entirely and absolutely wrong'. And relating this to the broader issue, though he was

as keen as anyone to see that reform should take place . . . what sort of people should we be,—what sort of a person would I be—if, because we wish to see a reformed House, I trimmed my sails on every issue which I regarded as being of major importance? I think that people outside would be justified in saying that a body composed of people like that is not worthy of reform or of perpetuation as a Second Chamber.

An important part of his speech, however, was taken up with specific stress on the measure which the House was considering. This was ingenious because it implied, in the first place, that it was this particular Order to which his Party was objecting and, moreover, that though the Tory benches were overflowing, there were no cohorts of backwoodsmen. 'There is' he said 'not one Peer on the benches behind me whom I do not know by name.' Avoiding the treacherous waters of the Lords v. Commons, Peers v. People, issue he thus anchored his argument to the question of the merits of the Order itself. This offered secondary advantages, arising from technicalities of procedure.

The 'Same Question/Same Session' Rule

Chapter 2 drew attention to the special problems growing out of the postwar increase in delegated legislation. Not only are such procedures excluded from the provisions of the Parliament Acts, so allowing the Lords an effective veto over measures requiring the affirmative resolution of both Houses, but, as Lord Carrington pointed out, this also permits the Executive to lay and re-lay Orders before Parliament, time and time again.

In this particular case, the Sanctions Order that had originally been made would remain in force until 8 July. If in the meantime the Lords rejected the Order, refusing an affirmative resolution, the Government could perfectly well introduce a fresh Order, bringing it before both Houses again before the original Order expired. Sanctions would not lapse with the rejection of the original Order but would continue to operate against the Rhodesian regime —and meanwhile the Government would have time for reflection.

It was crucial to the Conservative Leaders' arguments that though their party might force the rejection of the Order, the Government would nevertheless be able to re-lay it before the expiry date. In this way the Tories would be delaying the issue without actually sabotaging sanctions. If they were to agree to a fresh Order, having once made their demonstration of opposition (as the front bench hinted they might), they would not even have frustrated Government policy or the U.N. resolution.

This was the tenor of Lord Carrington's speech. But in reply the Labour Leader, Lord Shackleton, remarked 'the noble Lord seems terribly worried about the possibility of not re-laying exactly the same Order so that your Lordships can pass it . . . (Lord Carrington: 'No.') For in fact there was a complication here. On advice from the Clerks, Lord Shackleton suggested that, in theory, the Government might not be able to reintroduce the original Order 'in the present form'. There might be legal difficulties. The consequences of rejection might be technically difficult. The Labour Leader had some solemn fun teasing the Opposition. One Backbencher recalled in 1970 how 'Carrington was hanging on to the edge of his seat. I shall never forget the atmosphere in the Chamber. The Tory front bench were on absolute tenterhooks.' Lord Carrington anxiously sought elucidation; Lord Shackleton could only be drawn to say darkly that it might be necessary to have a new type of Order. It was not simply a question of re-laying the Order. While it might be a similar Order, 'we shall be taking a serious and definite step'.

This was fair. The Leader of the House was in no way misleading the Opposition, for the Clerks had brought to his attention the technicalities of the 'same Question/same Session' rule. While it was open to the Government to lay a fresh Order with similar, or even identical, effect, this had to be significantly different in some respects to circumvent the rule that no Question be brought before Parliament for reconsideration in the same Session in which a decision had already been taken. The Commons' Clerks would not be satisfied with an Order that was exactly the same as the one to which the Peers might disagree, as Lord Shackleton correctly explained.

Now although the new Order might satisfy procedural requirements even if it differed from the original in only minor respects (in this case, provisions about timing), nevertheless this was a clever tactical point to make. (And one which cannot have been much of a surprise to Lord Carrington, who would also receive the detached advice of the Clerks and who had in fact consulted a senior Clerk on this very point.) It rattled the Conservative Peers at the very end of the debate, just before the Division was to be taken, and even at this very late stage it offered Lord Carrington a loop-hole by which he could save face and advise his supporters to accept the Order. The fact that it could not be re-laid in identical form, as the Conservatives had imagined and had set out as the core of their argument, would make its rejection an explicit frustration and complication of Government policy. This would attract to the Conservative Party more disrepute and embarrassment than they had bargained for. As Lord Shackleton declared, the Tory Peers 'have unleashed a whirlwind . . . which the noble Lord, Lord Carrington, was riding so skilfully . . .; we know the job of Leader of the Conservative Opposition is not the easiest one in the world. He has lost control of the situation and I want to emphasize the consequences.'

The Consequences: The Vote and its Repercussions

Altogether fifty-one speeches were made in the debate on 17 and 18 June, twenty-six broadly in favour of the Order and twenty-five against. The chamber was packed with Peers, and the two days of debate were also memorable for the ingenuity with which miscellaneous temporary sleeping facilities were arranged in odd corners of the Palace.

When the House divided, 184 peers voted Content and 193 Not-content. There was strong whipping and, as far as the Conservatives were concerned, once it was accepted that the Tory diehards would vote against the Order, it was important to make as forceful and united a showing as possible from those benches.

It is interesting that the vote was lost so very narrowly. The Labour Whips were gratified to find that the Contents were made up of 84 Labour Peers, supported by 18 Bishops, 23 Liberals, 1 Communist, 50 Crossbenchers, and 8 Conservatives. As the number of Labour Peers among the working House was anyway only 95 (increasing to only 108 if the 5 per cent to $33\frac{1}{3}$ per cent attenders are included) this was an impressive showing.

The 193 Not-contents were all Conservatives, except for 15 Crossbenchers, and 4 more Crossbenchers who habitually voted Conservative. Thus 174 Conservatives voted against sanctions. There were at this time 125 Peers taking the Conservative whip among the working House and 235 including those who came between 5 per cent and $33\frac{1}{3}$ per cent of the time. It is fair to assume that only a few of these were unavoidably prevented from coming to vote, so about 50 or 60 Conservatives abstained from supporting the party either by not voting or by staying away from the House. There were only about half a dozen unfamiliar names on the Division List—certainly nothing like 300 backwoodsmen arrived.

But the narrowness of the Conservative victory, and the absence from the Not-content lobby of the sixty or so Tories who might have been expected to vote with their party, made the Division a political as well as a moral triumph for the Labour party. They had nearly won in terms of numbers and the Opposition had certainly lost in terms of face.

The immediate repercussions had been forecast. The Government reintroduced the Order, in virtually the same form. The Peers passed it, with some grumbling by the Conservatives, who nevertheless conceded that by now the Government had had sufficient time for reflection. And on the question of the talks about reform the prophetic warnings were fulfilled. Two days (20 June) after the Lords' vote, the Prime Minister announced to the Commons that, as a result of 'the deliberate and calculated decision of the Conservative Party' to reject the Order, there could be no question of the all-party talks continuing. What is more, he told the House that it was now the Government's intention to introduce at an early date comprehensive and radical legislation to revise the powers and composition of the Upper House. As the last chapter of this study explains, a short and drastic Bill to curb the Lords' powers was subsequently prepared by the Lord Chancellor's Office. That was no idle threat made in a fit of pique.

The talks had already achieved a real measure of agreement and promised an excellent basis for the introduction of a useful reform. It had not been a simple matter to establish a confident working relationship between representatives divided on political, practical, and ideological principles, and the party Leaders in the Lords, who had co-operated especially closely, were sorry at the decision to break off negotiations. It seemed to be an act of petulant folly, but in public Labour had a case for the decision. As Lord Shackleton said, with deep regret, 'if someone with whom you are in daily communication suddenly decides to cut your throat, even though he only succeeds in scratching it, you do not at that moment continue talking with him'.[2]

Post-mortem

The choice of this issue for the Conservative stand against the Government was an unfortunate one and, considering their Leaders' own interest in the all-party talks, somewhat puzzling. How far was this a deliberate and calculated decision by the Opposition? To answer this tantalizing question, it is necessary to consider the pressures on the Tory Leaders and the coincidence of timing and personalities influencing events.

Discussion of the matter with many of those involved gives good reason to believe that the Conservative Leader was unwilling to advise his Backbenchers to reject the Order. He was under strong pressure from the diehards, who had been so repeatedly frustrated in their wish to embarrass the Government. The Shadow Cabinet, too, suggested that an appropriate time had arrived to demonstrate that Labour could no longer expect a smooth ride for their legislative programme in the Lords. The Government's standing was as low in the country as it could possibly be, the morale of their Backbenchers in the Commons was enfeebled, and the momentum of Labour's Administration seemed to ebb away visibly as the summer sweltered on. To the Shadow Cabinet and eager Tory backbench Peers it must have appeared an irresistible opportunity to strike.

Lord Carrington did not judge it a good moment. It might be better to reserve the Lords' energies for the forthcoming Committee Stage of the ponderous Transport Bill. But he knew that his Backbenchers would be hard to restrain. As an outlet, he offered the Shadow Cabinet the alternative course of a vote of censure, instead

[2] *HL Debs.*, vol. 293, col. 867.

of a vote on the Order itself, but this was refused. Edward Heath did not press Lord Carrington to divide the House and reject the Order; it was now a question of whether the Tory backbench Peers could be persuaded to hold back.

There were, in the estimation of the Conservative Whips, about two hundred backbench Peers on whom the Leader could rely, but this was perhaps too optimistic a forecast. Loyal though these Peers were to Lord Carrington, who commanded great authority in the party, the matter rapidly became for the Conservative diehards a question of the prestige of their party and the House. The fact that the Marquess of Salisbury led the recalcitrants was extremely important. He was an influential elder statesman of the party and, moreover, had been Leader of the House after 1945 during the Labour Administration. He therefore spoke with some experience on the question of Opposition tactics against a minority Government in the Lords. Yet another accident was that Lord Harlech, a former Deputy Leader greatly respected by backbench Tory Peers, was in the U.S.A. at the beginning of June for the funeral of Robert Kennedy, and could not lend his support to Lord Carrington in the efforts to modify backbench opposition.

When it became apparent that a sizeable number of Peers were determined to reject the Order, the Leadership was forced to make the best of it and justify the action as one where the Lords were exercising their proper role as a delaying chamber, sanctioned by the provisions of the Parliament Act. In public discussion Frontbenchers loyally continued (in 1973) to use this argument to explain the Opposition's stand.

But private conversations suggest that Lord Carrington was indeed propelled by impatient Backbenchers into a difficult corner. The Leader and his Chief Whip could only hope that there would not be an embarrassingly large number of unknown backwoodsmen appearing to reinforce the Conservative vote. Fortunately this did not happen; in a way it was also fortunate that the Labour, Liberal, and crossbench Peers, and certainly the eighteen Bishops, made such a good showing that the Tory majority was not overwhelmingly large—indeed, was so minute. Moreover, the Order could be, and was, reintroduced.

But from every point of view the episode was lamentable. By breaking off the talks the Government lost some sympathy in the country, though not much, because it was the Peers who attracted most public odium. The Press presented the issue as one where the Tories had taken the side of the right-wing Rhodesian settlers and this, added to the Peers *v.* People aspect, did the Conservatives little good. The all-party talks were set back; thenceforth negotiations were to be more awkward and prickly.

The Labour Peers had scored a moral victory and rejoiced that they had so nearly outvoted the Opposition. The Conservatives had fired their shot—and misfired. This particular episode was a sorry failure, but better days were to come.

6

THE SEATS BILL

THE 1968–69 Session was an unhappy one for Labour. Support in the country was flagging—in May some 917 seats were lost at the borough and rural district council elections. In Parliament the Government were floundering. Combined opposition from Back-benchers of all parties had forced them to drop the House of Lords Reform Bill in April. When the Prime Minister announced this decision to Parliament, he used as a face-saving explanation the urgency of important legislation to improve industrial relations, but this too provoked trouble with the unions and the P.L.P., and in mid June the Industrial Relations Bill was the next to be abandoned. Since the beginning of 1969 there had been the Ford strike, the issues of Anguilla's revolt and the Biafran war, increased charges for false teeth and spectacles—truly the Government were accident-prone. Amidst this background of evident decline there erupted the Redistribution of Seats Bill.

Background to the Bill

It did not take the Government by surprise. Preoccupied though they were between 1964 and 1969, M.P.s of all parties had long known that their constituency boundaries were due to be realigned. The Report of the Parliamentary Boundary Commission loomed on the horizon like a dormant volcano. As early as May 1966 some Ministers had lightly wondered how Parliament, including the Lords, might react to various expedients for sidestepping the most injurious of the Commission's recommendations.

By the terms of an all-party agreement of 1958, the Commission reported every fifteen years. Accordingly, in 1969 the Home Secretary was statutorily required to lay before both Houses Orders implementing its recommendations 'as soon as may be'. There was good reason for M.P.s to fear for their individual seats and the fortunes of their parties, as the changes recommended by the Commission required, in all, alterations to 410 out of the 630 constituencies in the United Kingdom. Those who examined the proposals speculated that as many as thirty M.P.s might find their seats at risk. Subsequent events seem to have confirmed that the changes would have had a significant effect—a careful analysis has suggested that had the 1970 General Election been fought on the new boundaries, the net Conservative gain would have been eight seats and the net Labour loss three seats, giving an increase of eleven in the Conservative majority.[1]

It was therefore not surprising that while the Conservatives demanded that the Orders be laid forthwith, Labour members wished to find an excuse for delaying their implementation. The Government seized upon the Report of the Royal Commission on Local Government in England and Wales, and similar Reports and White Papers on Local Government Reorganization in Scotland and Northern Ireland, to provide a loop-hole. They argued that the changes these Reports proposed and the many months required for reorganization were relevant to the constituency alterations because it was on the local government boundaries that Parliamentary constituencies were based. The Labour Party attacked the Opposition for disregarding logical administrative procedures in their haste to implement proposals that would benefit the Conservatives at the next General Election; the Conservatives accused the Government of delaying the Orders to safeguard their own majority.

This was the background to the Bill which the Government introduced in June 1969, postponing the laying of the Orders. Its birth was unfortunately timed (the Industrial Relations Bill had just been dropped) and it was denounced as a swindle. But though the House of Commons (Redistribution of Seats) Bill had a contentious passage through the Commons it was passed with a three-line whip. Then it came to the Lords, where the Peers were unhampered by whips or a guillotine. High-mindedly democratic, they pounced upon it as the ideal issue on which to ditch the Government.

The Constitutional Trap—Again

Opinion in the country, even in Westminster, might have held

[1] D. E. Butler and M. Pinto-Duschinsky, *The British General Election of 1970* (1971), pp. 414-15.

that by rejecting the Bill the Lords were fulfilling their proper role as a Second Chamber curbing the excesses of the Executive. Nevertheless, they were pitching themselves into controversy again. By setting aside the expressed wish of the Commons they might be abusing their constitutional position. The date of the episode was important here.

It was now June 1969. Not only was the Government bogged down in a miry legislative programme but time was becoming short. At the very latest they had until April 1971 before being required to call a General Election. In theory this gave them sufficient time under the provisions of the 1947 Parliament Act to pass legislation rejected by the Lords, for on paper the Administration needed only two successive Sessions (1968–69 and 1969–70) with one year as the period of delay from Second Reading in the Commons, in which to pass a rejected Bill.

But, in effect, by the summer of 1969 the Administration had really run out of time. It was abundantly clear to Ministers that to secure the Seats Bill by using the Parliament Act would demand, first, that it run through all its Commons' and Lords' stages, a course that at this point would be expensive in terms of time and prestige and would inhibit the Prime Minister's freedom to choose the date of the General Election; secondly, that within this period necessary drafting would have to be done extremely quickly; and thirdly, that this would involve not only argument about the Bill itself but also controversy on matters of definition and procedure (what 'rejection' meant, what exactly was 'close of Session' and so forth) that the Opposition would exploit as thoroughly as they had done on the Parliament (No. 2) Bill. These were not risks that the Government wanted to take.[2]

Many Peers were unaware of this extra dimension to the issue but even the least subtle realized that there were limits to the extent to which they could provoke the Government. The reaction to the rejection of the Southern Rhodesia Order had been for the Prime Minister to break off talks on reform; throwing out the Seats Bill might goad him into abolishing the Lords altogether. However,

---

[2] Another explanation could have been that the Home Secretary introduced the Bill knowing full well that the Lords would reject it. Thus, even while the Bill ran its course through Parliament and before the Parliament Act could be invoked, a Dissolution might be proclaimed and the Election fought on the old boundaries. This reasoning is over-sophisticated. The Home Secretary's main concern was that the Orders should not be laid, no matter what device was used.

this time the Government were on very poor ground. They had been obtuse in deferring the Seats Bill until it was really too late to operate the Parliament Act's provisions, and the Bill they eventually proposed was so utterly condemned by commentators outside Parliament and in the Press that even action by the Lords had a good chance of attracting popular approval. The Lords had learnt from their experience over the Southern Rhodesia Order to tread softly. Tactics of diehard expostulation had not succeeded in that case; this time an attitude of reasoned, tactful protest might bring them credit.

Tactics—Second Reading

The Seats Bill was not covered by the mandate convention, by which Conservative Peers customarily acknowledged that legislation which was part of the electoral programme was entitled to a Second Reading. As soon as the Bill reached the Lords there was strong pressure on the Leader of the Opposition to reject it outright. Tory backbench Peers were supported by editorials that whipped the matter up into a constitutional issue and depicted the Government as cynical gerrymanderers.

Lord Carrington could only stave off the pressure by arguing, on the Clerks' advice, that to throw the Bill out straight away would provoke an unnecessary constitutional crisis. It would be a tactical mistake to 'swamp our protest with their protest'. Fortunately his authority was sufficiently firm to restrain the Backbenchers. They were also reminded that the subsequent Committee Stage would provide a much more fitting opportunity for opposition.

Simultaneously, the Government had set up a small ministerial Committee to consider the possible repercussions if the Lords rejected the Bill (including the introduction of a short Bill to curb the Lords' residual powers) and the tactical handling of the Seats Bill itself. Lord Shackleton and Lord Gardiner and, from the Commons, James Callaghan (Home Secretary), Fred Peart (Leader of the House), and Sir Elwyn Jones (Attorney-General) were among its members. It emerged that the Government would base a large part of their case on the administrative argument relating the realignment of constituency boundaries to the forthcoming reforms in local government areas.

On 17 July the Bill was given its Second Reading in the Lords and Lord Stonham opened the debate for the Government. He attempted to dispatch the argument that it was the Peers' duty to act as a constitutional watchdog—

As an exposition of democracy it will not stand up. This Government owe their so-called temporary majority in the Commons to the votes of the electors. The permanent Conservative majority in the Lords owes its preponderance to biological accident . . . I believe that the only Bill this House is entitled under the law to kill once and for all is one seeking to prolong the life of Parliament beyond its five-year limit; and by no stretch of the imagination does this Bill do that.[3]

Government speakers then tried to make the best possible case for the Bill, deploying, for example, the respected and upright Lord Longford to put a respectable face on the matter. His remarks were hardly enthusiastic. He was plainly unhappy at being involved in what he called 'this sort of discreditable nonsense' and sorry that it had fallen to him to speak so early. However, he sought to defend the Bill from the viewpoint of a dispassionate student of history. This was a role particularly appropriate now that he was speaking from the crossbenches, after resigning from the Government and from his position as Leader of the House.[4] Alluding to this he said: '. . . I do not think that I should be thought to be a slavish admirer of the Government of the day . . . nevertheless . . . I know that they are honest, I know that they are intelligent, and I know that they are too prudent to introduce a proposal that is totally indefensible.' But the defence on which he was obliged to rely was unfortunate and, by his own confession, depressing. According to a student of history it was that any Government is likely to choose the course that suits its own interests. The Government were acting entirely within their prerogatives in this instance, doing much the same sort of things as the Tories had always done and had believed to be absolutely right.

The Government were lucky to be able to rely on two or three distinguished Peers (Lord Silkin, Lord Mitchison, Lord Ritchie-Calder), who loyally supported the Bill but many of those whose assistance they would have welcomed remained silent. Lord Silkin nobly did his part, reiterating the 'two disturbances' argument that expediency and administrative logic required that Parliament

---

[3] *HL Debs.*, vol. 304, col. 478. Reference to proceedings on Second Reading run from this point.

[4] In Jan. 1968 he had resigned over the Government's postponement of the raising of the school-leaving age.

await the recommendations of the Redcliffe-Maud Report. Lord Popplewell and Lord Garnsworthy stressed the need for an M.P. to be able to win over a long period the confidence and loyalty of his electors and his party workers. The most succinct defence of all came from Lord Ritchie-Calder, who dismissed both the 'artificially devised' constitutional issue and the administrative arguments, staking everything on the question of motive. No Government, he declared, that were prepared to grant the vote at eighteen to two and a half million unpredictable young people were calculating on the gains they would receive from 'minor manipulations of a boundary'. This was spirited, if wishful, thinking.

But speeches in favour of the Bill were few. Both hereditary and created Peers, Liberals and Crossbenchers as well as Conservatives, felt that this was exactly the sort of issue where the Lords should intervene, and from every quarter there was opposition. Lord Ferrier observed that a Life Peer did not accept a peerage to act against his conscience; others took up Lord Stonham's remarks and replied that Life Peers certainly cannot be said to owe their seats to biological accident and that Crossbenchers are not always motivated by Conservative loyalties. One crossbench Peer of unblemished independence was Lord Robertson of Oakridge and it was a considerable *coup* for the Opposition when he declared that, if there were to be a vote on the Second Reading of the Bill, he would walk into the Lobby against the Government 'and as to the consequences, be damned to them!'

But perhaps the most devastating argument against the Bill was that set out by Baroness Sharp, speaking from the cross benches, as befitted a former civil servant. Lady Sharp had been Permanent Secretary at the Ministry of Housing and Local Government and after her retirement served on the Maud Commission. Her knowledge, objectivity, and judgement were respected in the House and her speech was crucial. While she agreed that it was important to align constituency boundaries with local government areas she was less optimistic than the Government in the time-table they envisaged for implementing the Maud proposals. She suggested that it might not even be until 1976-7 that the recommendations would be complete, at the earliest, and it was surely necessary to secure as soon as possible a satisfactory relation between Parliamentary constituencies and the distribution of the electorate. The Opposition seized delightedly on this argument and especially on the question of dates, for this implied that even if the Government were not intentionally gerrymandering, the delay sought by the Bill would have this precise effect.

It was easy for the Opposition to present the Bill as undemocratic and double-dealing but equally easy for them to be carried away on a wave of self-righteousness. The Conservative front bench had to guide the Opposition prudently and in this they were supported by the elder statesmen of the party. As Lord Conesford observed, to pass the Bill in its present form might do appalling injury to the good name of Parliament, but equally damaging to Parliament's reputation would be any indecorous and unconstitutional behaviour from the Lords.

Since they had learnt the lesson of their intemperate action over the Southern Rhodesia (United Nations Sanctions) Order, the sensible course this time was obviously that of firm remonstrance, determined resistance rather than intransigence. The advice of the Marquess of Salisbury, who had led the rebellious Tory Back-benchers in the earlier episode, was therefore particularly welcomed by those who advocated self-restraint. He confessed that he would personally have much preferred to throw out the Seats Bill on Second Reading, for it was bad and dangerous, and might even create a precedent that would justify some future Government in postponing a General Election. However, he agreed that other Peers of all parties and on the cross benches thought it preferable to 'adopt a rather less crude method for encompassing its destruction', one that would give the Government breathing-space in which to have second thoughts and alter their views. The method of preventing the Bill mattered less than the purpose itself and, moreover, it was frankly better to choose a course that would rally as many opponents of the Bill as possible into a single camp.

Lord Salisbury not only steered the backbench Peers but also voiced their feelings, reminding the front bench that if there was to be no Division on Second Reading the Peers required assurances that this would not prevent them from acting more forthrightly in subsequent stages. To give the Bill a Second Reading was in no way to capitulate to the Government. A careful Amendment had therefore been devised by the Conservative front bench to check the Lords from forcing a Division. This would allow the Opposition to preserve a statesmanlike appearance.

The course of action recommended by the front bench was set

out by Lord Brooke of Cumnor. This was to give the Bill a Second
Reading, without Division, in the hope that the Peers' admonitions
would induce the Government to change their minds and not seek
to pursue the issue. But should the Government persist in attempting to evade the statutory requirement to lay the Orders before
Parliament, Amendments would be introduced when the Seats
Bill reached its Lords' Committee Stage. These Amendments
would be moderate, obliging the Home Secretary to comply with
the law and lay the Orders, but granting him until 31 March 1970
to do so.[5] This would permit the Government to salvage some of
its reputation and would be a less drastic but equally effective
method of opposing the Bill than throwing it out altogether.

Lord Carrington took up this theme when he summed up the
debate for the Opposition. This course would give the Government
time for reflection—with indemnity and immunity for themselves
and the Home Secretary—during which they might consider the
discussions that had taken place inside and outside Parliament. It
would give them time to drop the Bill, albeit with some loss of dignity. Moreover, to reject the Bill outright by denying it a Second
Reading would in fact be a negative action, for though it would
remove the Home Secretary's indemnity it would do nothing to
oblige him to carry out his statutory duty. The right and proper
course, as well as the most prudent, was to give the Bill a Second
Reading and allow time for second thoughts.

Lady Sharp had sunk the Maud Commission argument without
trace, said Lord Carrington, leaving 'scarcely any bubbles'. It was
now the Lords' constitutional duty to express their concern. Arguments about the composition of the House were beside the point
for it was certainly not their fault that they were unreformed.
Opposition in the Commons had led the Government to discard
proposals for reform and consequently the Lords were left with the
same responsibilities and duties that they had always had. If they
followed the moderate course recommended by the front bench and
the procedure Lord Brooke had outlined, they would sensibly and
justifiably be doing their duty, within these careful limits.

It was obviously to the advantage of the Conservative front bench
to present the issue as a clash between a headstrong Government

---

[5] Lord Byers had a set of Amendments to indemnify the Minister by allowing him until
Nov. 1970 but the Liberals dropped these and joined the Conservatives in their more subtle
and effective Amendment.

and a high-principled Upper House. For the Government, on the other hand, tactics required that they present it as a party matter, where the Conservatives were being priggish. This strategy was used by Lord Shackleton in his speech closing the case for the Government. As a member of the Cabinet which had taken the decision to introduce the Bill, and as a determined politician, he was prepared to go ahead and push the Bill through the House. Neither he nor Lord Carrington nor their frontbench colleagues could tidily separate principle from political considerations in this affair. Neither side could be completely objective—politics was concerned with such problems of power. Lord Shackleton knew that, tactically, the Conservatives' moralizing approach could be made to work to their disadvantage by exposing their arguments about the constitutional duties of a revising chamber and the statutory obligations of Ministers as so much pious pontification.

In a similar position, he argued, Conservative politicians would, just as much as Labour, seek to defer the Boundary Commission's recommendations. In the case of the London Government Bill the Tories had arguably done so. Crossbenchers in particular should not be misled by the Tories, who were in this matter primarily motivated by political advantage and whose lofty arguments about the Lords' responsibilities were only a red herring in a partisan game.

In case this suggested that the Government's action was wholly one of cynical expediency the Labour Leader went on to explain that questions of boundary alignment were far more complex than the Opposition had made out. Their case had astonished him by a 'quite unbelievable barrage of innuendo', and lack of understanding of the relationship between local authority and Parliamentary boundaries. He emphasized his remarks by recollecting his own experience of narrowly losing his seat in the Commons (though in fact it was lost on a standard swing and redistribution had little to do with it). As an additional indication that the Government's policy was not irredeemably cold-blooded, Lord Shackleton explained that the Orders might even yet be laid. The introduction and passage of the Seats Bill did not make this impossible. Unfortunately this suggestion that procedural repentance could bring absolution was rather too much for most Peers, who only challenged it with cries of 'Oh, Oh'.

Whatever the rights and wrongs of the case, however, did it really concern the Lords once the Commons had passed the Bill?

The Leader asked whether the House, unreformed, should be able to exercise a veto 'only on behalf of one party' in the fourth and fifth years of a Parliament. This was not a constitutional matter and the Peers were using 'the fatal years' they always used for this purpose to hold up the House of Commons. Lord Carrington had talked about a bee sting but this, said Lord Shackleton, 'was not a very clever bee sting'.

Not only were the Peers 'a pretty odd emanation of the people' but the method recommended by Lord Brooke for avoiding the outright rejection of the Bill they had denounced so utterly also seemed somewhat curious. But as Lord Shackleton observed, 'It is certainly not for me to twit the Opposition on avoiding a head-on collision.' At this point, as it turned out, the collision was avoided and the Bill was given a Second Reading without a Division. Though the Lords took the advice of the Conservative front bench, however, it was obvious that a clash was inevitable and the Opposition looked forward to the events of the Committee Stage.

Tactics—Committee Stage

Here there was renewed pressure on the Conservative Leader and older Peers, egged on, it is said, by one school of proceduralists who said that Backbenchers were privileged to act as they saw fit and should disregard the Leader's advice. He was urged to take drastic action. One suggestion, backed by a leading article in *The Times*, was that the Opposition should propose an Amendment containing the very recommendations of the Boundary Commission—that is, putting back as part of the Bill the provisions it had been designed to circumvent. Lord Carrington sought expert opinion and his procedural advisers pointed out that since his supporters were attacking the Bill as a disreputable Parliamentary procedure, a wrecking Amendment of this sort would lay them open to the same criticism. (This, incidentally, is an excellent illustration of the way in which strictly procedural advice so quickly becomes tactical and, by extension, political.) Lord Carrington was warned not to seem 'to answer a trick with a trick'. In the event, the Amendment proposed was the moderate device suggested by Lord Brooke.

The Committee Stage on 21 July 1969 opened with this Amendment, No. 1, tabled in the names of Lord Carrington, Leader of the Conservatives, Lord Byers, Leader of the Liberals, and two highly regarded Crossbenchers, Lord Robertson of Oakridge and

Lord Tangley. It was significant that this was a consensus Amendment and the Conservatives were delighted to have the explicit support of the two Crossbenchers. The case that this was a matter of principle rather than party was notably reinforced.

In effect, the Amendment gave the Home Secretary another three months to lay the Orders, absolving him until the end of the present Parliamentary Session. Though such an Amendment had been the expressed intention of the Opposition since Second Reading they were still accused of inconsistency. Lord Mitchison, for example, pronounced it 'rather cheap and humbug' to pass a Bill on Second Reading and then amend it so substantially in Committee. From the front bench Lord Stonham declared that it sought not merely to wreck a Bill that the Peers had already approved in principle but to introduce a new Bill by the back door. Lord Donaldson too saw the Amendment as amounting to a direct negative and thus an assertion by an unreformed House of powers to reverse a major decision of the Commons.

But the Government were fighting a hopeless battle. Though their supporters were readier to speak in Committee than they had been on Second Reading, arguments against the Amendment were thin indeed. Baroness Gaitskell quoted an article by David Butler in the *Sunday Times* that had argued that Labour's proposals fell within the moderate tradition of the pursuit of self-interest in British party politics. She could not see them as justifying the excessive rhetoric they had evoked. Both parties were acting from partisan motives. Lord Champion, a Labour Life Peer and a former Deputy Leader of the Lords, appealed to the Committee not to let 'this reasonable Bill' become a source of conflict between the two Houses.[6]

It was clear that the majority of Peers in the House saw it as an issue affecting the Upper Chamber as a whole and if, as Lord Champion warned, it was to inspire a clash between Lords and Commons, no other question could have been more to the Lords' taste than this one. It drew together opposition from all sides; from the cross benches Lord Tangley explained:

for the first time in my life I have added my name to an Amendment tabled by the Tory party. I doubt whether this is ever likely to happen again ... I am not acting in concert with any of the other noble Lords who

---

[6] Quotations from the debate in Committee Stage are drawn from *HL Debs.*, vol. 304, col. 657 et seq.

sit on these benches, nor with either of the Opposition parties. But I have a strong intuition that what I am about to say accords with the secret thoughts of many noble Lords whatever benches they may occupy . . .

(Lord Tangley's words carried additional weight in this context as he had been Chairman of the Royal Commission on Local Government in Greater London, on whose report was based the Bill about which Labour had pessimistically expressed so much hostility in Parliament, only to be surprised when they won the subsequent local elections.)

Even if administrative tidy-mindedness rather than electoral advantage was the motive behind the Seats Bill now before the House, its consequences would still transcend any administrative convenience. They would express something alien to the whole spirit of our national life, said Lord Tangley. The Lords were offering the Government an honourable way out of a dishonourable situation and the Peers could show a growingly cynical population that Parliamentary institutions could rise above factional interests.

The Government were being attacked from all sides, by Conservatives, Liberals, and Crossbenchers. They were not even immune from defections by their own supporters. The Bishop of Southwark, for example, who took no whip but proclaimed his Labour allegiance from the Bishops' benches, announced that on this occasion he intended to vote for the Amendment. The standards implied by the arguments for the Bill, he felt, were incompatible with the values of Socialism and, because the Peers were a non-elected House, should they therefore 'have lockjaw and say nothing at all?'

Faced with opposition from every part of the House, Lord Shackleton did his best to rally Labour Backbenchers, attempting to undermine the Conservative and Liberal parties with friendly ridicule. He recalled 'the awful botched shot' over Rhodesia and reiterated that the very nature of the Lords deprived them of any right to strike what they believed to be a blow for constitutional freedom. Disavowing any threat of reprisals, he continued 'All I will say is this, that if this Committee passes these Amendments, as I suspect it will, it will be a bad day for the House of Lords'.

The Opposition were complacently self-righteous, however, and Lord Shackleton's warning seemed born of despair. Indeed, the Leader of the House confessed that in view of the Conservatives' serried ranks he wondered whether he should advise Labour Peers to go into the Lobby at all. Once again the Leader of the Opposition had shown that he controlled the Upper House.

The Government's case was so unsympathetic to the House as a whole that the Conservatives could disregard the allegation that the Opposition consisted of loyalist Tory lobby-fodder from the backwoods. Lord Carrington could disdain partisan quarrels. Drily he recalled that in the Second Reading debate 'at no time did we impugn the motives of the Government . . . Indeed, it is noticeable, if I may say so, that the only speeches which have contained Party political matter have been those from the other side. . . .' The Conservatives found ammunition enough in the arguments that administrative expediency and statutory obligation demanded the immediate introduction of new boundaries. None the less the moderate and conciliatory tone of Lord Carrington's speech did not conceal his enjoyment of the Government's discomfiture.

The Government had done all they could to rally their supporters and each of the 3 Labour Whips tried to coax his 30 Backbenchers into the Lobby. But when the House divided, the Peers voted decisively in favour of the Amendment, 270 Content and 96 Notcontent. Of the 96 Peers supporting the Government, 93 took the Labour whip and 16 held ministerial office. (One Minister, Lord Winterbottom, was ill and did not attend the debate.) The other 3 Not-contents were Crossbenchers: Lord Blackett, Lord Kirkwood, and Lord Platt. No Bishop supported the Government.

In favour of the Amendment were 207 Conservative Peers, 45 Crossbenchers, and 16 Liberals. Two Bishops, one of whom was the Bishop of Southwark, voted Content. As for the alleged backwoods contingent, the Division Lists admittedly contained the names of about 25 Peers who were otherwise very rarely seen in the House.

At least the Government could claim that Labour Peers had stood loyally behind the Administration. Their 93 supporters compared well with the 84 who had voted for sanctions against Rhodesia. But this time the Government were defeated by a far larger majority and, what is more, a majority that owed its superiority to Liberals and Crossbenchers rather than to implacable Conservatives. The Cabinet had awaited the vote anxiously and, though Labour Lords had been faithful, Ministers were disconsolate. They had lost the Division and had lost face as well.

In his speech Lord Shackleton had announced that his supporters would divide on the first Amendment only, treating the rest 'as at present drafted, with contempt'. Accordingly the other Amendments were carried consequentially without Division and the remaining stages of Report, Third Reading, and passage were merely a formality. The amended Bill was then returned to the Commons.

The Commons' Amendment

Though the Peers had scored one victory the last word still rested with the Lower House. Here the Government secured a repudiation of the Lords' Amendments and substituted their own. To some extent, this acknowledged that there had been some substance in the Lords' case, particularly in Lady Sharp's argument that waiting for the implementation of the Redcliffe-Maud Report would cause excessive delay. The Government Amendment attempted to conciliate the Lords by proposing that by March 1972—well after the next General Election—either a Boundary Commission should be reactivated or the 1969 recommendations laid before Parliament.

When the Bill came back to the Upper House, Lord Stonham had left the front bench and Lord Shepherd moved the Motion to agree with the Commons' Amendment. Lord Shackleton emphasized the Government's perfect rights in the matter, indicating that further interference from the Lords could only be futile. But this judgement was too harsh. Another defeat could put the Government in an awkward position from which they could only extricate themselves with more loss of prestige. Furthermore, the Lords were for once playing the role they had long coveted. As Lord Carrington pointed out,

The majority in the House of Commons can nowadays always get Bills through on a party basis, just as this Bill has come to us, guillotined, half-discussed and railroaded through their House. In this House, by the accident of its composition and by the independence of thought and mind of its members, no such thing is possible.[7]

The House remained hostile to what Peers saw as an affront to the dignity of Parliament itself and in demonstration of their independence divided upon the Motion to accept the Commons' Amendment. It was rejected. The Government ranks were as thin, thinner even, as in the earlier vote, for of the 78 Peers supporting

[7] Quotations from the debate on the Commons' Amendment in the Lords' Committee are taken from *HL Debs.*, vol. 304, col. 1543 et seq.

the Motion only 2 were drawn from the cross benches. Lord Kirkwood was one; Lord Blackett and Lord Platt did not vote. The other was Lord Helsby, who had voted against the Government in the Committee Stage but now felt that the Commons' Amendment had removed the taint of constitutional impropriety from the Bill. The 76 Labour Peers voting Content included 14 holding Ministerial office.

The Not-contents were also somewhat fewer but the majority was still as overwhelming. This time 229 Peers voted against the Government and 26 of these were Crossbenchers. The Bishop of Southwark obdurately voted against Labour and 13 Liberals joined in. Lord Shackleton's remark that again the Conservative Leader 'seemed to have a bit of overkill' amongst his Backbenchers was less justifiable than it had been in July. This time there were only half a dozen unfamiliar faces among the 189 Conservative supporters.

It was an indication of the moral defeat the Administration had suffered that they could attract the support of only 2 crossbench Peers and that as many as 26 voted with the Conservatives rather than abstaining. The fact that the Liberals turned out in such force against the Government and explicitly sided with the Tories underlined the contempt in which the Government's expedient was held. It was indeed the Peers' finest hour.

The Consequences

The Government were now in something of a fix, for procedurally as well as morally the Lords' gesture had not been entirely futile. The Seats Bill was now effectively delayed for a year by the terms of the 1947 Parliament Act and the Home Secretary was still obliged to proceed with laying the Orders before Parliament. So that the Orders need not be effected the Government adopted a suggestion which the Ministerial Committee had, it is said, seized upon as a 'most immoral' but most ingenious device. The Orders were laid before the Commons for affirmative resolution and the House was requested *not* to approve them. Labour M.P.s followed the advice of the Whips and voted against their own Home Secretary as he himself wished—a bizarre operation which the Conservative Opposition ridiculed delightedly.[8] Although the Administration

8 When the Conservatives returned to Office in June 1970 they announced their intention

succeeded in postponing the boundary alterations Labour's reputation was not enhanced in public eyes.

It was generally acknowledged that the Conservative Leadership in the Lords had played their hand opportunely and skilfully. The issue was certainly an ideal one on which to stand their ground. Unlike policy matters like the Iron and Steel Bill, the Land Commission Bill, or the Transport Bill, the legislation the Seats Bill proposed was not part of Labour's declared programme and they could not argue that the electorate had given them a mandate for it. Nor did the Government make out a very good case for the Seats Bill even though they had long been aware that this would be a sticky subject to deal with.

Whether or not the Peers' action was 'unconstitutional' as Labour alleged, whether or not the Conservatives would have behaved similarly in similar circumstances, the fact remains that the Tory Leaders in the Lords carefully played on the doubts of the informed public and successfully posed as constitutional watchdogs. The reasonable Conservative line drew together united opposition from Liberals, Crossbenchers, Bishops, and Conservatives, so that Labour could scarcely argue that the Amendment was passed by a horde of Tory backwoodsmen specially drummed up for the occasion. By restraining Conservative Backbenchers from throwing the Bill out on Second Reading or from proposing a sabotaging Amendment in Committee Stage, Lord Carrington, his Whips, and the elder statesmen of his party succeeded in clothing their demolition operation in a cloak of politeness and sensibility. Truly the Conservative Leaders made up for 'the botched shot' on sanctions against Rhodesia—they had, after all, more than one shot in their locker.

It is said that no mention was made in Cabinet of the difference that might have been made to the Government's position in the Lords had the Upper House been reformed on the lines of the Bill that had been abandoned earlier in the year. Even a House of voting Peers selected only from regular attenders might have refused to pass a Bill that seemed as cynical as the Seats Bill, according to the evidence of the Division Lists. It had, however, been a tactical mistake on the Government's part to break off the inter-party talks in 1968 and in April 1969 to drop the Reform Bill itself. When the

of proceeding with the implementation of the Boundary Commission's recommendations as soon as possible. The Orders were laid in Oct. 1970.

Seats Bill reached the Lords they were not only still piqued by the failure of reform but aware that now they had nothing to lose by outright opposition.

The Peers' conduct on the Seats Bill proved the need to reform the House. To those anxious to devise a useful and complementary House it provided further evidence that in the end, and after the time-consuming arguments about constitutionality had been reiterated, the Lords in their present form could never achieve more than a temporary victory. After all the fuss about the Seats Bill, eventually the Government had their way. To those who wished to remove the Lords' residual powers it implied that the Lords should be curbed once and for all. The majority of Ministers took the latter view and the Prime Minister was especially incensed. Not only had the Peers refused to accept the Commons' Amendment but they had placed the Home Secretary in an exceedingly unhappy position. This was to be of great significance in the months remaining until the end of the Parliament. For the present moment, however, the Lords could preen themselves on having exploited the limited opportunities of their role with the utmost skill.

7

THE ATTEMPT TO REFORM THE HOUSE OF LORDS; THE INTER-PARTY CONFERENCE

THE humiliation over the Southern Rhodesia (United Nations Sanctions) Order and the triumph on the Seats Bill amplified murmurs that the House has heard for years. If the Upper House never exercises its powers it is said to be redundant; if it does intervene it intrudes on the prerogatives of the Lower Chamber. Any bicameral system provokes problems of the division of powers but in this case the whole question of powers is intimidatingly entangled with that of composition. If the Lords' powers are to be made explicit and justifiable then simultaneously their peculiar composition has to be reformed. This was the intention in 1968 and 1969.

The story is a long one even when it is abbreviated to accord with private undertakings and official obligations.[1] However, it was so crucial an episode for the Lords that it is important to set out the history of the attempt and suggest reasons for its failure. In a sense, the lessons the fiasco taught were ones of general political strategy— that Parliamentary affairs also have their tide, which must be caught at exactly the right moment if a campaign is to succeed; that Governments are sometimes better advised to persist with unpopular measures than to weaken their own authority by abandoning them; that when legislative proposals are complicated they invite obstructive and prevaricating opposition.

These observations particularly concern the Government's procedure and practice in the Commons but the narrative also takes up themes that are specifically relevant to this study of the Lords. One significant feature was the contempt and suspicion with which many M.P.s see the Upper House as well as their reluctance to make the Lords a less ridiculous and thus a more dangerous rival. Another

---

[1] Official Cabinet papers are not yet publicly available. This account owes much to official papers in the keeping of the Lords' Journal Office, to the diaries of Richard Crossman, and to the recollections of some of the Ministers and officials most closely involved.

theme is that of the workings of the usual channels. Just as the early months of the campaign showed how productive inter-party consultation can be, so the breakdown of co-operation in the last phase, as the Bill struggled through Parliament, illustrates how fatal is the lack of conventional understandings between the party Leaders. Moreover the sorry tale of the Parliament (No. 2) Bill picks out another theme of this study. Earlier chapters have described the way in which the Lords rely on unwritten customs of political decorum rather than on the strict rules of time-tabling and procedure that usually constrain the Commons. It is not easy to see any particular advantages in depending on self-restraint rather than narrow rules for the conduct of Parliamentary business but this particular case provides an instructive contrast between the Commons' rigorous methods and the laxness of the Lords. Far from controlling and regulating proceedings in the Commons, the niceties of Standing Orders were a means for M.P.s to obstruct and frustrate and finally sabotage the Bill.

But this was the last stage in a complicated sequence of events that falls into three distinct phases: the Inter-party Conference, the publication of the White Paper, and, finally, the collapse of the Bill. Their beginning lies in the early years of Labour's Administration.

The Manifesto

Outright abolition of the Lords had once been a traditional part of Labour's programme but this aim disappeared after 1935. Very few party members felt that it was politically practicable but, nevertheless, as a party Labour were in favour of some change in the Lords' powers. The 1964 Election Manifesto included the phrase that 'Certainly we shall not permit effective action to be frustrated by the hereditary and non-elective Conservative majority in the House of Lords.'

Between 1964 and 1966 this was not put to the test. The Government's majority in the Commons was precarious and issues as contentious as Lords' reform or the renationalization of steel were prudently postponed. There was a more pressing programme of more urgent legislation. Furthermore, with self-restraint and caution any great difference between the Houses was prevented.

After the honeymoon, however, there was no surprise when the 1966 Election Manifesto announced that a Labour Government would introduce legislation 'to safeguard measures approved by the House of Commons from frustration by delay or defeat in the House of Lords'. But there was still small indication of what steps the Government were prepared to take and no unanimity among members of the party, in Lords or Commons. Some Labour members professed to be staunch reformers but others were less passionate about curbing the Lords' powers. This was not solely for the tactical reason that even with a Commons' majority of 99 such a drastic constitutional change might prove impossible. The preservationists had other motives. Some felt that the Lords still had a useful role to play as a complementary chamber with some authority. Some may have had lordly ambitions themselves, while others suggested that the best way to hasten the Lords' natural death would be to allow them to potter on into decrepitude.

Ministers were lukewarm at a time when more urgent departmental Bills were in preparation and, although a small Committee of officials met in February 1967 to work on a Bill to remove the Lords' residual delaying powers, the Cabinet showed little enthusiasm for such a measure.

None the less rumours of reform unsettled Conservative diehards in both Houses. They were particularly afraid of legislation by the Labour Party. Though Labour now had a sizeable number of their own supporters in the Lords, they were still considered unsympathetic to its traditions and activities. On the other hand, many Conservative Peers together with members of the other parties and the cross benches acknowledged that reform was necessary. If the Lords remained unaltered they risked either a catastrophic clash with the Commons or gradual etiolation as they lost all credibility and respect. On several occasions the Peers themselves had advocated various schemes of reform and the time seemed appropriate for another debate on the subject.

The Lords' Debate

On 12 April 1967 Lord Mitchison, a notable radical, proposed a Motion for Papers calling attention to the need for reform.[2] From the Labour front bench the Lord Privy Seal and Leader of the House, Lord Longford, said that while this was not the proper occasion to go into details of the Government's intentions, they

---

[2] *HL Debs.*, vol. 281, cols. 1287–1396.

held to the pledge given in the Manifesto and would take note of points raised in the debate. The official Labour line was therefore still obscure. The words from the Opposition front bench were more interesting.

Lord Carrington, the Leader, was abroad and Lord Harlech, the Deputy Leader, spoke for the Conservatives. He observed that the chief criticism that could be levelled against the Upper House at the present time was the built-in Conservative majority, and, on the question of the hereditary Peers, he admitted that

in this day and age [this] is not really a rational basis on which to run a second chamber in a democracy . . . If we are to achieve a fair balance between the parties in this House . . . then this particular nettle will have to be grasped.

Lord Harlech promised that the Conservatives would be very ready to discuss proposals for improving the Upper House and the way in which it worked. Although it was understood that his words in no way committed the party, the speech had evidently been carefully considered before the debate.

It was a godsend to Labour Ministers who wanted a constructive measure of reform for they could refer to Lord Harlech's remarks in explaining to their colleagues that a Bill dealing solely with powers might be unnecessarily destructive. If, as it now appeared, the Conservative front bench in the Lords were willing even to consider jettisoning the hereditary right to a seat, then legislation to reform both powers and composition might at last be possible.

The debate came at a particularly fruitful moment. For the best part of a year two of the Labour Ministers in the Lords had been urging the Cabinet to undertake reform of powers and composition together. They had prepared a joint paper, of which the first half argued that, with composition unaltered, the hereditary Peers would still be in control. Even with their residual delaying powers removed they would be in a position to frustrate Government legislation in the last year of a Parliament. This was a skilful piece of advocacy, especially as it came from an impeccably radical Minister.

The second half of the paper suggested a two-tier scheme of voting and non-voting Peers. One of the Ministers and his assiduous Private Secretary had adapted this from an earlier scheme. Apparently the Cabinet Secretariat were interested in their ideas

and the Prime Minister agreed that reforming the Lords' composition was worth while. Opinion in the Cabinet still favoured
a reform dealing only with powers. For this reason the Cabinet
Committee that was established in July 1967 was asked to consider
this aspect alone.

Those who sought to deal with both powers and composition
were not put off and at this point they acquired new allies. The
Labour Chief Whip in the Lords, Lord Shepherd, showed immense
energy in explaining the situation to business managers in the
Commons, and his discussions with the Chief Whip in the Lower
House were especially important. The Lords' Deputy Leader, Lord
Shackleton, became increasingly intrigued by the opportunity for
a constructive reform and, at the Commons' end, Richard Crossman
seized on its possibilities. Sympathetic personal relations between
these two proponents were to prove extremely valuable in the
coming months as they grew more influential in discussions.

In these first weeks of the summer of 1967, the Committee was
bombarded with papers setting out possible schemes of reform. The
Clerk and the civil servants who served the Committee were not
only thorough but imaginative and enthusiastic as well. Gradually
the Committee found themselves considering powers and composition as interconnected questions. By late summer it had
become apparent that opinion was divided over three schemes.

The Three Schemes

The most radical plan was for a House of three hundred Peers,
all appointed by some sort of committee. All would have voting
rights and there would be an assured Government majority. Two
members of the Committee favoured this 'one-tier' scheme.

The simple 'two-tier' proposal was for a House where some Peers
had only speaking rights, while others, selected initially from the
present Life Peers and Peers of first creation, would have voting
rights as well. This scheme was preferred by one of the early proponents of reform.

The refined 'two-tier' scheme was much more complicated. It
proposed a House of voting and non-voting Peers, with some of the
present hereditary Peers among those permitted to vote as well as
speak. The hereditary Peers would be permitted to serve out their
time (the natural death rate would gently but firmly ensure a

Burkean organic adaptation) and the power to create new Peers would remain. The number of voting Peers would be balanced among the parties to assure a 'sensible' Government majority. There would, however, be crossbench Peers and some scope for the Government to be defeated occasionally. To counter an inevitable tendency to conservatism the scheme would include some method for disqualifying Peers. Regularity of attendance might be the criterion for this. Four members of the Committee thought highly of these intricate proposals.

It was difficult to achieve agreement. Discussions were complex and meetings were between busy men preoccupied by departmental and Parliamentary business. No sooner did debate take a constructive turn than members would have to disperse. It was therefore an imaginative and generous stroke when one of the keenest supporters of reform arranged for the Committee to confer undisturbed at Chequers, borrowed from the Prime Minister, at his invitation. In these more leisurely surroundings three more supporters were won over to the refined two-tier scheme and consensus was achieved.

The Queen's Speech

No firm decisions had been taken at these early meetings but at least those concerned had now resolved to consider powers and composition and to explore the possibilities of the complex two-tier plan. This represented a victory for those Ministers like Richard Crossman and Lord Shackleton who wanted to use reform to shape a strong complementary Upper House rather than to trim the Lords' residual powers so that they would wither away into insignificance. Their success was reflected in the bald paragraph in the Queen's Speech on 31 October, at the beginning of the 1967–68 Session. It promised that

Legislation will be introduced to reduce the present powers of the House of Lords and to eliminate its present hereditary basis, thereby enabling it to develop within the framework of a modern Parliamentary system.

But more striking was the next sentence: 'My Government are prepared to enter into consultations appropriate to a constitutional change of such importance.' From this reference the Inter-party Conference was born. But the Government's offer had been by no means spontaneous. A week before the Queen's Speech the members of the Cabinet in the Lords, Lord Gardiner and Lord Longford, had approached the Opposition Leaders, Lord Carrington and Lord Jellicoe, to discuss the phrasing of the paragraph. To the Opposition's distress, there had been no mention of consultation in the Speech. Though inter-party discussions seemed intelligent and reasonable to those with a mutual interest in an acceptable reform and to Frontbenchers used to the working of the usual channels, M.P.s would be less accustomed to the idea of cross-party negotiations on important matters of policy. It was therefore necessary to explain to the Cabinet and the P.L.P. the implications and arguments for inter-party consultations before the sentence suggested by the Opposition could be accepted. Careful negotiation between the Chief Whips in each House persuaded Labour members to agree; thus the Government committed themselves.

The sentence duly appeared in the Speech, and in the Commons' debate the Leader of the Opposition's probing question clarified any remaining doubts. He asked whether full and proper consultations were meant or whether the Government would merely inform the Opposition of their intentions. The Prime Minister's reply established the Government's attitude. He said that

> It would have been a discourtesy to those who will be taking part if we had put forward cut-and-dried plans this afternoon before the consultations had taken place. We shall be ready to consider any alternative suggestions made by right hon. Gentlemen to achieve the same objectives and principles. The consultations will be real consultations.[3]

But he did warn that, if no agreement was possible or if the talks were so 'unconscionably delayed' that legislation would not be possible in that Session, the Government would proceed with their own legislation. The time-table was optimistic but the warning was plain.

Some of the Cabinet had doubted whether the P.L.P. would welcome these proposals but to some extent the shock had been softened by an exclusive and well-informed story by James Margach in the *Sunday Times*. At the lobby conference after the Speech, the Lord President (the post was now held by Richard Crossman) and Lord Shackleton explained that the Government were not yet committed to any precise plans for reform. This reserved statement was

---

[3] *HC Debs.*, vol. 785, cols. 27–30.

belied by the enthusiasm Lord Longford clearly showed for a two-tier scheme, but only the *Guardian* correspondent, Ian Aitken, noticed it. This was fortunate because Ministers did not want to alarm the Opposition in Lords or Commons nor to suggest specific proposals. Ideas held in reserve at this stage might be useful as 'concessions' later on.

At the Labour Party meeting a cheer was given when Lords' reform was mentioned. M.P.s seemed to approve provided that 'we don't give too much away' to the Conservatives. There was already a favourable nucleus of M.P.s in the Parliamentary Reform Group. Richard Crossman's role had by now become important. In September 1967 the Prime Minister had reshuffled his Cabinet, making Mr. Crossman Lord President of the Council and Leader of the House of Commons, encouraging him to undertake the procedural renovations in the Commons for which the Select Committee and some energetic young Labour M.P.s were so keen. Mr. Crossman himself had long advocated Parliamentary reforms for both Lords and Commons and, inspired by his own Introduction to Bagehot's *English Constitution*,[4] he believed that a reformed and justifiable Upper House might make the Lower House more rather than less effective. Some of the Commons' more tedious everyday preoccupations could appropriately be given to a reconstituted Lords. Mr. Crossman was also finding the duties of his new office intellectually less challenging than those of his former Department, the Ministry of Housing and Local Government, and he therefore grasped this chance eagerly. He began to sound out the Cabinet, the Cabinet Secretariat, and the Whips' Office on the possibilities of introducing not only such Commons' reforms as morning sittings and Select Committees but also a far-reaching plan for the Lords. After the Queen's Speech, he and the Chief Whip proceeded smartly with the arrangements for inter-party consultations.

The Inter-party Conference

The Leader of the Opposition, Edward Heath, and of the Liberal Party, Jeremy Thorpe, accepted the Prime Minister's invitation to take part in the talks and all three party Leaders showed some interest in the early stages of discussion. All possessed, it is true, a professional concern with patronage. The Prime Minister had

---

[4] Introduction to *The English Constitution* (1963).

the additional responsibility for explaining to the Palace what the Conference was trying to do. He and Edward Heath attended the first meeting of the inter-party group on 8 November 1967.

At this and subsequent meetings the Government were represented by the Lord Chancellor (Lord Gardiner), the Lord Privy Seal and Leader of the Lords (Lord Longford), and the Deputy Leader (Lord Shackleton). After January 1968, Lord Shackleton attended as Leader, having replaced Lord Longford.

From the Commons, the Government had the Lord President (Richard Crossman), the Home Secretary (Roy Jenkins), and the Chief Whip (John Silkin), who apparently attended once. After November 1967, James Callaghan replaced Roy Jenkins as Home Secretary.

The Conservative Party was represented by Lord Carrington and Lord Jellicoe, and from the Commons, Reginald Maudling and Iain Macleod. The Liberals sent Lord Byers and Jeremy Thorpe. The Conservative Chief Whip in the Lords, Lord St. Aldwyn, also came occasionally.

The official Committee was served by Secretaries drawn from the Cabinet Office, the Home Office, and the Parliament Office in the Lords and, in a curious combination of Minister and chief executive, this official Committee was chaired by Lord Shackleton. It is unusual to find a Minister chairing a committee of officials but in this case the peculiar abilities of its members blended well. As a working party it proved immensely industrious and productive.

Before the first meeting of the Conference a Ministerial Committee had to decide which department should take responsibility for the eventual Bill. The Lord Chancellor argued that his department was already overburdened and anyhow it was not really equipped for major legislative work. Civil servants agreed that a department with a Parliamentary branch was required to give technical advice and information to spokesmen, prepare notes on clauses, and so forth. (Had the Civil Service Department existed it would have been appropriate but at that time it had not yet been established.) The Committee therefore decided that the Bill would be undertaken by the Home Secretary, Roy Jenkins (later James Callaghan), and Richard Crossman. They would take responsibility, leaving the Lord Chancellor to act not as a Government representative but as judicial Chairman of the full Inter-party

N

Conference. The decision to send the Bill to the Home Office for preparation was to have unfortunate repercussions later on.

The Lord President, not the Lord Chancellor, thus acted as the advocate of the Government's proposals but no official Labour line was laid down before the Conference met. Richard Crossman himself felt that some Commons' business—subordinate legislation and Private Bills, for instance—could be shunted on to the renovated Upper House but the other Government representatives had not entertained ideas of such scope. Nevertheless, they were broadly agreed that the Lords' powers for delaying legislation and vetoing delegated legislation should be curbed. As for changing composition, at least one Minister had his own fanciful schemes for a sort of exotic Privy Council, others were by now in favour of some two-tier scheme and some wished to keep the proposal in reserve. Lord Longford, at least, was publicly committed to it. Nor had the Government representatives any definite mandate from the P.L.P. A straw poll of Labour M.P.s in December 1967 showed no particular preference for any specific scheme.[5]

The representatives of the other parties were also unconstrained by a formal mandate. It was clear, though, that the Conservatives were most unhappy at the idea of ending the hereditary right to a seat in the Lords. As this was a matter that concerned Peers of all parties, it was the especial task of the Lords' party Leaders to discuss with their House and amongst themselves. Meetings of the Conference went smoothly and by Christmas 1967 it was firmly established that all parties would agree to the Bill's covering both powers and composition and that the question of the Lords' delaying power would be a crucial one.

The Sub-Committee

Before the full Conference met again in January, there were many meetings of a small Sub-Committee of the party Leaders in the Lords: Lord Shackleton, Lord Byers, and Lord Jellicoe (taking the place of Lord Carrington, who was in Australia). Not surprisingly, there was an interesting contrast between the way in which this group and the full Conference worked. At the Conference, where the Government had the upper hand, there was more of a disposi-

---

[5] M.P.s were asked six questions on Lords' reform. The bulk wanted a reform based on an agreed solution and did not care deeply about delaying powers, Life Peers only, or a determining Government majority.

tion for members to regard themselves as representatives of political parties, sitting very much as delegates and bargaining for concessions. In the smaller group, however, the three Leaders were familiar colleagues, accustomed to making mutual accommodations in managing their own House. Moreover, as Peers themselves they realized how unpredictable the reactions of their Backbenchers could be and how important it was that reform proposals had the support of the Lords as a collective House, where all are theoretically equal. The Lords' debate on the White Paper was to show how successful the Leaders were in coaxing the House along. (Had there been a representative of the Commons on the Sub-Committee, Minister or Backbencher, it might have been easier to appreciate the qualms M.P.s were feeling.)

The Sub-Committee also understood that the Crossbenchers' opinions had to be considered and, although they had no official representative on the Committee, their views were sought at every stage. Whenever it was possible the interested Crossbenchers were given information that could be passed on to the others. Whilst all three Leaders on the Sub-Committee were intensely politically minded (Lord Shackleton and Lord Byers had been in the Commons and Lord Jellicoe had had youthful aspirations to sit there), they had a genuine affection for the Lords and were sensitive to its problems. The Sub-Committee almost formed in itself a delegation to the full Conference.

Lord Shackleton's Model House

The group was given no research facilities but fortunately the three Leaders and the two Secretaries, one from the Home Office and one from the Lords' Parliament Office, who had been assigned to the full Conference, were energetic and inventive. Like the proceedings of the Conference those of the Sub-Committee were confidential. Much of the work of the smaller group was informal and it is said that the Secretaries would often take notes of the discussion rather than formal minutes, themselves injecting new ideas or an occasional cautionary word into conversations. Academic authorities are said to have been uninterested and to have made few useful suggestions; no doubt the group's sense of isolation, as they spontaneously generated schemes and models, made it more difficult for them to avoid being carried giddily away.

The Sub-Committee had many informal meetings during the spring and summer of 1968 and prepared quantities of papers and statistical notes for the full Conference. Since the early discussions in the autumn of 1967, Lord Shackleton had criticized the unsystematic way in which the Lords' composition and activities had been examined hitherto. He was particularly eager to apply techniques of quantitative analysis in studying the performance of the House. His suggestion that a model of a reformed House should be devised was coolly received by the Home Office. Those whom he consulted at the Ministry of Defence advised him that a complete analysis could cost as much as £15,000–£20,000. However, the Home Office eventually gave their help in running some simple analyses and different models of a reconstituted Upper House were prepared.

These were based on the full figures for Peers' attendance: age, party affiliation, type of peerage, and so forth, among those who were entitled to attend the House, those who actually did so, and those who performed its various activities.[6] Models were devised which showed the effect that different retiring ages, as well as the natural death-rate, would have on a reformed House. They illustrated the possible influence of systems of renominating voting Peers at successive General Elections. The small group, in particular the two Secretaries and the Leader, studied the flow of business between the two Houses, the exercise of the Lords' various powers, their procedural problems, timing of sittings, claims for expenses, and pattern of Divisions.

It is certainly true to say that their persistence was justified and Lord Shackleton vindicated at a later stage. Although the models were insufficiently sophisticated to deserve official publication, much of the statistical work provided indispensable ammunition when the Parliament (No. 2) Bill was struggling through the Commons. What is more, the Peers themselves needed reassuring that the implications of a reformed House with a definite retiring age had been thoroughly explored.

On the other hand, there were drawbacks to a situation where a small group of enthusiastic reformers grew to know so much more about the scope of a renovated House than their colleagues in the Conference or in Parliament. All too frequently, those who devise theoretical models are apt to lose touch with the sceptical world

---

[6] Many of these statistics have been cited in previous chapters.

outside. Refining and perfecting their brainchild, they become increasingly captivated by its potentialities, growing immune to criticism, and dismissing the doubts of mere practical men. In such a way, the ultimate scheme for a reformed House became more and more complex. This was a factor in its undoing.

Despite the Sub-Committee's industry, progress was slow and negotiations delicate. This proved the extravagance of the original hope that the Conference would complete its work within two or three months so that its recommendations could be introduced as legislation during the 1967-68 Session. By March 1968, however, two major points had been settled.

The Delaying Period

When it had been decided in the first weeks of January 1968 that the reformed House would operate a two-tier system of voting and non-voting Peers, it was agreed that in return for abandoning the hereditary principle the Conservatives would be given generous arrangements for the delaying period. It was ironic that intellectually and emotionally the Tories should set more store by the Lords' delaying power while Labour representatives at the Conference now appreciated that it was the Lords' composition, that is, the sizeable hereditary element, that could in fact make life difficult for the Government. Indeed, the two Labour Frontbenchers, Lord Shackleton and Lord Shepherd, knew from experience that the Lords' delaying powers were more apparent than real, and that the longer the Peers were entitled to hold up legislation, the less likely they might be to use such embarrassing stratagems.

At the Conference it emerged that the Government wished to give a reformed House the power to delay Bills for six months from Third Reading in the Commons; the Conservatives wanted nine months from the point of disagreement with the Commons, which was tantamount to a year from Commons' Third Reading. Bargaining indicated that six months from the point of disagreement was the most acceptable compromise and this scheme was eventually adopted and announced to the public. A 'carry-over' principle was also devised, whereby disputed Bills could be presented for Royal Assent at the end of the period of delay, even if this ran over a Prorogation at the end of a Session or a Dissolution at the end of a Parliament.

By spring 1968, therefore, at least the two-tier principle and the six-month delaying power had been settled. This, however, seemed small progress, for these had been features of earlier measures of Lords' reform. Many intricate points still required solution. Some of these were dealt with in March and April.

Details of the Scheme

The Party Balance

By March it had been roughly agreed that in a reformed House the Government should have a majority over all parties of at least ten. The Liberals would have about twenty members, Conservative and Labour would be almost equal, with the small majority for the Government. However, the inclusion of thirty to forty cross-bench Peers with no affiliation would permit an occasional Government defeat in the face of united opposition from the rest of the House. Provision was made for three parties—Labour, Conservative, and Liberal—but the scheme could be revised if circumstances changed.

A Government majority of ten seemed small and was to disappoint dedicated members of the P.L.P. The Labour representatives at the Conference were willing to settle for this to avoid a situation where an incoming Administration would be obliged to make an unwieldy number of new creations. And if a combination of the Crossbenchers and the other parties could occasionally defeat the Government, albeit narrowly, the House would not appear to be the creature of the Administration.

It was suggested that there might be a Selection Committee to choose the crossbench Peers and to pay special attention to regional and Scottish Peers. The Conference itself might be perpetuated as such an advisory body. Eventually, though, the members decided to retain the Prime Minister's normal selection procedure for creations and hope that sensible choices might be made.

Bishops

The Bishops were also concerned about their position. Early in April three or four, led by the Archbishop of Canterbury, came to the Conference to seek reassurance on the matter of their voting rights. They agreed with a proposal to reduce the twenty-six Lords Spiritual to sixteen, with five being allowed to vote as well as speak, but they were anxious lest these five should somehow turn out to be the more idiosyncratic members of the Bishops' Bench. The Conference would not agree to the delegates' request that they be allowed to choose their own voting Bishops but suggested instead that the five should be the *ex officio* Bishops (the two Archbishops of Canterbury and York and the Bishops of London, Durham, and Winchester). The delegation appreciated the fact that it was arguable that no Bishops should be included in a reformed House at all and agreed to accept the offer, especially as the Conference promised to look closely at the recommendations of the Church's own forthcoming Report on Church and State.[7]

Remuneration

The question of Peers' remuneration was a delicate one. When various schemes for reform had been discussed by Labour Ministers the previous autumn, one suggestion had been for a House of voting Peers selected by the Whips and, like M.P.s, paid a salary. The objection to this was that public opinion as well as the Conservative Opposition would never accept the principle of an Upper House of acquiescent Peers first chosen by the Whips and then paid for their work. Indeed, the Prime Minister eventually announced to the Commons that the whole issue of payment for Peers would be dropped from the Parliament Bill, so resentful were the criticisms of M.P.s.

In a reformed House, though, it seemed sensible to provide an expenses allowance to cover fares and so on for speaking Peers and it was generally accepted at the Conference that voting Peers would be offered substantially more. Whether this would be an annual or a *per diem* allowance, and how it was to be calculated, were difficult questions to decide. One view was that 'the old warhorses', the solid phalanx of voting Peers, might prefer an annual allowance rather like a salary and Lord Shackleton described an ingenious scheme (borrowed from the Canadian Senate) by which those who failed to fulfil their attendance quota would have to repay a proportion. Another view was that Peers would prefer an expenses system, particularly the more affluent members of the House who paid a high rate of tax. This sensitive matter was left unresolved.

[7] The Bishops were fortunate. The White Paper ultimately remained ambiguous and it was not clear whether all sixteen Bishops could qualify as voters if they were frequent attenders. According to an official source, the ambiguity was 'smuggled in'.

Qualifications for Voting Peers

Instead of spending time on these important but fiddly questions, the Conference gave much of March and April 1968 to the stiffer problems of reform, one of which was the criterion by which Peers would acquire voting rights. The Conference was divided. The Labour Peers (Lord Gardiner and Lord Shackleton) were the most moderate. They suggested a Sessional arrangement so that Peers who at the beginning of a Session opted only for speaking rights could request voting rights at the beginning of a subsequent Session.

Richard Crossman was more strict, maintaining that a Peer's decision should hold for the life of a whole Parliament. By far the most severe was Lord Carrington, with his preference for 'worker-bees'—Peers who would say what they wanted and stick to it. Though he preferred that once a Peer had chosen only speaking rights the ban on his voting should be for life, he did allow that Peers wishing to re-qualify for voting rights could ask to be put on a waiting list. However, other members of the Conference pointed out that this would give even more patronage powers to the Prime Minister or the Lords' Whips. Not only would there be the task of nominating voting Peers in the first place but also that of reallocating voting privileges to those who had lost or originally renounced them. The 'waiting list' suggestion was not adopted but the Session v. Parliament dispute was not settled either.

Privileges of Speaking Peers

The Conference was equally undecided on the matter of rights of speaking Peers and by the end of April 1968 this question became a central part of the Labour case in the inter-party discussion. The Conservative representatives took the view that much of the everyday work of the House was done by an 'excellent bloc' of hereditary Peers and the three Lords' Leaders at the Conference agreed. They argued that these Peers by succession should retain the right to move Resolutions and Motions, but also, still more controversially, to vote both in Committee and in any joint Committees that might be held between Lords and Commons. This proposal was re-inforced by the argument that if the Commons' system of taking legislative Committees 'upstairs', rather than as Committees of the Whole House, were to be extended to the Lords, then any deciding vote would still be taken on the Floor of the House. It would thus be decided only by Peers with full voting rights. The Lords' party Leaders maintained that unless speaking Peers were permitted to vote in Committee it would be impossible to man Committees on Private Bills, for instance, because the pool of full-voting Peers would be too small.

Although Lord Shackleton and Richard Crossman had some sympathy for this view, other Labour representatives at the Conference suspected that it masked an attempt by the Conservatives to consolidate the position of a rump of hereditary Peers. Certainly a great number of the faithful attenders, with time to give to Committee work, were hereditary Peers who would be disqualified from voting, despite their assiduity, because this would upset the party balance in a reconstituted Lords. The radical view was that to draw upon the hereditary Peers in this practical way would be an impossible departure from principle.

Meetings at the end of March had shown that Labour M.P.s and Labour Peers were unhappy with the proposals and felt that they promised little political advantage for the party. Committed Labour backbench Peers thought that the proposed Government majority of ten was too small and the compromise plan for a six-month delaying power seemed to be a sacrifice of principle. The radical delegates to the Conference were therefore anxious to placate the party by remaining adamantly opposed to any erosion of the strict voting/non-voting distinction; the practical reformers felt that any apparently arbitrary discrimination between Peers by succession and by creation was unfortunate; and Lord Shackleton was obliged to warn the Conference that the Conservatives would hold out on this point. It could break the Conference or lead to deadlock. However, this was not the only major obstacle.

The Operative Date of Reform

There was also the question of the date from which reform would come into effect. The unreformed House could either continue to sit as it was constituted at present until the beginning of the next new Parliament or only until the end of the Session during which the Reform Bill was passed. There was some suspicion that the Conservative representatives at the Conference who were not keen on reform wished to postpone its implementation so that it might ultimately be avoided altogether. After a two- or three-year interval the momentum of the inter-party talks would have vanished and there might even be a Conservative Administration which could repeal reforming legislation.

Certainly to delay the operative date of the Act would allow a rump Conservative House to frustrate Labour legislation in the last years of the old Parliament—a tactical point which had not escaped the Conservatives at the Conference. Iain Macleod in particular was sceptical towards Lords' reform of any kind and adhered unshakably to the point of principle that the operative date should be later rather than sooner. In Macleod's absence, for he was an exceptionally skilled advocate, the Conference came near to agreement on one occasion during the summer. The other Conservative representatives seemed to approve of a complex suggestion of Lord Shackleton, based on the idea of a transitional period.

The Labour Leader argued that if implementation were postponed to the new Parliament at least a hundred new Peers would have to be created at a stroke, a break which Tory Peers would never accept. Immediate reform, however, would allow the new House to evolve smoothly from the old and the shock could be cushioned by a two-stage retirement age. During the transition period until the new Parliament, the retiring age could be put at 75, allowing forty or fifty older, experienced Peers to stay for the remaining Sessions. After the General Election the age could then be lowered to 72 for subsequent Parliaments. Lord Shackleton was able to demonstrate the subtleties of his scheme with the models prepared by the working group.

The Conservative Peers at the Conference (Lord Carrington and Lord Jellicoe) were anxious for a sensible reform and were ready to compromise. Nevertheless they were overridden by their colleagues from the Commons (Reginald Maudling and Iain Macleod) who were less determined to reach an agreed solution and more preoccupied by tactical considerations. It is important to remember that at this time the Government seemed to have lost the confidence of the country and the Conservatives wished to have little truck with Labour as the Administration's fortunes fell.

The issue of the operative date had still not been agreed when the implacable Iain Macleod returned to the Conference. In the previous week Labour had suffered defeat in four by-elections,[8] three

8 Acton, Dudley, Meriden, and Warwick and Leamington.

of which had been lost on a single day. Macleod argued that it would be grossly improper for the Government to implement Lords' reform when they lacked any popular support and that though, if pressed, he would agree to have a White Paper and a Bill, the Bill would only be acceptable if the operative date of reform were postponed to the beginning of the new Parliament.

The Press made out that Macleod was backed by the Shadow Cabinet and he refused to give way. Although by the beginning of May 1968 the Conference had sufficiently agreed on the other details of reform to prepare a draft White Paper, at a meeting on 7 May he declared that the Conservative representatives would refuse to sign it unless implementation were postponed. Richard Crossman, it was said, suggested that the White Paper could contain a dissenting paragraph signed by the Conservatives, on which the Commons could have a free vote. This was generous and ingenious and one Conservative delegate concurred, but the other alleged that a free vote would not in fact be 'a fair operation'.

This was a crucial question because the purpose of holding the Inter-party Conference had been to try to secure an agreed scheme. If all participants were to sign the White Paper it would be evident that all three parties were in favour of the Bill and committed to its success. Backbench M.P.s and Peers of all parties would then be expected to follow their Frontbenchers' recommendations and support the Bill. The intransigence of the Shadow Cabinet was therefore extremely worrying. There was little hope that the Labour representatives would give way in return for a Conservative pledge of good behaviour, for not only was it central to Labour's strategy that the House should be reconstituted well before the last year of the Parliament but even the most reasonable Labour delegate was anxious that the reformers' campaign should not lose momentum. Those who had pressed for a constructive reform were naturally eager to bring it to birth; they were also well aware that the longer the transitional period took the more dubious their schemes would appear. Neither Labour nor Conservatives would give way and on this issue the Conference was deadlocked. Later on, when the Parliament Bill reached the Commons, this issue was to become a focus of partisan conflict. At this point there was no further advance. Meanwhile events outside the world of the inter-party talks were becoming critical and they were to have a devastating effect on proceedings.

The Political Climate

As the Government's stock slumped so the Tory delegates from the Commons became even less enthusiastic towards the idea of an agreed reform. The Conservative Peers, on the other hand, wanted to debate a White Paper as soon as possible, lest the chance of reform elude the Lords again. Lord Carrington definitely wanted the Upper House to discuss the measure before the contentious Transport Bill reached the House in June and July.

This division between the Conservative representatives from the Lords and from the Commons was only one straw in the wind. The Peers of all parties wanted reform; the Commons' delegates, on the whole, were less eager. Richard Crossman was alone in his keenness to modernize the Lords, for his Commons colleagues were comparatively uninterested. Michael Stewart, who would have been a solid ally, could not be spared from his preoccupations at the Foreign Office; Roy Jenkins, whose book on the 1911 Reform Bill made him a natural proponent of reform, had left the Home Office for the Treasury. His successor, James Callaghan, was according to reports in the Press 'hardly an enthusiast'. Moreover, his acute political antennae warned him that the measure was unpalatable to M.P.s and parliamentarily uncertain. While Fred Peart had overcome his initial doubts and, once involved in the Conference, had become stalwartly loyal to the scheme, his other duties left him, like James Callaghan, with little scope to bother with the detailed drafting of the White Paper.

But it is too simple a diagnosis to attribute the difference in attitude to differences in personalities. Even if the world of the Peers was only half removed from the party distractions of the M.P.s at the Conference, this was enough to explain the contrast in their approach. For the Commons' delegates, reform was not a central part of their legislative lives; for the Lords it had become a vital and urgent duty. Richard Crossman, too, had invested so much energy and imagination in Lords' reform that it was for him much more than a tedious distraction. Indeed some weeks later he was to incur the disapproval of the Cabinet for his close fraternization with the Conservative Peers, an association which the Cabinet, unsympathetic to reform, understood only as co-operation with the enemy.

As May wore on, pressure of business made M.P.s more irritable and the Government's increasing unpopularity was reflected in by-election results and opinion polls. The Cabinet struggled within the constraints of Britain's unhappy financial situation and the problems resulting from taking the Finance Bill in Committee upstairs brought the Crossman Parliamentary reforms into increasing disrepute. Lords' reform and inter-party co-operation were anathema equally to both Cabinet and Shadow Cabinet and to both left- and right-wing M.P.s. The Peers' Leaders and Richard Crossman became gradually more depressed about the prospects of passing a Parliament Bill at all—but if they tried to rush the operation they might attract even more hostility.

The small group of vigorous reformers (as the Lords' Leaders and Mr. Crossman could be called) therefore hoped to take the White Paper through Cabinet before the Whitsun Recess and to the Shadow Cabinet immediately after the Recess, so that it could be put to both Houses for debate as soon as possible after that. The White Paper was drafted in great secrecy, for both Cabinet and Shadow Cabinet believed it was to be the work of the Peers' Sub-Committee. In fact Lord Shackleton, Lord Carrington, and Lord Byers appreciated that the draft would be more swiftly and professionally prepared if it was the responsibility of only one Minister, working with the two indispensable Secretaries. It was left in the hands of Richard Crossman.

The draft White Paper was ready by mid May but the reformers' despondency grew as the Parliamentary atmosphere became ever less propitious. One Minister disliked the authority that was apparently given to the crossbench Peers; another declared that the Bill would never be accepted by the P.L.P.; the Chief Whip, according to well-informed Press accounts, was pessimistic. Lord Carrington reported that Conservative Peers were equally unhappy. Mr. Crossman and the Sub-Committee of Peers anticipated a hard task when Parliament reassembled after the summer.

The Counter-plot

They would have been even more troubled had they known that a counter-plan was already being prepared. It is difficult to uncover the whole history of this affair but it has been suggested that during the Whitsun Recess, while Mr. Crossman was abroad, officials had been asked to prepare a short Bill to trim the Lords' remaining powers but with no provisions for reforming their composition or extending their functions. Those who had been working on the draft schemes and the White Paper were carefully excluded. The Labour Leader in the Lords had heard some mention that a short 'powers-only' measure could be drafted, using a chopped-up draft of the full scheme and curbing the Lords' delaying powers from three to six months. But he considered this no more than ill-informed speculation. In their ignorance, the Peers' working party and Mr. Crossman at least believed there was no ready alternative to their own scheme.

The Vote on the Southern Rhodesia (*United Nations Sanctions*) Order

As chapter 5 showed, it was the Southern Rhodesia Sanctions vote that brought things to a head. Until the middle of June, the Lords had displayed great self-restraint and their Leaders had been most careful not to jeopardize the talks by any ill-considered action. But the Government's rapid decline in the early summer of 1968 nourished feelings that Labour had lost its grip and will to govern. The Opposition in the Lords could no longer take the Government seriously. In these circumstances, as the earlier chapter describes,[9] the Leader of the Opposition in the Lords came under heavy pressure to use his majority. When the Shadow Cabinet refused to adopt the device of a vote of censure instead of voting down the Southern Rhodesia Order he finally capitulated and agreed to support the vote against sanctions with a whip.

It was against this background of an intolerably crowded Parliamentary time-table, sweltering hot weather, and mutual suspicion between those favouring and those opposed to Lords' reform that there occurred the curious incident of Roy Jenkins's Birmingham speech (to which chapter 5 referred).[10] Lord Shackleton had been hinting for some time that by rejecting the Southern Rhodesia (United Nations Sanctions) Order the Tory Peers might thereby sabotage the inter-party talks and the opportunity to secure an agreed reform scheme. He once again made this point at a lobby meeting and the reference was taken up by *The Times*.

The storm intensified when the Chancellor of the Exchequer, Roy Jenkins, repeated the threat to break off the talks in a speech on Saturday, 15 June. Press reports varied in their comments on the speech. Some speculated that the Chancellor had interpreted

[9] See p. 142.   [10] See p. 143.

Lord Shackleton's very sensible warning as the official No. 10 briefing; others even suggested that the Prime Minister had not cleared the speech and was troubled by the Chancellor's remarks. Roy Jenkins seemed to be more radical than Harold Wilson and this, it has been hazarded, spurred the Prime Minister on in his determination to attack the problem of the recalcitrant Peers even more drastically and, as then seemed likely, to break off the talks.

This may have been an extravagant analysis. However, it can certainly be said that the Cabinet's hostility towards the Peers increased when the Tories' decision to oppose the Order became known. As for the Conservatives, the diehard Peers grew even more violently opposed to the Government in the face of the Cabinet's minatory remarks. As Lord Shackleton had feared, the suggestion that the talks might be broken off was counter-productive in that, far from deterring the diehards from rejecting the Order, it perhaps induced some Conservatives to attend the debate who would otherwise have stayed away.

The Commons were to debate the Order on Monday, 17 June, and the Lords over two days, Monday, 17 and Tuesday, 18 June. Those in the Cabinet who saw this as an appropriate opportunity to break off the talks drew some comfort from a Gallup Poll published on 18 June which showed that a majority of the sample disapproved of the Lords' 'interference' on the sanctions question. While the Lords debated, the group of reformers anxiously awaited the Division. This was a rare Parliamentary occasion when the outcome of a vote was genuinely in doubt.

When it was announced that the Government had been defeated by only nine votes, Richard Crossman and Lord Shackleton jubilantly analysed the result. It augured well for the future of a House reformed according to their scheme. The bloc of predominantly hereditary Conservative Peers who had turned out against the Order were of the same group whose voting rights would probably disappear in a reformed House. On this occasion they had nearly been outvoted by the sort of Peers, of all parties and largely of first creation, who would retain voting privileges in the reconstituted Upper House.

But while they celebrated over dinner in the Commons, Lord Shackleton and Richard Crossman received a shattering blow. At this point the counter-plan was revealed. As they speculated about the consequences of the Government's defeat, a source in the Whips'

Office remarked that there need be no delay in introducing a Bill to end the powers of the Lords as it had already been prepared. Indeed, the protagonists of constructive reform seemed to have been outmanœuvred and the Peers' vote against the Order had finally ditched their campaign.

The Prime Minister himself, who had not realized that the episode was one where Lord Carrington had bowed under extreme pressure, believed that Edward Heath and the Shadow Cabinet had used the Lords to engineer a humiliating Government defeat. There was an outburst of popular indignation against the Lords and a section of the P.L.P. was furious. (William Hamilton was already dashing down an Early Day Motion demanding instant abolition.) In such circumstances it was impossible to proceed with an all-party proposal.

It is said that on the following day, Wednesday, 19 June, Mr. Crossman telephoned the Chief Whip, but he too felt that there could now be no question of carrying through an agreed scheme. The reformers had lost another ally. At a meeting of Ministers with the Prime Minister that morning, the constructive reformers argued against the proposal to introduce forthwith a short Bill to curtail the Lords' remaining powers, in response to the drastic retaliatory action for which Government supporters in the Commons would undoubtedly press. The Prime Minister, according to some accounts, attacked the dream world of the Inter-party Conferences and confidences. The real political climate had undoubtedly grown more bitter since the days of the Queen's Speech in October 1967. It now seemed that the only way to remove the obstruction of the Lords was to curb their powers immediately, postponing indefinitely any tinkerings with composition.

In reply the practical reformers apparently argued that it would not only be a repudiation of the original agreement, if powers were trimmed without altering composition, but that the two reforms were in fact inseparable. The Lords' delaying powers, they emphasized, were not their major weapons of obstruction. Their real power lay in possessing an overwhelming number of Conservative Peers with the capacity to filibuster, to hold up all legislation, if they were provoked by an angry and hasty Parliament Bill. In this sense, 'composition' was at the root of 'powers'.

Moreover, from a business point of view, the Lords could put the Government in some difficulty if Amendments were added to the short Bill dealing with powers. Furthermore, the proposed short Bill did not sidestep the provisions of the 1947 Parliament Act. Though the Government could pass a Bill in twelve to thirteen months, during that time the Conservative Peers could, by an intelligent use of their powers, hold up business indefinitely, including the Prices and Incomes Bill and the Transport Bill. By the end of what was by all accounts a stormy meeting the reformers had won the acquiescence of the Prime Minister but it was still not clear whether or not the talks would be resumed and what kind of constructive Parliament Bill could now be introduced. These matters were to be discussed at Cabinet on Thursday morning.

The End of the Inter-party Conference

In the interval, on Wednesday afternoon, those who had been particularly concerned to achieve an agreed scheme had a melancholy and secret meeting on the neutral territory of the Lords. It was plain that the talks could not be resumed nor an agreed plan implemented. Just as the Conservative Leader had had to allow backbench Peers to have their way so Mr. Crossman was vulnerable to similar pressure from his Backbenchers in the Commons. Once partisan considerations had entered the affair any co-operative solution was impossible.

Not only had backbench Labour M.P.s been assured that the agreed plan would be dropped but the Press overwhelmingly expected that on Thursday, 20 June the Prime Minister would announce a Bill to abolish the Lords. The question was fought out as the first item on the Cabinet agenda that morning. One opinion was that Edward Heath should be strongly denounced for the Lords' outrageous rejection of the Order, an action completely contradicting the spirit of the inter-party talks and fraught with dangerous complications for Britain, embarrassing us in the eyes of the U.N. and the world. The talks should be broken off and the Government's freedom of action retained for carrying out 'a comprehensive radical reform of the Lords'.

This line was opposed by Ministers who were either convinced unicameralists or who had their own intricate schemes for reforming the Upper House. Several Ministers agreed that talks must not be abandoned. One staunch ally argued that they must be resumed. The constructive reformers who had fought so hard retained the

full support of three other Ministers. The arguments of the previous morning were repeated and it became clear that at least the
case was won for abandoning any Bill dealing with powers only and
not composition. Had it not been for their efforts on the Wednesday
morning, the Cabinet might have been presented with a short and
drastic Bill as a *fait accompli* on the morning of 20 June.

The Announcement to the Commons

The Prime Minister's bitterness was evident when he made his
announcement to the Commons on the afternoon of 20 June.[11]
There could be no question, he said, of the all-party talks continuing, and (as chapter 5 described) he promised comprehensive
and radical legislation 'to give effect to the intention announced in
the Gracious Speech'.

So, just as Wilson's answer to the Queen's Speech in October
1967 had implied, the impossibility of reaching agreed reform meant
that the Government would resort to unilateral action. But what had
wrecked the talks had been not the impossibility of securing agreement but the climate in which the negotiators had had to operate.
The pressure of outside events had finally proved overwhelming.

The Prime Minister's statement was welcomed by Labour Backbenchers, of whom 132 were soon to vote in favour of William
Hamilton's ten-minute-rule Bill proposing outright abolition of
the Second Chamber. There was strong feeling in the Cabinet and
the P.L.P. that idealistic reformers—Richard Crossman, Lord
Gardiner, and Lord Shackleton—had become entranced in a world
aloof from the partisan actualities of Parliament. To the Backbenchers they seemed carried away by fanciful schemes of reform,
indulging in informal conversations with the Opposition, and
working in cahoots with the Conservatives. A new Parliament Bill
would have to be prepared and a new Cabinet Committee formed
to devise it.

[11] *HC Debs.* vol. 766, cols. 1314-16.

8

THE ATTEMPT TO REFORM THE
HOUSE OF LORDS; THE WHITE PAPER
AND THE PARLIAMENT BILL

A. *The Cabinet Committees*

THOUGH the new Committee was reinforced by two noted opponents of the draft reform scheme, five of those who had attended the now defunct Inter-party Conference were members. They were Richard Crossman, Lord Gardiner, Lord Shackleton, Lord Beswick, and James Callaghan. All but the Home Secretary were still enthusiastic reformers. Their strength was further improved when the Prime Minister agreed to their request that the Minister who had so stoutly argued for the continuation of talks (at the Cabinet meeting on 20 June) should be included in the new Committee. It was fortunate too that they retained the services of the two Secretaries who had been attached to the Conference.

The Committee preserved other features of the Conference. Lord Gardiner was still the official chairman and nominally its proceedings were still the responsibility of the Lord Chancellor and the Home Secretary. Richard Crossman remained the leader of the discussions and Lord Shackleton maintained his odd role of Ministerial executive director.

Understandably, the disadvantages of these arrangements had been less apparent at the larger Conference where Conservative and Liberal delegates had taken part as well as Labour. Now that Ministers from the Government front bench only had the responsibility for drawing up and carrying through a Government Bill, the defects of this division of labour should have been more obvious.

In the first place, it was a tactical mistake that the Minister who was politically in charge of the operation had no department to support him. Naturally Richard Crossman wished to press on with the measure that was so substantially his brainchild but it became increasingly difficult for him to push through Parliament a Bill prepared by another department. This was especially so when he left the Lord Presidency and handed over the Leadership of the Commons to a successor who was less vigorously dedicated to Parliamentary reform.

Again, it was tactically unwise to give charge of preparing the Bill to the Home Office. That department is accustomed, it is true, to a variety of responsibilities, but none the less it is unused to constitutional measures of this magnitude. It would not be surprising to find that the official from the Home Office whose task it was to work so closely with the Parliament Office felt himself somewhat cut off from his colleagues' everyday world. Nor was the Home Secretary himself keenly interested in the Bill. It was perhaps James Callaghan who first sensed that the measure was doomed in Commons' terms.

There was a fundamental justification for this awkward state of affairs. Since the Government intended to press their own Reform Bill it was sensible and, from the enthusiasts' point of view, important for the Committee to preserve as much continuity as possible with the Conference. Keeping the original Labour membership and the original allocation of responsibilities was a step in this direction. At the same time, however, the 'dream world' of the passionate reformers was perpetuated, so that it was hard for them to see the ominous faults in its foundation.

Tactics

Meanwhile the reformers' tactics were to lie low. They were particularly concerned that the Lords should not incur the further wrath of the Cabinet and the Commons by insisting on their Amendments to the Transport Bill and this warning was effectively delivered by Lord Shackleton. It was also important to try to preserve some contact with the Conservative representatives at the Conference who had favoured reform, if the agreed proposals were to be sustained, but any conversations would now have to be covert and informal. Despite the bitterness of the reaction to the rejection of the Southern Rhodesia (United Nations Sanctions) Order, friendly relations had been maintained by those on the Labour and Conservative front benches whose reforming zeal was unimpaired. Within the Lords, too, the three party Leaders were obliged to discuss everyday business together and doubtless the question of reform crept occasionally into their conversation.

In such a fashion, therefore, Richard Crossman was given to

understand that if the Committee hoped to proceed with a Bill to which the Conservative Party had given tacit support, he must ask the Shadow Cabinet for this himself. Such an initiative would have some chance of success, or so his soundings implied. The Labour Ministers had been pessimistic, the more so because the Royal Commission on the Constitution had just been established and they feared that the Conservatives would seize on this as an excuse to postpone further talk of Lords' reform. But if it should prove possible to proceed with the agreed scheme, disguised as the Government's own measure, they imagined that this could only be to its advantage.

There were three reasons why the reformers had decided to try to keep the scheme set out in the draft White Paper. To start with, it seemed an honourable way to proceed. To those who attached more importance to crude realities of politics they could reply that a strict Labour scheme would obtain little support from the Conservatives in the Commons—and it would certainly arouse the antagonism of the Lords themselves. The Lords had originally given their consent to an agreed measure, not to a partisan Government Bill. Finally, since the reformers had laboured so long to devise a scheme so comprehensive and sophisticated, it seemed impractical to jettison it and start again.

The Committee accordingly asked the Shadow Cabinet for assurance. Relations between Labour and Conservative business managers in the Commons were at this time of glacial formality but letters were exchanged and the Opposition proved surprisingly helpful. The Government representatives asked if they might be released from the original pledge of confidentiality so that the recommendations of the inter-party talks could be published. They also requested an acknowledgement that the Cabinet Committee's new scheme was a faithful conservation of the principles agreed in the original draft White Paper. Thirdly, they asked for an undertaking that if the scheme became law, the Conservatives would in their turn attempt to operate it. The Shadow Cabinet then considered these somewhat optimistic requests. The Leader of the Opposition was able to give the Government a 'reasonable letter' in reply, which encouraged the Committee. The Opposition proposed that talks could be held with Conservatives and Liberals to discuss the scope of Amendments to the Bill, with particular attention to the conventions for nominating future Peers. Such discussions, however, were forestalled. Simultaneously the Prime Minister asked the Committee to publish the White Paper as soon as they could, to anticipate a possible leak from the Press.

If the determined reformers on the Committee had been given more time to reflect, they might have realized that the course on which they had embarked was intrinsically hazardous. Hindsight made them wiser; at this point they saw only reassurance in the Shadow Cabinet's reply. This was an error. The Conservatives had not promised to give official support to the Reform Bill and they did not give the assistance of their Whips when the Bill undertook its Parliamentary career. To drive the agreed scheme through the Commons, the reformers needed all-party support. Without official assistance from the Conservative frontbench managers and the help of the Opposition Whip, the Bill's success would depend on the support of Labour Backbenchers. Their approval was uncertain. In fact, it was more likely that Labour M.P.s would be hostile to a Parliament Bill based on the agreed proposals. They might have acquiesced in a severe, radical scheme but not in what they saw as an inter-party conspiracy masquerading as a Government Bill. The reformers' dilemma was that only a very different measure would have been acceptable to the Labour left, but only the original scheme would have won wide agreement in both Houses.

A tough and dispassionate critic would have indicated three possibilities. The whole idea of a Parliament Bill could have been dropped altogether. At that time this seemed an unrealistic forfeiture of Government credit. Or a drastic Labour Bill could have been proposed—but this would antagonize the Lords. Or the Conference could have reassembled after a discreet interval—but the Prime Minister's words after the sanctions episode had been so angry, and he and his Cabinet were so intransigent that this was a hopeless suggestion. As it was, the enthusiasts tried to press an agreed scheme through a House riven by disagreement, a nonpartisan measure through an essentially partisan assembly. Their miscalculation became all too apparent later on.

B. *The White Paper*

At the very beginning of the 1968-69 Session the Prime Minister urged the Committee to publish the White Paper. This was on

29 October. The final draft was prepared at speed, a more straight-forward task than it might otherwise have been because during the lying-low period and the Summer Recess the two Secretaries and the determined reformers had worked over successive versions of the original draft White Paper in order to make its wording slightly more fitting for a left-wing Government Bill. It has been said that the draft went through as many as fifteen editions before it struck the appropriate note of a constructive reform inspired by a sensitive but none the less cool approach to the Upper House. Once again the various talents of the two Secretaries and Richard Crossman and Lord Shackleton made a productive combination of imaginative notions, coherent and energetic editing, and patient attention to minutiae.

The White Paper was squarely based on the proposed draft that the Inter-party Conference had considered. Some points were properly diluted, those concerning patronage, for example. A few points were emphasized rather more strongly and a tone of detached, slightly contemptuous objectivity towards the Lords was allowed to infuse its phrases. But no new provisions were introduced and the White Paper of November was basically similar to the original draft of May.

Its authors feared that the scheme would be derided by M.P.s and the Press. Not only was it complex and the refinements of the two-tier principle extremely subtle but the provisions concerning patronage had been deliberately left somewhat vague. The device of a Selection Committee, which the Conference had envisaged, had been discarded. The White Paper implied that the customary methods would be continued, with nominations made by the Prime Minister and the conventional acceptance of the Leader of the Opposition's nominees. To secure as thorough and favourable a Press coverage as possible the reformers put out an embargoed brief, and saturated lobby correspondents with explanations of the scheme. The White Paper, Cmnd. 3799, was sent to the Cabinet, the Leaders of the Lords were briefed on 31 October, and on 1 November it was published.

Provisions of the White Paper

Press reaction was polite but generally favourable, though the proposals were certainly complicated. Nor had M.P.s much inkling of the refinements of the scheme, for until 1 November the proceedings of the Conference had been confidential. At the beginning of the Session, on 30 October, the Queen's Speech had informed them that legislation would be introduced on both the powers and composition of the Lords, and in his speech on the Address the Prime Minister had announced that the reforms proposed in the White Paper were in fact based on the outline agreed at the Conference. The actual provisions of Cmnd. 3799 were therefore a surprise to the majority of M.P.s.

The White Paper set out the objectives of reform: to eliminate the present hereditary basis of membership; to ensure that no one party should possess a permanent majority; to allow the Government of the day to secure a reasonable working majority, in normal circumstances; to restrict the Lords' powers to delay public legislation; and to abolish their powers to withhold consent to subordinate legislation against the will of the Commons.

It continued with an account of the present functions of the House and went on to discuss its existing composition, in terms of party affiliation as well as type of peerage, illustrating with tables how these factors were related to attendance. Powers were then treated, with particular mention of those areas of Parliamentary business where the present House had 'co-equal power with an elected House of Commons'. The case for comprehensive reform of both powers and composition was described, drawing attention to the problems caused by the overwhelming Conservative majority. Scotching the abolitionist argument and the proposals of those who wanted to reform only the Lords' powers, the two-tier scheme was given.

The summary of the proposals is given here:[1]

(*a*) The reformed House of Lords should be a two-tier structure comprising voting Peers, with a right to speak and vote, and non-voting Peers, with a right to speak.

(*b*) After the reform came into effect, succession to a hereditary peerage should no longer carry the right to a seat in the House of Lords but existing Peers by succession would have the right to sit as non-voting members for their life-time.

(*c*) Voting members would be exclusively created Peers, but some Peers by succession would be created Life Peers and therefore become qualified to be voting Peers.

---

[1] Cmnd. 3799, pp. 28-9.

(*d*) Non-voting Peers would include created Peers who did not meet the requirements of voting membership, and Peers who at the time of the reform sat by right of succession.

(*e*) Peers who at the time of the reform sat by right of succession would have an opportunity to withdraw from the House if they wished to do so.

(*f*) Voting Peers would be expected to play a full part in the work of the House and required to attend at least one-third of the sittings; they would be subject to an age of retirement.

(*g*) The voting House would initially consist of about 230 Peers, distributed between the parties in a way which would give the Government a small majority over the Opposition parties, but not a majority of the House as a whole when those without party allegiance were included.

(*h*) Non-voting Peers would be able to ask questions and move motions and also to serve in committee; but not to vote on the Floor of the House or in any committee for the consideration of legislation.

(*i*) The reformed House should include a suitable number of Peers able to speak with authority on the problems and wishes of Scotland, Wales, Northern Ireland, and the regions of England.

(*j*) Voting Peers should be paid at a rate which would reflect their responsibilities and duties, but the question should be referred to an independent committee.

(*k*) The reformed House should be able to impose a delay of six months on the passage of an ordinary public Bill sent up from the Commons on which there was disagreement between the two Houses; it should then be possible to submit the Bill for Royal Assent provided that a resolution to that effect had been passed in the House of Commons. The period of delay should be capable of running into a new Session or into a new Parliament.

(*l*) The reformed House should be able to require the House of Commons to reconsider an affirmative order, or to consider a negative order, but its power of final rejection should be removed.

(*m*) There should be a place in the reformed House for Law Lords and Bishops.

(*n*) All Peers should in future be qualified to vote in Parliamentary elections.

(*o*) Future Peers by succession and existing Peers by succession who chose to renounce their membership of the House of Lords should be enabled to sit in the House of Commons if elected.

(*p*) A review should be made of the functions and procedures of the two Houses once the main reform had come into effect.

(*q*) A committee should be established to review periodically the composition of the reformed House; it should have a chairman of national standing but without party-political affiliations and its members would include representatives of the political parties and persons without party-political affiliations.

To those who had followed the inter-party talks and knew of the manœuvres of the reformers (and the activities of the 'powers-only' group), the paragraphs in the White Paper represented a substantial victory for those who had wanted to consider powers and composition together, to evolve a complementary House out of the old, to dismiss for good the notion of complete abolition. The White Paper definitely discarded other suggestions for reform proposals that the Upper House be elected by popular vote, or by election or nomination from regional or local authorities. The scheme for a House of Peers nominated only for the life of one Parliament, with party balance broadly reflecting that of the Commons, was firmly rejected on the grounds that this would erode the independence of the individual Peer and of the Whole House. The authors also declared that such a scheme would be open to attack from those anxious about the increase of patronage that this would give 'party managers'. Perhaps the authors hoped that these remarks would mollify the Peers themselves when they came to consider the provisions of the scheme. However, the question of patronage was only one of those which continued to bedevil discussion until the last days of debate on the Parliament Bill.

In a tactful attempt to reconcile the two main principles of reform —a degree of independence combined with an effective contribution to good, democratic government—the two-tier scheme was advanced. As the summary shows, the detailed points differed very little from the conclusions of the Conference. On the matter of the small majority and the Crossbenchers' crucial role (para. *g*), and of the substantial powers retained by a reformed House (paras. *k*, *l*), the authors embodied in their recommendations their preference for a Second Chamber with real independence. On the thorny question of the privileges of non-voting Peers to vote in Committee, the White Paper was promisingly vague (para. *h*). The final paragraph (*q*) hinted at the inevitable criticism, that unsupervised nominations would vastly increase the Prime Minister's patronage and that an unmonitored House would always tend to conservatism. The original suggestion for an elaborate Committee of scrutiny was dropped, leaving only the impression that from time to time some body would examine—not nominations beforehand but—'composition'.

The other difference was that ideas for further developments in functions and procedure were relegated to an appendix,[2] and prudently described only as the kind of change which 'might be made after the reform had come into effect'. It was considered too risky to specify the suggestions the Conference had considered for such plans as joint Committees on subordinate legislation, the introduction of specialist or Select Committees, and new procedures for Private and Public Bills.[3]

Only in the last pages of the White Paper was the idea advanced that such proposals might be examined by a Joint Select Committee, institutionalizing the device of the Inter-party Conference, after the implementation of the main reform. Even when the proposals for Lords' reform were skilfully presented in the context of general Parliamentary innovation, it would have been impolitic for the authors to refer too openly to the days of inter-party collaboration.

Reaction to the White Paper

The Shadow Cabinet had given only tacit approval to the White Paper and the reformers now discerned that the Conservative front bench intended 'to play it easy and let us make the running'. Tory Backbenchers, in the 1922 Committee and in the Lords, were not unsympathetic, according to well-informed accounts in the Press, but some observers sensed that a feeling of antipathy to reform was beginning to emerge. Apart from one speech by Enoch Powell, however, there was little open protest from M.P.s until the second week of November. Ominously, this came from the Labour side.

A P.L.P. meeting was held on Wednesday, 13 November, when, *The Times* reported, 'only one backbencher and one obscure Peer' had a kind word to say. A witness of the meeting has said that only about thirty-five people were present at the beginning, over half of them Labour Peers, for Labour M.P.s were largely indifferent to the scheme. Even at the end, when the Prime Minister was there, only about eighty members had come. It was said that the Home Secretary, who opened the discussion, commended the scheme but

---

[2] Cmnd. 3799, Appendix 2.

[3] Many of these proposals were to be implemented in 1971 and 1972 under a Conservative Administration. Once the impetus had been given, gradual reform became feasible.

disclaimed any expert knowledge. The recommendations were denounced by older party members like Michael Foot, William Hamilton, Charles Pannell, and Emanuel Shinwell. In answer, Richard Crossman stressed that the negotiators' refusal to give way to the Conservative demand to delay the implementation of reform represented a victory for the Labour Party. It proved, he said, that the Conservatives did feel that the scheme would deprive them of the advantages they had hitherto gained from the unreformed House. But backbench M.P.s were unimpressed by this argument. Their moodiness was deepened the following day when the Chairman of the party, Douglas Houghton, publicly revealed his hostility to the scheme in conversations with the Press. The reformers became increasingly pessimistic about the reception the White Paper would receive in the Commons. Public reaction had been puzzled but approving; now the debate centred on Parliament.

The Commons' Debate

This was held on 19 and 20 November and the Motion had originally been 'to take note of the White Paper', without a Division. But at the beginning of the debate the Speaker allowed William Hamilton to propose a Motion to reject the White Paper; this required a Division and thus changed the character of the proceedings. Some accounts suggest that the Chief Whip accordingly sent out a three-line whip, others that no whip was issued. Whatever the case, the Whips apparently made little effort to encourage Backbenchers to attend the debate or speak in support of the proposals. This was understandable on the Conservative side, for the front bench were now plainly lukewarm about the whole enterprise, but it was odd in the case of the Government.[4] Attendance was poor, with a maximum of seventy M.P.s hearing the opening and closing speeches, but with only thirty to forty present at some time during the main part of the debate.

Richard Crossman opened the debate on the first day, putting forward a powerful case for the White Paper. On his own admission he needled Backbenchers through his confidence in the scheme itself and through the assumption that they would be as intellectually

---

[4] It was suggested that the Chief Whip's difficulty stemmed partly from the Prime Minister's ambivalence on Lords' reform and partly from his own loyalty to his father, Lord Silkin, who seemed critical of the scheme when he spoke in the Lords' debate.

quick to appreciate its merits. His speech was often interrupted and he was somewhat downcast. From this moment, the officials in the box sensed that all would not be well.

It soon became clear that the reforms would have a rough passage in the Commons; a succession of backbench speakers were overwhelmingly critical. This was the first stage in a campaign in which extreme right- and left-wing M.P.s would join in attack. Michael Foot, Enoch Powell, Maurice Edelman, and William Hamilton echoed the criticisms of the 'frontbench Mafia' that had devised the proposals, alleging that they promised a paid and nominated House that would open the way to an iniquitous extension of Prime-Ministerial patronage and a decisive role for a group of politically fickle crossbench Peers.

Only the frontbench speakers really supported the scheme. Reginald Maudling skirted any explicit Conservative commitment, but he, Iain Macleod, and Sir Peter Rawlinson gave general backing from the Shadow Cabinet. Iain Macleod was said to have been particularly impressive. Never an enthusiast for reform and certainly opposed to its early implementation, he now stood firmly by the Opposition understanding and spoke effectively in favour of the scheme. James Callaghan, too, gave what has been judged an extremely able speech, of great debating skill. Precisely because he was known not to be a diehard reformer, his argument that Labour needed the scheme to overcome the Lords' capacity for obstruction was all the more convincing to Backbenchers.

Nevertheless the debate was not a success and M.P.s remained sceptical. The reformers considered themselves fortunate that the Motion to reject the White Paper was defeated by 270 votes to 159, a majority of 111 (with, perhaps, a Government three-line whip). In all, 47 Labour M.P.s voted against the scheme, 40 abstained, and 233 gave their approval. This was less encouraging when the votes of the other parties were inspected. All 8 Liberals voted against the scheme and of the Conservatives, who had a free vote, only 47 voted for the White Paper, 50 abstained, and as many as 104 voted for rejection. So with a large number of Tories and a sizeable number of Labour M.P.s hostile to the proposals, and almost 100 M.P.s abstaining altogether, the Division did not promise well for the Bill itself.

The Lords' Debate

The Commons' Division may have had some bearing on the Lords' debate. The Peers discussed the Bill for three days, 19, 20, and 21 November, on a Motion to approve the proposals. There were 101 speakers from all parts of the House and most of them favoured the scheme. Reassurance came from both front benches and party Leaders stressed that all parties had agreed to the measure. Speeches for the Government by Lord Gardiner and Lord Shackleton, for the Opposition by Lord Carrington, and for the Liberals by Lord Byers were supported by those of their respective Whips, Lord Beswick, Lord St. Aldwyn, and Lord Henley. From the cross benches, too, came a remarkable series of constructive speeches by respected figures in the House.

As their leaders had expected, Backbenchers gave their reservations on a number of detailed points. They deplored the carping tone of the Commons' debate but, though their remarks were courteous and moderate, some were frankly critical. Anxious about patronage, some Peers suggested racial, religious, professional, and regional categories from which nominations could be made. Others, particularly those of ancient peerage, felt that the end of the hereditary system spelt both the elimination of ancient rights and also the loss to their counsels of ordinary men, selected by accident of birth, and younger men, selected by accident of death. (In answer, it was pointed out that very few Peers under 40 attended regularly anyway.)

Peers gave examples of those surviving to a useful dotage, in criticism of the proposed retiring age of 72, and Scottish Peers and others living at a distance described the drawbacks of regular attendance as a qualification for voting privileges. However, the two-tier scheme was generally commended, though some found it hard to choose between being 'a dumb voter or an impotent spouter', and there were suggestions for even more tiers to try out young hereditary Peers or accommodate apprentices to a Commons' career.

Many Peers were baffled by the scheme to maintain the balance of parties with a small Government majority, despite Lord Shackleton's assurance that these matters (including wastage rates resulting from death, retirement, etc.) had been worked out by careful quantitative techniques. They were troubled, too, about the Crossbenchers' status, for though their independence could check the Executive, it might be inappropriate for them to hold the balance of power. Other speakers discussed the rights of Law Lords, of Bishops, of Ministers, and whether these should be entitled to vote. It was also felt that speaking Peers should perhaps be able to vote in Committee. A more delicate matter on which the Lords had qualms concerned the need to provide adequate and dignified remuneration without introducing a House of paid placemen.

A six-month delaying power met with approval, though some Peers wished to retain their right to reject subordinate legislation. They were somewhat appeased by 'the honey in Appendix two' suggesting an extended role for the Upper House. The timing of the reform bothered the Lords less than the Commons; still, the few Peers adamantly opposed to the measure argued that Lords' reform was surely inappropriate in advance of the Report of the Royal Commission on the Constitution. A handful condemned the proposals as a 'political sham', a disguised abolition. From the right, the Marquess of Salisbury feared that the Commons wanted to make the Lords a copy of the Lower House. From the left, the Communist, Lord Milford, wanted abolition (as did Lord Archibald), and Baroness Wootton approved of the scheme only because it seemed a step in that direction.

Overwhelmingly, however, the Peers welcomed the White Paper. They saw the need for reform and felt that at last the time had come for a measure long promised and long debated. Indeed, there were echoes of earlier debates, in 1909 and 1911, in which they or their parents had spoken, and reminders of the investigatory Committee chaired by the Marquess of Salisbury in 1938 and of an earlier two-writ scheme devised by Commander Burrows.[5] At last the proposals might alleviate the problems of the Lords' 'twilight period', and the White Paper's elegant paragraphs suggested to the majority of the House 'sensible' reforms, happily devised by frontbench agreement.

The Lords' Division was more heartening to the reformers than the Commons' vote had been. The White Paper was approved by 251 votes to 56, with only a minority disapproving in each party. No Labour Peers voted Not-content; 72 approved. Of the Liberals, 13 voted Content and only 3 Not-content. Among crossbench

---

[5] Commander Henry Burrows, who entered the House of Lords as a Clerk in 1925 and retired in 1963 from the office of Clerk-Assistant of the Parliaments.

Peers, Bishops, and Law Lords, 58 voted Content; 10 Not-content. And of the Conservatives, who might have been particularly expected to distrust the proposals, 108 gave their support and 43 opposed. Altogether the Lords gave the White Paper a five-to-one vote of consent, and the reformers felt they had surmounted another hurdle.

The next stage was the Parliament Bill itself, and this was less straightforward.

c. The Parliament (No. 2) Bill[6]

As this account has unfolded from the first inklings of an attempt at reform in the early months of the 1964 Parliament, it has become clear that at every stage the committed reformers (as Lord Gardiner, Lord Shackleton, Lord Jellicoe, Lord Byers, and Richard Crossman can conveniently be called) were sowing trouble for their campaign. The awkwardness of Mr. Callaghan's and Mr. Crossman's divided roles, and of the allocation of responsibility between them, emerged at the Conference and was perpetuated at the second Cabinet Committee. Though it was no fault of the reformers, the breaking off of talks had been a major mistake. And to proceed with the 'agreed' non-partisan measure in an atmosphere of party rancour, without the declared support of the whip on both sides of the Commons, was indeed imprudent. Furthermore, whether in unconscious escapism or remote preoccupation, or even sheer failure of political sensitivity, the reformers were unaware of the strength of backbench hostility. Their scheme was itself incredibly complicated and, to those who had not created it, probably bizarre. To many members of the Commons, the Lords might have been inhabitants of some other planet; a similar separation now seemed to exist between the world of the reformers and that of down-to-earth backbench M.P.s. The career of the Parliament (No. 2) Bill had brought the two worlds into collision and every tactical error reached fruition.

After the debate on the White Paper, the first decision had to be on the timing of the Bill. The formal First Reading had been fixed for 19 December and, although one proponent at least was anxious that Second Reading should be taken before Christmas, the Recess

---

[6] The Government Bill was entitled the Parliament (No. 2) Bill because Lord Mitchison had earlier that Session introduced a Private Member's Bill into the Lords, which was entitled the Parliament Bill. It made no progress after First Reading.

was too near to make very much start. On Thursday, 21 November, the Government's business managers discussed the legislative time-table for the forthcoming Session with the Prime Minister and decided that Second Reading should be postponed until after Christmas. Somewhat sinister was the suggestion that the diffi-culties of the economic situation (the international monetary system was turbulent) might make a Parliament Bill seem so irrelevant at this point that it might be necessary to drop it altogether in the New Year. Doubt and vacillation about the Bill were troubling the Government already. The reformers perceived that, like the Leader of the House, the Chief Whip, and the Chairman of the P.L.P., the Prime Minister was no unwavering friend of the Bill. Intellectually he perhaps approved of the scheme, but his political instinct warned him that an expensive struggle lay ahead.

Nevertheless, the Prime Minister had promised a measure to reform the Lords in the Manifesto and reiterated it in his speech after the sanctions vote. Assuming that he would be reluctant to abandon this undertaking, the reformers were encouraged. There were still divisions in the Cabinet: one over-wrought Minister demanded that the Bill be dropped altogether, others felt that it should be pushed as swiftly as possible. The Cabinet meeting on 5 December 1968 saw the first discussions of Government strategy and the reformers set out their tactical proposals.

The Cabinet agreed that two concessions should be made in an effort to placate some potential critics. The first concerned the rights of Peers, and particularly the complicated issue of Scottish Peers and their rights under the Act of Union. It was agreed that reference to this should be made in a Preamble, but matters which could be dealt with by the Royal Prerogative or the Peers themselves should be left aside, the Bill itself dealing only with changes in the law necessary to implement its proposals. This device seemed sensible, but it was to prove a miscalculation. The Preamble offered irresistible scope for M.P.s to filibuster and delay discussion of the main Clauses.

The Government also hoped to allay some of the backbench con-cern that a paid and nominated House implied a dangerous degree of patronage. Accordingly, the Cabinet decided to abandon the suggestion for a Committee of Remuneration to consider salaries for Peers, retaining in the meantime the customary expenses allowance. This was a substantial concession, but insufficient, as the reformers realized when sixteen or so M.P.s at a meeting of the Parliamentary Reform group[7] expressed their own unease.

Such tactical expedients were a necessary part of advance planning, but it was perhaps significant that even at this early stage the Cabinet considered such large concessions. Already, it seemed, their conviction was trembling. It was possible, too, that from instinctive caution some Ministers explained the Cabinet's decision publicly, risking the betrayal of the Government's uncertainty. Thus, although Cabinet had decided that there should be no publicity before the Bill was introduced on 19 December, Fred Peart did give a small briefing meeting to explain the remuneration concession and Lord Shackleton met the Press to kill once and for all rumours that the Government would drop the Bill. Parliament rose for the Christmas Recess and the reformers prepared for the struggle in the New Year.

Second Reading

The Prime Minister moved the Second Reading on 3 February 1969. Some of his audience discerned a hurried, somewhat flat note in his delivery, which suggested that it was not without reluctance that he had been persuaded to propose the Motion. The Home Secretary, nominally responsible for the Bill, wound up the debate. The Liberal Leader approved the scheme and, from the Opposition front bench, Reginald Maudling (the Deputy Leader) supported the Bill. The speech from Sir Alec Douglas-Home, himself a former Leader of the Lords, was said to have been particularly delightful and it was undoubtedly persuasive in commending the Bill to Conservative Backbenchers.

The Prime Minister announced the decision to continue the system of tax-free expenses and the Government's decision to preserve an open mind on the question of payment for voting Peers, but, more surprising, he also suggested a concession on the vexed matter of the operative date of reform. This had been the cause of deadlock. Now Mr. Wilson mentioned that those parts of the Bill dealing with the Lords' delaying and other powers and those dealing with composition could possibly be separated, with a different timing for each. This was in answer to a reasoned Amendment from the Conservatives (who were already beginning to play politics with

[7] On 19 Dec. 1968.

the Bill) demanding that implementation be postponed to the next Parliament.

The Home Secretary, James Callaghan, also took up this idea. It was not entirely unexpected, for such an expedient had been mentioned in earlier deliberations and private talks. Still, some members of the Cabinet (including, it is said, the committed reformers and the Government's business managers) afterwards expressed their surprise at the Prime Minister's remarks. A plausible interpretation was that Mr. Wilson assumed that this suggestion was a devious tactic agreed by the Cabinet Committee, or that the Committee assumed that the Prime Minister had reached some private arrangement with the Opposition (which was unlikely, for the usual channels now restricted their discussions to matters of time-tabling alone). Anyhow, the incident reveals how poor were communications between the Ministers involved, how diffuse the responsibility for the Bill, and, perhaps, how preoccupied was the Prime Minister with other distractions, leaving him little time to scrutinize his brief in advance.

The debate on Second Reading was less disastrous than that on the White Paper; nevertheless, as discussions continued, there were rumours of a mass abstention by Labour Backbenchers, despite a Government two-line whip. The reformers were the more worried because those who still pressed for a short stringent Parliament Bill suggested that this would be justified if the Government were defeated on Second Reading of the elaborate, 'soft' Bill (At every stage that argument was to harry constructive reformers.) However, on this occasion, the Government carried the Division.

The majority was larger than the front bench had expected, 285 votes to 135. Labour M.P.s had after all responded to the urgings of the whip, and 226 voted for the proposals, with a hard core of 25 against. Sir Alec Douglas-Home's speech had helped to rally the Conservatives, and on a free vote, 58 supported the Bill, with 105 against. This was still a two-to-one vote in opposition to the scheme. This time the Liberals were divided, 3 for the Bill, 3 against, with one abstention. A Welsh and a Scottish Nationalist also voted against the measure. The Government majority was 39 more than that secured in the Division on the White Paper, but Second Reading had not been the greatest test. It was the Committee Stage that would see the success or failure of the Bill.

Committee Stage

Bills on constitutional matters are not sent to a Standing Committee but referred to a Committee of the Whole House. One pessimist in the Whips' Office is reported to have suggested that on this occasion convention might be broken, and the Parliament Bill sent upstairs, but the suggestion was not taken seriously. As *The Times* reported, the Government originally allowed five days for the Committee Stage on the Floor of the House. This was bitterly optimistic.

The Commons sat in Committee on six days in February (12, 18, 19, 20, 25, 26 February) and 18 and 19 March, and on 1, 12, and 14 April, but by 17 April only the Preamble and five Clauses had been debated. The Government's time-table was seriously upset, and a first-class Parliamentary crisis developed. The cause was plain. Business is normally managed by agreement through the usual channels of the Government and Opposition Chief Whips and their officials, who fix a time-table for debates and divisions. In return for conceding adequate time for the Opposition to allow their members to oppose aspects of a measure, the Government secure agreement that business will be curtailed at convenient intervals within a definite period of time. In this case, there was no co-operation.

This state of affairs was the direct result of breaking off the inter-party talks and, in consequence, inter-party arrangements for getting the Bill through the House. Though Edward Heath had implied that the Opposition would support the White Paper, no promises were given on the handling of the Bill itself. Frontbench Conservatives had indeed spoken in favour of the Second Reading of the Bill, but even so they were not all wholeheartedly eager to see it through. Reginald Maudling, for example, seemed to sense that this would be an appropriate measure on which the Opposition could launch a full-scale attack; Iain Macleod, on the other hand, continued to give unflinching support. It was reliably reported that the Opposition Chief Whip, William Whitelaw, was sympathetic to the Bill, but he could not commit the Shadow Cabinet to its support.

Conservative Whips were not instructed to discipline Backbenchers in Committee Stage. In fact, the Shadow Cabinet would not have been able to deliver the support of Tory M.P.s, for the party Leaders had already agreed that members would be entirely free to vote as they saw fit. The usual channels had collapsed and, in the absence of the customary arrangements, the Government could only hope that they might limit discussion by imposing a guillotine. But this too was impossible for it required the support of a majority of the House. Conservative M.P.s would very probably have voted against a guillotine, arguing that it would be inappropriate for such an important constitutional measure; the thirty or so Labour M.P.s opposed to the Reform Bill would, at best, have abstained. In this situation, the Government were forced to permit the debate to drag along its interminable course.

Unhampered by any agreement between the Whips, and unrestrained by the Chairman, backbench critics gleefully seized the opportunities offered by the need to take the Bill on the Floor of the House. United in opposition, the Bill's opponents were divided in their motives. Some wanted to leave the Lords as it was, either because they approved of it, or because they hoped that it would wither away. Others wanted outright abolition; some had alternative schemes of reform. Moreover, Backbenchers had recently been vociferously complaining of the impotence of Parliament and of the individual Backbencher, treated only as lobby-fodder by the Government and the Whips and as food for powder in the private skirmishings of the usual channels. The fiasco of morning sittings, the struggles of the Finance Bill, even the controversial experiments in lenient discipline with which Richard Crossman and John Silkin had antagonized authoritarian members of the P.L.P., had done little to mitigate backbench crabbiness. The Parliament Bill gave ample scope for M.P.s to retaliate. An all-party alliance of able Backbenchers, from Michael Foot on the left to Enoch Powell on the right, enthusiastically exploited every procedural device to hinder the Bill's passage in Committee.

Backbench strategy was evident from the first day in Committee, 12 February. As early as 14 February, the Cabinet Committee on the Bill began to consider the possibility of asking the Opposition for a guillotine agreement in return for postponing the operative date of reform until the next Parliament. During the ensuing days, they worked for this—morale was now very low. Meanwhile M.P.s filibustered energetically, spending hours on points of order, Motions to report progress, vast catalogues of Amendments. The addition of the Preamble proved to be a costly mistake. The fact that more complex and obscure Clauses dealing with composition preceded those concerning the powers of a reformed House provided further ammunition. Opposition was not constructive—it was clear that both Labour and Conservative M.P.s, reactionary preservationists or fundamental abolitionists, were indulging in a filibuster of uncommon scale. (Robert Sheldon, for example, spoke for two hours and twenty minutes on an Amendment which he then withdrew without a Division; three hours were spent merely challenging the Preamble.) Behind the scenes, too, Backbenchers complained. One recurring argument was that at a time of more urgent legislation (the Merchant Shipping Bill was a favourite example) the Parliament Bill was a futile irrelevance.

The long days and 'ghastly nights' of the Committee Stage were the despair of the Government Whips. On 26 February, for instance, the Government needed 100 members for the closure on Clause 2, and so many Labour Backbenchers had left the House that the Whips sent out a desperate summons at 5.45 a.m. Only at 7.45 a.m. were 102 members rounded up. One observer has described the management of the debate and the Divisions in terms more fitted to a floundering, demoralized military campaign, with dutiful but cynical old soldiers doggedly shambling through the lobbies, lacking will, lacking encouragement.

Some Frontbenchers did their best to give direction. Richard Crossman staunchly sat through discussion and defended his Bill. But even so, it has been suggested that his intellectual detachment and the grandeur of his new position as Secretary of State detracted from his efforts to rally Backbenchers and explain the importance of the Bill. James Callaghan was much closer to the ordinary backbench Member, but his warnings had been disregarded by the reformers as inspired by his hostility for the measure. He was now angered by the Government's failure to anticipate backbench reaction and, on the other hand, by M.P.s' determination to sabotage a Bill sponsored by his department. As a Parliamentarian, he wanted to drive the Bill through; lukewarm to reform, he wanted to abandon it altogether. M.P.s sensed, and resented, this ambivalence.

The emptiness of the Opposition front bench showed that the Conservatives had removed any semblance of official support. The negligible and disconsolate support on the Government front bench indicated the Government's loss of will and lack of determination. *The Times* reported that Backbenchers were again demanding that the Bill be dropped and if necessary the short Bill to curb the Lords' powers introduced instead. The more M.P.s suspected that this course might be forced upon the Government, the more futile the Bill appeared and the more resolutely it was opposed. Thus the Bill had plunged into a vicious downward spiral.

Escape-hatches

Even those in the Cabinet who hankered for a short Bill were aware that this would unite the Tory Party against the Government, and, if it passed the Commons, provoke line-by-line opposition in the Lords. On 27 February, Cabinet considered the Parliamentary situation, and the committed reformers urged the Prime Minister to soldier on. But in the absence of tacit collaboration through the usual channels, Committee Stage could now last at least another fifteen or sixteen days, well into the Whitsun Recess or even into August.

Soldiering on, therefore, would upset all the Government's legislative plans, and the need for some arrangement with the Opposition front bench became ever more urgent. While the Conservative leaders in the Lords were obviously still sympathetic, matters had not been improved by an attack that James Callaghan had made on the Conservative front bench for 'ratting' on a pact of tacit support. The Home Secretary was coming to feel that it might now be preferable to risk defeat once and for all on a guillotine Motion than to drive ahead with a Bill that was rapidly becoming anathema to him.[8] The reformers were tentatively working towards some arrangement for a voluntary agreement between the parties, but this was hopeless. The Tories could not coerce their Backbenchers or offer any sort of 'deal' on a guillotine Motion. Conversations between business managers made it plain that there was no chance of the Shadow Cabinet patching up any sort of arrangement with the Opposition, and that, in fact, a guillotine Motion would be opposed by a Conservative three-line whip.

Cabinet assessed the situation on 6 March. The first course, a guillotine, was impossible, in the face of a backbench revolt and probable defeat. If the Bill reached the Lords, this would provoke further difficulties. The alternatives were equally dismal. The short Bill was ruled out—the Lords would never agree and the rest of the Government's legislative programme would be mauled. The

---

[8] James Callaghan discussed the possibility with Reginald Maudling at a private meeting.

proposal to send the Bill upstairs to a small Committee of fifty members, breaking all precedent, was also ruled out, for there the Government's majority would, proportionately, be even smaller. Dropping the Bill altogether would not only be an admission of failure but might set a dangerous precedent. If the Government capitulated to Backbenchers on this issue, forced by thirty or forty Labour rebels, then the proposed Industrial Relations Bill would surely be defeated. Cabinet had already recognized that Prices and Incomes legislation would have to be abandoned, and more than thirty Labour members had voted against the Defence Estimates with impunity. The dropping of the Parliament Bill would be a symbolic lowering of the flag.

Cabinet therefore agreed to fight on, with all-night and morning sittings, and on Monday, 10 March, Ministers considered how extra time could be found in the programme. But despite their decision to run the Bill for ten to fifteen days more, it continued to languish in the House. On 18 March the House debated points of order, on 20 March M.P.s discussed the confidentiality of Lords' attendance records. On Thursday, 20 March, Cabinet decided that instead of taking odd days here and there the Government should try to 'take a good crack' at the Bill over consecutive days. This attempt to show a determined front was undermined by Ministers' obvious gloom and indecision; the Home Secretary's lack of faith was now apparent to the House and the remaining Government supporters were exhausted and disheartened. Just before the Easter Recess, on 2 April, critics cheered as debate was abandoned at 10 p.m. because the Whips feared that they could not muster the necessary quorum. The strategy of ploughing on seemed ever more onerous.

Dropping the Bill

The decision to drop the Bill altogether was apparently taken before the Easter Recess. Ministers had other important matters to consider, notably the forthcoming Budget and the state of the Prices and Incomes Bill. Barbara Castle wished to introduce the Industrial Relations Bill and this required both debating time in the House and a sympathetic, acquiescent party.

During the Easter Recess, Roy Jenkins, Richard Crossman, and Barbara Castle met privately at the Chancellor's cottage to discuss legislative priorities. They agreed that, as part of the package abandoning the 1968 Prices and Incomes legislation and introducing a short Industrial Relations Bill, it was inevitable that the Parliament Bill should be dropped. When the Prime Minister returned from the Scillies on Thursday, 10 April, they put their tactical suggestions before him. It is plausible to assume that he not only agreed that the Parliament Bill should be jettisoned as soon as possible, but that he realized that the Conservatives could usefully be blamed for breaking off the co-operative agreement.

The loss of the Parliament Bill was therefore considered as a necessary corollary of the Industrial Relations 'package' when Cabinet met again on Monday, 14 April. Quite apart from finding time and approval for the 'package', if the Parliament Bill were now to be carried through at all the Prime Minister would have had to demand the party's support for a guillotine. This he would have been reluctant to do.

Meanwhile, on the Floor of the House discussion continued. By this time the Bill had spent twelve days and over eighty hours in Committee and only the Preamble and five Clauses had been debated. On 14 April proceedings followed the now customary pattern—the Government failed to secure a closure Motion on the proposal that Clause 6 be deferred until after consideration of Clause 15. It was clear, however, that these exercises were a mere formality until the Prime Minister should announce the dropping of the scheme.

Before the Cabinet meeting on Wednesday, 16 April, two of the committed reformers and one of the Secretaries met for breakfast in a last attempt to devise an expedient for salvaging the Bill. The only solution—a desperate one—would have been to rest content with the five Clauses that had already been secured, omitting the Clauses on powers. But it was just these provisions in which Labour Backbenchers were most interested, and so they would not have consented to this. There was no alternative way to save the Bill. At Cabinet later that morning the reformers themselves therefore argued that the announcement should be made immediately, and the Lords' reform, including any mention of a snap Bill, indefinitely deferred.

On 17 April the Prime Minister announced to the House, and later to the P.L.P., that the Bill was to be abandoned; he emphasized that this was to ensure more time for essential Parliamentary legislation, including the Industrial Relations Bill and the Merchant

Shipping Bill. The Commons were told that the Leader of the House would at the appropriate time inform Parliament of the Government's further intentions on the matter of the Bill. (In fact future proposals were mere window-dressing.) Though Labour's Election Manifesto in May 1970 warned that proposals would be brought forward, House of Lords' reform was a question which Governments now hesitated to touch.[9] In the event, the Conservatives returned to Government in June 1970, so the Labour Party were unable to show how they had intended to fulfil their promise.

D. *Post-mortem*

It is easy to moralize retrospectively but it is useful to understand the lessons of this débâcle. The Bill failed because departmental responsibility was too diffuse and ministerial roles confused. It failed because those who had devised the scheme were carried away by its beauty and suppressed their doubts that Backbenchers would fail to appreciate its intelligence. Those who realized how hostile Backbenchers might be were ignored. Whipping from both front benches and a programme agreed via the usual channels would have assisted its passage through the Commons but this was impossible once the talks had been broken off. The Chairman was insufficiently ruthless. The Government vacillated between hesitancy and insistence. They seemed ready to entertain concessions and the next moment determined to plough on with the measure. The Bill was far too complex—a four-clause Bill would have been safer. And forced to procrastinate, both by external circumstances and by their desire to perfect the scheme, the reformers missed the political tide, launching the Bill only as the Government's programme entered the doldrums.

Labour's 1970 Election Manifesto referred to the situation where 'the House of Lords can nullify important decisions of the House of Commons and with its delaying powers veto measures in the last year before an election'. This paragraph was ironic to those who recalled that it had been the Commons, not the Lords, that had defeated the Parliament Bill and nullified the Government's measure. Hitherto the Lords had always represented themselves

---

[9] After the Announcement on 17 Apr. of the dropping of the Government Bill, Lord Alport introduced an identical (No. 6) Bill in the Lords. It received only a First Reading, and was carried on Division by 54 to 43 votes—the first Lords' Division on a First Reading since 1933.

as the defenders of the Constitution; this time it had been M.P.s who had thereby justified their opposition to the Bill, showing just that hostility that the Peers had demonstrated against earlier Parliament Acts. Certainly the Bill's career had borne out the case for Parliamentary reform. As Richard Crossman had pointed out, it was necessary to bring Backbenchers more closely into the workings of Parliament or they would indeed feel frustrated by lack of effective power and rebel against Government legislation and the obscure procedures and conventions of the usual channels. And as it had been the shortage of Commons' time that finally spelled the death of the Parliament Bill, this too supported the case for a complementary Upper House to remove legislative pressure from the Lower Chamber.

The issue of Lords' reform allowed a renaissance of backbench independence in the Commons (and was to become a permanent part of M.P.s' lore). It was a valuable lesson for the Government to endure the Backbenchers' campaign and the front benches no doubt understood M.P.s' motives. Members seized the chance to exercise their unaccustomed freedom from the Whips and from ministerial direction and enjoyed the opportunity to play politics with an exotic Bill. They had other motives too that were perhaps of more concern to friends of the Upper House. M.P.s were suspicious of a Bill which the Peers seemed to favour; there must, they felt, be something dubious about it. The Commons were jealous of the Lords and more jealous of a scheme to create an even more comfortable House of 'paid and nominated Peers'. Underlying all this was fear that an Upper House remade, reconstituted, justifiable, and efficient, would inevitably rival their own. No longer ridiculous, the Lords would become dangerous.

To some extent the episode proved the superiority of the Lords' way of proceeding about their legislative business. It was paradoxically the very procedural devices used by the Commons to expedite and regulate business that allowed M.P.s to prolong their objections to the Bill. And on this occasion the closure and the guillotine could not be used in the Commons' Committee Stage. In the preceding four years, the Peers' unsophisticated methods of self-restraint had been far more successful.

It was an unfortunate affair altogether and uncomfortable in the longer term as well. Dropping the Parliament Bill did set a precedent—the Industrial Relations Bill was also abandoned after pressure from Backbenchers who had now tasted blood. The Government's credibility and the Cabinet's authority were seriously impaired. The Lords were also annoyed by the Commons' treatment of the scheme. The Peers had approved the measure and were disappointed that their 'twilight period' was not to be thus suddenly illumined. In this mood, their attitude towards the Government in 1968 and 1969 was even less helpful than it might have been and they now had some justification for being not only hurt, but recalcitrant. Chapter 6 described their action on the Seats Bill—here it is enough to repeat Lord Carrington's remark: 'After all, it is not your Lordships' fault that you are unreformed.'[10] Nor was it the fault of the reformers. They had certainly made tactical errors but without the initiatives of Lord Gardiner and Lord Longford and the impetus given by Richard Crossman and the Leaders in the Lords with their Secretaries, the scheme would never have been devised nor the effort sustained. The Commons, having wrecked the Bill, thereby assumed the blame for frustrating Lords' reform.

[10] *HL Debs.*, vol. 304, col. 538.

CONCLUSION[1]

The House of Lords 1964–70

IN 1974 the House of Lords remains unique among European legislative bodies. Its members are not elected and the majority still sit by hereditary right. Its survival is perhaps surprising. When Labour came to power in 1964 the Government had been determined to suffer no obstruction to their radical programme and they suspected that the Lords might prove particularly stubborn. The Government were hostile to an Upper House with an established Conservative majority and a tendency to conservatism among its aged members. Moreover, though nowadays the Lords' powers to delay and veto legislation might be vestigial, the Labour Party traditionally opposed hereditary privilege. This attitude might have suggested that the Lords' extinction was inevitable.

As at the end of Labour's term of office in 1970, the Lords are still there and still unreformed. They are not unchanged—for by now the cumulative effect of the introduction of Life Peers and the provision of attendance and expenses allowances has noticeably altered their composition, party balance, and pattern of attendance. Increasingly, and with some justification, the Peers draw attention to their own progressive outlook. Self-consciously they assure the world that the Upper House has become an indispensable auxiliary in the overburdened Parliamentary process.

Six years of Labour Government also affected the House in less obvious ways. New tensions have been created by the presence of the large number of Labour Peers nominated by the Prime Minister. Old problems have been revived by the socialist legislation with which Peers have had to deal. The Conservatives devised fresh strategies and adopted familiar conventions so that they could oppose legislation. Taking 1964–70 as a whole, it is plain that the Lords

[1] This study has described the House of Lords during the years of the 1964–70 Labour Government, and the Conclusion brings that history to a close with some reflections on the role and standing of the Upper House as it appeared in 1970. When the Conservatives came to power in 1970 the House of Lords continued to change and adapt itself but it would be unwieldy and confusing to incorporate further observations here. A sketch of the House under the 1970–74 Conservative Administration has therefore been appended in the Epilogue.

unfailingly, if sometimes regretfully, acknowledged the prerogatives of the Lower House and the authority of the Government's majority there. The Opposition kept largely to the principles their Leaders reiterated in 1964, conventionally giving a Second Reading to all Bills which had the backing of the Manifesto and Commons' approval. Attempts to erode and alter them by Lords' Amendments were reserved for Committee and Report Stages, such Amendments not being insisted upon if the Commons ultimately disagreed. Contentious legislation passed into law with far less fuss than earlier Labour and Liberal Governments had encountered and even in the two salient exceptions of the Southern Rhodesia (United Nations Sanctions) Order and the Seats Bill the Government eventually had their way. Though Labour's programme was ambitious the Conservatives in the Lords gave them a good innings.

This study has indicated the more decorous methods the Peers use in order to oppose with least risk to themselves. Tactics range from the most general and implicit criticism, subtly revealed in rhetoric and manner, to the most explicit and open opposition, expressed by the hostile Question or Motion, insistence on selected Amendments, or disapproval of delegated legislation until the Commons have reconsidered it. However, the Lords understand that responsibility for checking or goading the Executive now lies primarily with the Commons and, conscious of their own attenuated role, Peers almost always restrain themselves whenever they are tempted to intervene.

Guarantees of 'Good Behaviour'

Why have the Peers been so sensible? The answer lies in the themes that emerged in the Introduction and have recurred throughout this narrative. They are restrained by self-discipline, public duty, and agreed convention. The Lords are aware that their House is a collective body whose precarious status can easily be jeopardized by ill-considered action from any Peer or party or from the Whole House in confrontation with the Commons. Nor is it too fanciful to suggest that a desire to see fair play also reconciles the Lords to their subordinate role. When it was Labour's turn to govern, wrecking Bills would have been ungentlemanly as well as hazardous.

Compared with backbench M.P.s, the Peers are less suspicious and resentful of co-operation between the party managers. Their leaders have fortunately sympathized with each other and the usual channels have worked well. With only rare exceptions, Backbenchers have deferred to the wisdom of their party Leaders when time-tables are arranged, strategies planned, and tactics of self-restraint advocated for minor as well as major issues. Undoubtedly, however, the most powerful curb on any hotheaded impetuosity has been the threat of reprisals from the Commons.

The Ultimate Deterrent

An innocent approach supposes that over-zealous backbench Peers might be suppressed by the threat of either outright abolition or drastic reform of their residual powers. Indeed, during the period of Labour rule the Government front bench did warn the Opposition of reprisals and the Conservatives' own leaders did remind their followers that they could not strike the Government with impunity more than once. Though dubious, such advice was effective and forestalled rash opposition on such issues as the War Damages Bill and the Land Commission Bill.

But oddly enough the emphasis of the Government's sanction changed. It was not so much that if the Lords misbehaved they might be reformed as that if they misbehaved they might *not* be reformed—certainly not with a scheme agreed by all parties. Back-benchers were told that revolt would jeopardize the inter-party talks and, until the Southern Rhodesia (United Nations Sanctions) Order, they heeded the warning. Ironically, the bogy of reform was finally exorcized when the scheme devised by the Inter-party Con-ference was published in the White Paper, for the proposals were far more palatable than Peers had originally hoped. They had long felt that their legislative and debating contribution had been insufficiently appreciated and the scheme would remedy this. They need worry no longer about their delicate and ambiguous consti-tutional position because the proposals would end hereditary legislative privilege and simultaneously establish the precise role of the Second Chamber. Although there would be only a token delaying power, this was no more revolutionary than the terms of the earlier Parliament Bills. Moreover, the 1968 White Paper promised to leave speaking and voting Peers considerable Parlia-mentary work to do and the suggestions in Appendix 2 were especially attractive.

Backbenchers therefore generally welcomed the agreed scheme and were as sorry as their leaders when the Parliament Bill was discarded. The episode did nothing to improve relations between the two Houses; between 1969 and 1970, too, the party Leaders required a substitute deterrent. The Government still had a year to run before the end of the Parliament and for the remainder of Labour's term the Conservative Peers might resort to unrestrained opposition, arguing that since three years had elapsed since the General Election the Government no longer enjoyed a mandate. The Labour Leader in the Lords sought to intimidate the Opposition; his Conservative counterpart also looked for some way to persuade his Backbenchers that outright opposition would not be in their best interests. Since the rejection of the Southern Rhodesia (United Nations Sanctions) Order had been a botched shot, changing Government policy not a whit, Tory Peers could argue that at least no harm would come of opposition in the remaining months of Labour's Administration. Even token demonstrations against Government legislation would be more dignified than conventional acquiescence. Labour might in any case lose the next General Election and a victorious Conservative Government could then abandon any legislation that had been delayed by the Lords.

A simple view therefore suggests that this time the party Leaders found the appropriate convenient deterrent in the tacit threats to abolish the Lords or, alternatively, in hints of measures to remove their residual powers without reforming composition. It is true that the Government did declare their intention to bring forward proposals to secure reform, without specifying what form these were likely to take. As this study has shown, when the Peers nevertheless defied the Government on the Seats Bill, it provoked as much reaction as if the Lords' opposition had come only from the Tory benches. Once again the Government stated that they would kill or cure the Upper House. But in 1974 the Lords has not been reformed—and it is easy to feel a sense of anticlimax at the end of the story.

However, there is an important lesson in these events. They show how much of an irrelevance the Cabinet, Shadow Cabinet, and the Commons considered Lords' reform to be. The failure to revive the measure indicates how low a place it took in the legislative programme. This uninterested, even disparaging, attitude seems to accord with the views of the reasonable critic who examines the status of the Upper House.

The Reasonable Critic

A dispassionate observer could argue that the real sanction obliging the Lords to behave 'sensibly' is not the threat of reform but the Peers' own awareness that their powers are, ultimately, negligible. For the most part the Commons have both the initiative and the final word in disposing of Government legislation; the Lords can revise or delay it only in response to Commons' decisions. Lords' Bills or Amendments eventually need the approval of M.P.s and even Lords' Private Members' Bills are not automatically given a hearing.

The two exceptional cases of the Rhodesia Order and the Seats Bill, where the Lords insisted on exercising their privileges, in fact prove how vestigial their powers now are. The Government re-laid the Order, after very little delay, and the Lords accepted it. The Commons rejected the Lords' Amendments to the Seats Bill and the Home Secretary eventually circumvented the Boundary Commission's recommendations. The Lords may assure themselves that they were performing a useful function but they are certainly sadly aware that many cynics in the outside world do not share this view.

The reason, of course, is that any power they have possessed has been based upon their prestige. They do not share with the Commons the authority or 'the audacity of elected persons'. When the Lords as a body no longer command respect as a social, economic, political, and even spiritual élite, their right to take part in legislative proceedings can be questioned with impunity. The composition of the Upper House is no longer justifiable (to some, it is absurd) and so their essential prestige has slipped away. The Lords lack credibility. They are no use as a hindrance to bad government and very little use as an agent of good.

Like the reasonable critic, those who have been committed to Lords' reform have understood that questions of 'powers' are rooted in those of 'composition'. They have sought to remedy an anachronism by phasing out the hereditary right to a seat, establishing the two-tier principle of voting Peers and speaking Peers, and reserving for the Lords clearly defined functions that nevertheless respect the prerogatives of the elected House. The reformers have seen their scheme in the whole context of Parliamentary reform. Their opponents have considered it an irrelevant measure, consuming valuable Parliamentary time only to prop up a moribund and redundant chamber.

The dispassionate analyst can suggest that even a reformed House organized on rational principles would be superfluous. An Upper House stripped of its panoply and mystique, lacking honours, hereditary dignities, aristocratic virtues and snobberies, arcane circumlocution, and archaic mumbo-jumbo would simply be a committee of nominated elder statesmen. They would not be elected and therefore could not encroach on the electoral responsibilities of M.P.s. They would have no further Parliamentary ambition but would be willing to devote some of their time and expertise to public debate. Among their duties might possibly be the discussion and completion of the less controversial details of legislation for which the Commons have insufficient time; much of their proceedings would be devoted to deliberating the scope for new enactments and perhaps the operation of existing legislation.

And such a reconstructed House, a cynic might argue, would be redundant. With its powers, dignities, and the whole game of writs and creations removed, a nominated committee would not even serve as a handy source of Prime-Ministerial patronage, a means of remembering old friends and clearing out lumber. (If, on the other hand, there were any honour in belonging to such a body it would perpetuate regrettable but inevitable class distinctions and snobberies.)

Revision and deliberation could be done as well by the Lower House, reinforced by more Parliamentary draftsmen and by procedural reforms. The speeches of elder statesmen could be relegated to letters in the newspapers, broadcast remarks, or conversation in their clubs. The real world being a world of party government and of partisanship, it is important that this should be seen to be the case. The better and the more efficiently a Second Chamber performs its legislative function, limited though this might be, the more it legitimizes non-partisanship. A reconstructed Upper House that distracts the electorate from the hard world where party battles are fought, where representatives are accountable, and decisions actually investigated, will only prove at worst pernicious and at best superfluous. In such a fashion the reasonable but tough-minded critic would make his case against a Second Chamber, reformed or unreformed.

A Modest Reply

Many of those who unflinchingly support the House of Lords would none the less agree that no constitution-maker today would invent a chamber so curious. But it exists, and a sympathetic but objective observer can find arguments in its favour. A realist, he might argue, appreciates that patronage is convenient (and snobbery endemic). Furthermore, it is prudent to ensure that there are successive stages in the legislative process, and the existence of a Second Chamber through which legislation must pass, if only formally, helps to retain such a time-lag. The executive and their administrative advisers are all too liable to press their enactments into force and two chambers, better than one, hinder any dangerous tendency to expedite legislation unnecessarily.

The reasonable supporter does not seek to judge the House of Lords by House of Commons' standards. The Lords do not have comparable weight as a legislative body and do not need to. Reconstructed and legitimized, they could relieve the Commons of some of their more tedious detailed work and non-controversial technical and legal points could also be referred to the Upper House. They could usefully examine the intricacies of subordinate legislation, reporting their conclusions to the Commons for criticism and resolution, or, if such a role were suspect, some sort of joint Committee could be established. Private Bills could be dealt with by the Lords; Private Members' legislation could still have a trial run in the Upper House. Separately, or in joint Committee, the Lords could examine recommendations for future legislation or investigate how Bills that have passed into law are working in practice. None of these functions needs to trespass on the preserve of the Commons and, though limited in scope and apparently innocuous in effect, they would allow a reconstructed, legitimate House of Lords to act as a useful adjunct in the Parliamentary process. The Lords would be a complementary House, but as auxiliaries rather than as co-equals.

This would not be a contrivance devised only to keep elder statesmen happy, to reward distinguished men and women, or to give retired but nostalgic politicians something to do. The House of Lords in recent years has served another purpose that closely resembles the 'dignified' function Bagehot ascribed to Parliament a century ago. Real power has passed elsewhere and no one would suggest that fundamental divisions between political parties are resolved in the Lords. The reasonable critic is right—a nominated deliberative and revising committee would not exemplify the partisan conflict which is an intrinsic part of political activity. The reasonable defender would reply that perhaps this is just as well and that the very value of a milder, less controversial and contentious House might be as a foil and a reminder to the electorate and to the Commons that there are other, indeed complementary, ways to conduct affairs.

A Darwinian Parable

The British Parliament has developed organically. The habits and responsibilities of each chamber have gradually, often imperceptibly, been modified in response to changes in its complementary half. The two Houses have remained in partnership and continuity has been preserved.

Simultaneously, the Commons have adapted to the times in one fashion and the Lords in quite another, so that each House has followed a separate and distinct evolutionary path. As the first part of this study showed, by 1964 the Lords had changed substantially. Though not extinct, however, they were none the less anachronistic; the coming years were to test their adaptive capacity still further.

Part Two described how they sustained this delicate and difficult task. The Lords had to curb some of their natural inclinations and adopt tactical compromises so that they should not be swept aside. With dignity and good sense they have managed to survive.

Perhaps it is symbolic that radical reform failed. No completely new House was created—but the Lords have continued to alter their procedures and the scope of their activities at a discreet and even pace. Their survival in the face of sustained and varied pressures suggests, not bemused detachment, but an evolutionary resilience of which Darwin himself would have approved.

EPILOGUE

AFTER the 1964 General Election the Lords had a lively appre-
hension that they continued to exist only on sufferance. The Labour
Party, which explicitly set little store by the Upper House, was now
in a position where they might seek to abolish it and, moreover, in
any confrontation with the Peers the Government would now enjoy
far more public sympathy than, say, in 1911 or the 1945–51 period.
Between 1964 and 1970 there was only one major occasion when the
House as a whole asserted itself and that was at the very end of the
Parliament on an issue, the House of Commons (Redistribution
of Seats) Bill, which they could confidently denounce as a trick.
The Peers realized very well that though their House had changed—
with Life Peers acting as an important catalyst—so had public
attitudes.

And despite the changes, the Conservative Opposition in the
Lords still enjoyed a large majority. (The party imbalance persisted
even in 1970, for Harold Wilson carefully kept an upper limit to
the number of new creations.) As this study has shown, the paradoxical state of the parties made it all the more necessary for the
Lords to behave discreetly in their relations with the Commons and
with the parties in their own House. Government legislation survived, the Labour benches were adequately manned, and the Conservatives mustered the appropriate strength to protest but not to
protest too much. Day-to-day business was managed not so much
by careful whipping as by the Peers' voluntary, conscious self-
restraint and the sensible working arrangements between the party
Leaders and their Chief Whips. The Leader of the House, for
example, was very much a father-figure in the House rather than
just the Leader of his party. Altogether, the Peers discovered during
this period the scope—and limits—of their authority and they
became even more eager for reform.

In 1970 the Conservatives won the General Election and they
were (in 1974) in Government for three years. It is a suitable
footnote to this study to ask how, during the new Administration,
the Conservative and Labour Parties in the Lords behaved towards

each other and, tentatively, whether there was very much change in the relationship between the Commons and the Lords.

If some Conservative Peers were taken aback by the party's defeat in 1964, Labour were as surprised to find themselves in Opposition in 1970. One or two embittered Labour Peers (newly created or newly deposed from office) were ready to make life as difficult as possible for the Conservative front bench and there was hot talk of snap Divisions, Divisions on Second Reading, wrecking Amendments, filibustering, and obstruction. More thoughtful Labour Peers saw that such tactics could be futile and might even set dangerous precedents for frustrating a future Labour Government. The Conservatives still enjoyed a majority in the House, even if it was somewhat diminished among the everyday working House. The Lords depends on self-discipline and, if Labour Peers were to abuse its procedures, the Conservatives could use their majority to silence them, curtail proceedings, and carry their legislation.

More to the point, it was important for the Labour Party in the Lords and for the standing of the House in public eyes that Labour follow the same conventions which the Tories had kept to during the previous Administration. Legislation for which the Government had a mandate should be given a Second Reading and amended, if possible, in Committee. Self-indulgent exploitation of the procedural freedom of the House could bring Labour into disrepute and even bring about the introduction of a Commons-like Speaker and an end to flexible self-government. These points were made in a paper which Lord Shackleton, now Leader of the Opposition, put before the front bench, and they supported his policy without dissent.

To some extent it was a test for the Conservatives too. On issues of major controversy when there might just be an Opposition victory on a surprise Division it was essential for the Government to ensure that their benches were fully manned, but, as a general rule, they enjoyed the advantage of numbers. Naturally the Conservative Leader, his Chief Whip, and their front bench, would coolly exact the benefits of their preponderant majority but, on the other hand, they had to be prepared to accommodate the Opposition sympathetically, in House-of-Lords-like fashion. Up to a point, the Conservatives were obliged to tolerate Labour's obfuscations and objections, always resisting the temptation to impose rules and expedite Government business.

An important trial came on the 1971 Industrial Relations Bill. Acting in the spirit recommended by Lord Shackleton, the Labour front bench did not actually oppose the Bill on Second Reading, for the Government had a mandate for this legislation. Instead, the Opposition concocted with great ingenuity a Motion that Second Reading be deferred and on the first day of the Committee Stage they proposed another Motion that that stage be deferred. Thus a protest was made, but it required some skill to draft Motions to satisfy Labour Peers who were passionately opposed to the Bill without abandoning the convention that Government legislation, mandated and already passed by the Commons, should be given a Second Reading in the Lords.

This convention did allow the Opposition to press Amendments in Committee and Labour exploited this to the full, extracting considerable concessions from the Government. At first the usual channels failed to work and there were no time-tabling arrangements. There was persistent opposition from a vociferous group of Labour Peers whose tactics frequently verged on the filibustering and at one point Lord Byers wrote an admonitory article in *The Times* stressing the advantages of Lords' procedure and warning how easily it could be abused. The Government steadily refused to adopt any uncharacteristic guillotine procedure and sensible Front- and Backbenchers dedicatedly 'slogged it out'. The Conservatives ensured that they had enough support to sit through the Opposition's interminable disquisitions and to carry Divisions; Labour Peers remained to discuss serious Amendments (sometimes long after the ostentatious filibusterers had gone home). The House often sat until very late at night and the Bill took a record thirty days of discussion, of which seventeen were in Committee and eleven on Report Stage. Altogether the Industrial Relations Bill was a great strain on the House and it was only through the exercise of amazing goodwill that business was carried on without the adoption of rigid procedural rules.

In a way, this Bill was something of a purgative. Virulent Labour extremists vented their hostility to the new Government. The procedures of the House bore the strain and when the Bill was disposed of the usual channels continued to work smoothly for most of the time. (That this is very much a matter of personal relationships, of Leaders and Whips who are accustomed to working with each other, was evident in the early summer of 1972, at the time of the Housing

Finance Bill. Some key Frontbenchers were absent from the House and their representatives were less experienced. Time-tabling arrangements almost broke down again and proceedings became temporarily much more awkward.) By 1974, however, much of the early partisan bombast had expended itself. Bitter skirmishes took place from time to time, Question Time was sometimes ragged, but the House quickly settled down to work.

The description of the House between 1964 and 1970 showed that party lines were also blurred by the presence of Liberals, Cross-benchers, and other groups sharing some, perhaps temporary, sympathy. This is still very much the case. Indeed, in a House where, since 1970, Peers continue to attend at the rate of 200-250 a day, the Liberal and Crossbench element has grown slightly and, simultaneously, new and influential groups of Peers have emerged. The four or five disabled Peers, for example, are effective and attractive lobbyists.

It is also astonishing to see how women Peers have blossomed as a self-conscious and forceful minority. There were no women in the House before 1958; now there are forty-three Peeresses by succession and creation, of whom at least thirty-five attend regularly. They take a particularly lively part in debates on matters of social conscience. A recent example has been their effort on the National Health Service Bill to rally the Lords to insist on their Amendment to provide free contraceptive services. Their increased numbers have encouraged the women. So, possibly, has the climate which has produced and fostered the Anti-Discrimination Bill, drawing attention to the disadvantages women experience on grounds of sex. Indeed, there were complaints that the Select Committee taking evidence on this Bill did not include enough women, and when it was reconstituted at the beginning of the 1972-73 Session women outnumbered men by four to three.

In any case many items of business do not inspire division on party lines, though they may be controversial. The Anti-Discrimination Bill itself is such an issue, one where a Private Member's Bill has drawn enthusiastic support from all quarters of the House. Where Public Bills are concerned, the 1972 Local Government Bill provides an interesting case where coalitions of Peers joined to secure Amendments to the Government's original proposals. They fought for alterations to the boundaries proposed for the new local authority areas and sometimes won. Two other cases, again *sui generis*, show the strength which an all-party combination can exercise. One is the 1971 Immigration Bill, where Liberals, Cross-benchers, and Bishops joined the Opposition front bench to defeat the Government on an important Amendment; the other area, where the House has overwhelmingly assented to the Government's policy, has been on legislation concerning Northern Ireland.

But it is perhaps the 1972 European Economic Communities Bill that has demanded the Peers' utmost in political and practical toleration and good sense. While the majority of the House were in favour of the resolution to join the E.E.C., the small group of anti-Marketeers who valiantly spoke to their Amendments and provoked Divisions were naturally given a respectful hearing. It was the pro-Marketeers, of all parties, who had to control their exasperation. The Bill was brief and incomplete and many of those in both Houses who supported entry were concerned that the Government had omitted provisions for Parliamentary scrutiny of European legislation, for procedures to keep the United Kingdom fully informed of proceedings at Strasbourg, and the like. Conservative frontbench Peers tried to persuade the Cabinet of the need to accept some such Amendments but the Government were adamant, as much towards its own supporters as towards the Opposition. Pro-Marketeers in the Commons worked on the Bill and supplied the Lords with drafting assistance but to no purpose. In their anxiety to pass the Bill into law, the Government had allowed no time for Amendments, even on a drafting point. To yield to a single Lords' Amendment, however reasonable, would mean that the Bill would have to return to the Commons and this would delay its enactment. The Conservative Leader, Lord Jellicoe, and his Chief Whip were requested to persuade Tory Peers not to propose or support Amendments and the strain this caused was to have repercussions in the following Session, 1972–73, when some disenchanted backbench Conservatives began to chafe at self-discipline.

It was therefore left to pro-Marketeers on the Labour benches to draft and press constructive Amendments, a frustrating exercise, for they knew that they enjoyed much sympathy for pro-Marketeers on the Conservative benches, that nevertheless Government supporters were obliged to vote against them, and that their defeat was assured. The E.E.C. Bill thus imposed a special strain on the House —and it was also infuriating in practical terms. Like the Local Government Bill, it did not reach the Lords until very late in the

1971-72 Session and they were unable to do very much work on it before the Summer Recess. While the Commons were still on holiday, the Peers reassembled in September for more Committee work on the Local Government Bill and the final stages of the E.E.C. Bill. This made demands not only on the Peers' stamina and good temper but also on that of the Officers and officials of the House, including the Doorkeepers, the catering staff, the Hansard reporters, the Printed Paper Office, and the Clerks. Renovation and repair work was going on in the House at the same time so that the Peers were almost bivouacking in their quarters. The Lords grumbled surprisingly little once they had reassembled for, to be honest, they felt rather proud of themselves. Attendance was good, averaging some two hundred a day, and not only were the Lords visibly at work while the Commons were in Recess, but they also managed to inject some useful and well-publicized discussions on Government Statements into their days of Committee discussions.

Still, the Peers have felt slightly put upon. Although it is true that the end of the Labour Government in 1970 removed their anxiety that the Lords' residual powers would be pruned, and possibly that the House would be abolished altogether, the attitude even of a Conservative Government towards the House sometimes seemed cavalier. With the failure of the wholesale Lords' Reform, the Lords' Leadership have attempted to carry out as many of the Bill's proposals as they can, piecemeal and with the acquiescence of their own House. Lord Brooke of Cumnor's Joint Select Committee on Delegated Legislation made some important recommendations and the White Paper's proposals for more Select Committee work have been put into effect. In the spirit of the White Paper, too, have been the efforts to redress the balance of the legislative time-table, although, as ever in the early years of a Parliament, too much tends to fall on to the Lords too late. A long-overdue concession from the Commons was achieved in November 1972, when a new Standing Order, No. 58A, was approved, allowing some relaxation of the Commons' financial privilege. Some legislation that has hitherto been jealously guarded by the Commons may in future be permitted to start in the Lords. Although the number of Conservative Cabinet Ministers in the Lords was only three, a Conservative Government is accustomed to disparage the Upper House and its spokesmen less than the Labour Government was inclined to do and for this reason one would imagine that between 1970 and 1973 Lord Jellicoe found more sympathy for the Lords' problems than Lord Shackleton enjoyed when he was Leader.

On balance, however, the Conservatives, like any new Government, presented Parliament with an ambitious legislative programme to which the Lords conscientiously addressed themselves without obtaining very much in return. But undoubtedly the House has continued to change with the times, even in the short period since 1970. The Leadership has secured the important changes mentioned above; there have also been a number of minor innovations, on the lines of the Tenth Report of the Procedure Committee, based on the investigations conducted by Lord Hood and his Committee. Some procedures have been streamlined, including the conduct of Divisions. Topical debates have been introduced and the practice of taking some less politically controversial Bills upstairs in Committee has been continued. Unreformed but determined, the Lords have for the past three years steadily carried on their deliberative and legislative work. In recent months it has even seemed to some of the informed public that the Lords have become more self-assertive. In the case of the Anti-Discrimination Bill, for instance, the coincidence of the Lords' initiative and public opinion persuaded the Government to propose legislation of its own. Another example is the stand that the Peers took on the National Health Services Bill Amendment (where the Government met the Lords' demands to the extent that contraception was included in its provisions). In a more minor, but none the less significant, area, they passed in one Session and over innumerable hurdles, a Private Member's Bill putting an end to the hunting of badgers and, in consequence, of other forms of wild life. Even where departments are lukewarm and where no drafting assistance is forthcoming from the Government, individual initiative and the backing of a dedicated group of Peers can achieve much.

Though the Lords remain a voluntary assembly of elders, attendance is still high, and an energetic group of Peers and Officials continues to reappraise its procedures and structures, searching for ways to extend its function. The Lords, in workman-like fashion, are adapting to their Parliamentary and public circumstances and treading carefully, in 1974 as in 1964.

APPENDIX

TABLE 1

Life Peerages Conferred, April 1958–June 1971

Year	Creations
Apr. 1958–Aug. 1959	18
Oct. 1959–Oct. 1960	7
Oct. 1960–Oct. 1961	17
Oct. 1961–Oct. 1962	0
Oct. 1962–Oct. 1963	3
Oct. 1963–Oct. 1964	16
Oct. 1964–Oct. 1965	39
Oct. 1965–Mar. 1966	20
Mar. 1966–Oct. 1967	34
Oct. 1967–Oct. 1968	17
Oct. 1968–Oct. 1969	5
Oct. 1969–May 1970	2
June 1970–June 1971	20
Total	198

(At the beginning of a new Parliament, viz. in 1964, 1966, and 1970, the number was also swollen by Dissolution and Resignation honours.)

Source: HL Journal Office.

TABLE 2

Life Peerages by Party, April 1958–June 1971

Year	Con.	Lab.	Lib.	No affilia-tion	Total
1958 Macmillan	3	6	—	3	12
1959 Macmillan	1	—	—	4	5
1960 Macmillan	—	—	—	1	1
1961 Macmillan	3	6	—	1	10
1962 Macmillan/Home	1	4	1	1	7
1963 Home	2	—	—	1	3
1964 Dissolution/Wilson	4	21	2	2	29
1965 Wilson	—	6	—	14	20
1966 Dissolution/Wilson	4	9	2	7	22
1967 Wilson	1	15	3	8	27
1968 Wilson	—	1	—	12	13
1969 Wilson	—	—	—	9	9
1970 Dissolution/Heath	4	13	—	9	26
1971 Heath	5	—	2	7	14
Total	28	81	10	79	198

Source: Vacher's *Parliamentary Companion.*

TABLE 3

Attendance at the House of Lords, 31 October 1967–1 August 1968

Party	Peers attending more than 33⅓% sitting days (working House)			Peers attending 5%–33⅓% sitting days		
	Created Peers	Hereditary Peers	Total	Created Peers	Hereditary Peers	Total
Conservative	38	87	125	24	86	110
Labour	81	14	95	8	5	13
Liberal	8	11	19	2	6	8
Peers not receiving a party whip	26	26	52	61	24	85
Total	153	138	291	95	121	216

Source: Cmnd. 3799, p. 5.

TABLE 4

Attendance at the House of Lords, 31 October 1967–1 August 1968

	Peers who attended up to 5% sitting days			Peers who did not attend		
	Created Peers	Hereditary Peers	Total	Created Peers	Hereditary Peers	Total
Conservative	4	1	5	2	1	3
Labour	9	70	79	6	31	37
Liberal	2	8	10	1	3	4
Peers not receiving a party whip	22	56	78	32	307	339
Total	37	135	172	41	342	383

Source: Cmnd. 3799, p. 5.

TABLE 5

Hours for which the House sat, 1955–71

(Excluding days on which the House sat for judicial and formal business only.)

Session	No. of sitting days	No. of hours	Average sitting time to nearest $\frac{1}{4}$ hour
1955–56	136	484	$3\frac{1}{2}$
1956–57	103	401	4
1957–58	103	395	$3\frac{3}{4}$
1958–59	109	465	$4\frac{1}{4}$
1959–60	113	450	4
1960–61	125	599	$4\frac{3}{4}$
1961–62	115	544	$4\frac{3}{4}$
1962–63	127	698*	$5\frac{1}{2}$
1963–64	110	534	$4\frac{3}{4}$
1964–65	124	593	$4\frac{3}{4}$
1965–66 (short)	50	264	$5\frac{1}{4}$
1966–67 (long)	191	1,001	$5\frac{1}{4}$
1967–68	139	$802\frac{1}{2}$	$5\frac{3}{4}$
1968–69	109	550	5
1969–70	83	$396\frac{1}{2}$	$4\frac{3}{4}$
1970–71	153	966	$6\frac{1}{4}$

* London Government Bill.

Source: HL Journal Office.

TABLE 6

Late Sittings, 1945-71

(Footnotes indicate major causes of late sittings)

Session	Sittings after 10 p.m.	Session	Sittings after 10 p.m.
1945–46	0	1958–59	5
1946–47	26[a]	1959–60	1
1947–48	9	1960–61	5
1948–49	8	1961–62	11
1949–50	2	1962–63	22[b]
1950–51	1	1963–64	3
1951–52	1	1964–65	8
1952–53	4	1965–66	5 (short Session)
1953–54	6	1966–67	17 (long Session)
1954–55	0	1967–68	31[c]
1955–56	5	1968–69	8
1956–57	2	1969–70	5
1957–58	1	1970–71	38[d]

[a] Transport Bill; Town and Country Planning Bill; Electricity Bill.
[b] London Government Bill.
[c] Transport Bill.
[d] Industrial Relations Bill.

Source: HL Journal Office.

TABLE 7

Monday Sittings, 1959–71

1959–60		14 out of 33 sitting weeks		
1960–61	21	,,	36	,,
1961–62	18	,,	33	,,
1962–63	23	,,	34	,,
1963–64	15	,,	32	,,
1964–65	15	,,	38	,,
1965–66	8	,,	14	,,
1966–67	37	,,	53	,,
1967–68	25	,,	38	,,
1968–69	10	,,	33	,,
1969–70	6	,,	26	,,
1970–71	22	,,	44	,,

Source: HL Journal Office.

TABLE 8

Public Bills Introduced in the House of Lords, 1952–70

Session	Government Bills	Consolidation Bills	Total
1952–53	7	5	12
1953–54	7	5	12
1954–55	5	0	5
1955–56	5	6	11
1956–57	3	8	11
1957–58	3	9	12
1958–59	6	13	19
1959–60	11	4	15
1960–61	9	2	11
1961–62	8	5	13
1962–63	11	6	17
1963–64	14	4	18
1964–65	5	15	20
r965–66	7	3	10
1966–67	18	16	34
1967–68	14	10	24
1968–69	9	5	14
1969–70	12	3	15

Source: HL Journal Office.

TABLE 9

Amendments to Public Bills in the Lords, 1946–70

Session	No. of Bills introduced in Commons, Lords	No. of Bills Amended by HL	No. of HL Amend-ments	No. of HC Amend-ments	No. of Amendments rejected by other House	% rejected
1946–47						
HC	43	17	996	—	53	5
HL	10	6	431	236	—	—
1948–49						
HC	76	29	533	—	41	6
HL	15	10	666	428	—	—
1951–52						
HC	44	7	30	—	—	—
HL	10	4	75	31	—	—
1962–63						
HC	33	13	456	—	—	—
HL	5	3	283	377	—	—
1964–65						
HC	45	18	203	—	11	5
HL	6	6	101	117	—	—
1966–67						
HC	70	30	732	—	48	4
HL	18	9	246	386	—	—
1967–68						
HC	42	23	1,009	—	29	6
HL	14	9	361	454	—	—
1968–69						
HC	39	16	490	—	29	6
HL	10	5	101	186	—	—
1969–70						
HC	30	11	119	—	8	5
HL	12	8	136	121	—	—

Source: HL Public Bill Office.

TABLE 10

Private Members' Bills Introduced in the Lords, 1952-71

Session	Introduced	Passed	Session	Introduced	Passed
1952-53	1	0	1961-62	3	1
1953-54	3	0	1962-63	8	2
1954-55	2	0	1963-64	8	7
1955-56	5	1	1964-65	13	4
1956-57	5	0	1965-66	3	0
1957-58	5	1	1966-67	15	5
1958-59	4	1	1967-68	10	0
1959-60	2	1	1968-69	14	2
1960-61	0	0	1969-70	13	3
			1970-71	14	3

Source: HL Journal Office.

TABLE 11

Motions for Papers, 1955-71

Session	Con.	Lab.	Lib.	Cb.	Total
Conservative Government					
1955-56					57
1956-57					43
1957-58					33
1958-59					46
1959-60					46
1960-61	16	27	4	3	50
1961-62	10	24*	4	3*	42
1962-63	14	25	3	2	44
1963-64	12	19	2	1	34
Labour Government					
1964-65	24	6	3	4	37
1965-66	7	8	2	3	20
1966-67	25	7	7	10	49
1967-68	16	4	4	4	28
1968-69	14	6	4	4	28
1969-70	11	3	2	3	19
Conservative Government					
1970-71	5	14	2	6	27

* Excluding one joint Labour-Crossbench Motion.

Source: HL Public Bill Office.

APPENDIX

TABLE 12

Motions debated in the House 1967-68, 1968-69, 1969-70

Day	Government (Labour)	Other frontbench (Conservative and Liberal)	Backbench (all parties and crossbench)	Total
Wednesday	6	26	44	76
Other days	11	1	6	18
Total	17	27	50	94

Source: HL Journal Office.

TABLE 13

Unstarred Questions, 1960-71

Session	Con.	Lab.	Lib.	Cb.	Total
1960-61	3	8	0	1	12
1961-62	5	6	0	1	12
1962-63	5	4	0	0	9
1963-64	10	11	1	1	23
1964-65	23	11	3	0	37
1965-66	4	6	1	1	12
1966-67	31	19	5	6	61
1967-68	17	8	2	1	28
1968-69	19	11	3	2	35
1969-70	17	10	4	1	32
1970-71	17	15	1	4	37

Source: HL Journal Office.

TABLE 14

Typical Divisions on Government Business, 1965–68

Business	For Government						For Opposition					
	Lab.	Con.	Lib.	Cb.	Bps.	Law Lords	Lab.	Con.	Lib.	Cb.	Bps.	Law Lords
Housing Ctee.												
9 Dec. 1965	28			9				66	4	2		
W. Midlands Order												
22 Dec. 1965	30	25	2	8				11		1		
Trade Descriptions Cttee.												
21 Feb. 1966	23	2		3			4	32	8	7	1	
Milk Order												
22 Feb. 1966	19	21		3			2	5	6	9		
Industl. Dvlpt. Ctee.												
2 Aug. 1966	51			2				52		2		
Prices and Incomes Ctee.												
11 Aug. 1966	62	2		8				19				
Land Commission Rept.												
17 Jan. 1967	42			4				72	1	3		1
Companies Bill Rept.												
24 Jan. 1967	35		1					60	5	12		
Iron and Steel Ctee.												
28 Feb. 1967	40		8	7				55		4		
Agric. Bill Rept.												
21 Mar. 1967	39			3				71	10	8		
Marine Bdcasting Ctee.												
1 May 1967	38		2	4				58	2	5		
Criminal Justice Rept.												
3 July 1967	49	5	5	6				49		2	1	
Leasehold Reform Ctee.												
10 July 1967	44			2			5	59		13		
Defence Est. Motion												
5 July 1967	51		6	4				76		9		
Economic Policy Motion												
24 Jan. 1968	87		9	11				130	1	17		

Source: HL Public Bill Office.

TABLE 15

Typical Divisions on Private Members' Legislation, 1965–67

Business	Con. Pro	Con. Anti	Lab. Pro	Lab. Anti	Lib. Pro	Lib. Anti	Cb. Pro	Cb. Anti	Bps. Pro	Bps. Anti	Law Lords Pro	Law Lords Anti
Abortion Second Reading 30 Dec. 1965	15	4	30	1	7		13	3	4			1
Abortion Report Amdt. 22 Feb. 1966	11	52	27	8	4	4	9	9	6			2
Christopher Swabey Motion 5 May 1966	36	19	19	2	3	3	6	10	2			
Sexual Offences Second Reading 10 May 1966	18	20	22	5	10		13	4	7			
Televising HL Motion 15 June 1966	27	27	16		7	2	6	2				
Sexual Offences Passage 28 June 1966	23	41	30	10	7	2	13	4	4		1	3
Matrimonial Homes Report 7 July 1966	7	35	36		3		6	2	2			
Protectn. Birds Committee 31 Aug. 1966	8	32	18	6	4		7	3			1	
Racial Discrimination Second Reading 10 Feb. 1967	1	37	15	16	3		1	7	3			
Sunday Entertainments Report 24 Apr. 1967	21	24	40		4	3	13	4	1	2		
Sexual Offences (No. 2) Second Reading 13 July 1967	40	29	42	12	10		14	6	3		2	1
Medical Termination of Pregnancy Second Reading 19 July 1967	46	10	47	2	13	1	18	7	3	1		
Brighton Marina Instruction 20 July 1967	3	16	19	3	3		6	4				
Medical Termination of Pregnancy Committee 26 July 1967	10	70	39	12	10	2	8	25	6			1
Abortion (No. 2) Report Oct. 1967	25	51	50	5	11	3	23	12	3	4	1	4

Source: HL Public Bill Office.

BIBLIOGRAPHICAL NOTE

EXTRAORDINARILY little of lasting value has been published on the House of Lords and the scholarly work that exists deals mainly with the origins of the House and schemes for its reform. Full references to all these books and articles are set out in a comprehensive list prepared by the House of Commons Research Division, *Bibliography No. 35*, covering the period 1856–1957, with supplementary bibliographies continuing the references to April 1969 (*Reference sheets 67/30* and *69/11*). The majority of the items are of limited or ephemeral interest, and this narrative has therefore relied mainly on official documents and private accounts to test and illustrate oral evidence.

Of official documents, the most helpful are:

HL Debs., vols. 254–329 (1964–72).
Companion to Standing Orders, revised edition, 1972.
HL Journals, 1964–72.
Cd. 9038, Conference on the Reform of the Second Chamber, Letter from V. Bryce to the Prime Minister (1918).
Cmd. 7380, Parliament Bill 1947. Agreed Statement on Conclusion of the Conference of Party Leaders (Feb./Apr. 1948).
Cmnd. 3799, House of Lords Reform, Nov. 1968.
Reports of the HL Procedure Committee, notably the Tenth Report, 1971.

The professional journal of the Clerks of the Parliaments of the United Kingdom and Commonwealth, *The Table*, contains much valuable miscellaneous information on procedural precedents and innovations. The volumes covering 1950–70 are particularly useful. The Clerk of the Parliaments, Sir David Stephens, has provided a factual account of the Lords' activities and powers in *Constitutional and Parliamentary Information* (Apr. 1967). The intricacies of procedure are also set out in:

Erskine May, *Treatise on the Law, Privileges, Proceedings and Usage of Parliament*, 18th edition, 1971.
Sir W. I. Jennings, *Cabinet Government*, 3rd edition, 1959, chapter 13.

General information about Peers themselves comes in the first instance from customary works of reference like *Who's Who* and *Vacher's Parliamentary Companion*. Official records, including the Lords' own confidential *Guide*, provide further detail.

Among the few published sources, by far the most valuable is Professor Bromhead's book: *The House of Lords and Contemporary Politics*

1911-57, 1958. This describes the composition, function, and procedure of the Lords as well as their activities in the first part of the century. The early difficulties of the Upper House are also fully depicted in Roy Jenkins's *Mr. Balfour's Poodle: an account of the struggle between the House of Lords and the Government of Mr. Asquith*, 1954. The earliest origins of the Lords are the subject of an exact and elaborate study by J. Enoch Powell and Keith Wallis, *The House of Lords in the Middle Ages*, 1968. Much of its detail falls outside the scope of this study but the Introduction provides a powerful insight into the place of the Upper House in an ever-developing constitution. Another historical work that is of special assistance is P. D. G. Thomas, *The House of Commons in the Eighteenth Century*, 1971. This deals with the embryonic procedural devices once customary in the Commons and, in 1971, still followed in the Lords. On the Lords' judicial activities, L. Blom-Cooper and G. Drewry have provided a complete study, in *Final Appeal*, 1973.

The dilemma faced by a non-elected House empowered to intervene in questions of constituency boundaries is described in D. E. Butler's *The Electoral System in Britain 1918-1951*, 1953; the consequences of more recent arrangements and the Lords' intervention in D. E. Butler and M. Pinto-Duchinsky, *The British General Election of 1970*, 1971.

Bernard Crick's book *The Reform of Parliament*, 1964, is now a classic; chapters 5 and 6 deal with the House of Lords. Occasional articles in *Parliamentary Affairs* also offer important and sensitive analyses of various aspects of the Upper House. For example:

P. Bromhead, 'The Peerage Act and the New Prime Minister', vol. 17 (1963-4).
H. Burrows, 'House of Lords—Change or Decay?', vol. 17 (1963-4).
V. Weare, 'The House of Lords—Prophecy and Fulfilment', vol. 18 (1964-5).
J. Vincent, 'The House of Lords', vol. 19 (1965-6) and 'A Correction and Reconsideration', vol. 20 (1966-7).
P. Bromhead and D. Shell, 'The Lords and their House', vol. 20 (1966-7).
P. Henderson, 'Legislation in the Upper House', vol. 21 (1967-8).
G. Drewry and J. Morgan, 'Law Lords as Legislators', vol. 22 (1968-9).
G. Drewry and J. Brock, 'Prelates in Parliament', vol. 24 (1970-1).
R. Borthwick, 'An Early Experiment with Standing Committees in the House of Lords', vol. 25 (1971-2).

Skirmishings between Lords and Commons, minor measures of reform, and attempts at major schemes have from time to time provoked well-informed articles in daily and weekly newspapers. Some of the most interesting are:

B. Crick, 'Tackling the Lords', *New Society*, 6 May 1965.

H. Burrows, 'How the House of Lords might reform itself', *The Times*, 26 May 1966.

Lord Alport, 'A new House of Lords', *Guardian*, 17 June 1966.

D. Wood, 'Lords withdraw from the constitutional trinity', *The Times*, 20 Feb. 1967.

R. Butt, 'A shake-up for the Lords', *Sunday Times*, 29 Oct. 1967.

'Giving the Lords a worthwhile role', *Financial Times*, 31 Oct. 1967. 'Mr. Wilson and the Lords', *Spectator*, 3 Nov. 1967. 'My Lords, go home', *The Economist*, 4 Nov. 1967. 'Hogg urges a Senate', *Observer*, 5 Nov. 1967. 'How the accidental axe fell on the Peers . . .', *Sunday Times*, 5 Nov. 1967. 'Our Lords, right or wrong', *Sunday Telegraph*, 5 Nov. 1967.

I. Trethowan, 'Beware a too radical Lords reform', *The Times*, 9 Nov. 1967.

J. Grimond, 'What kind of Second Chamber?', *Guardian*, 27 Nov. 1967. 'Focus on Reform of the Lords', B.B.C. Transcript of Radio 4 broadcast, 12 Dec. 1967.

In 1968 there was a flurry of articles in the Press when the Peers rejected the Sanctions Order; in the last months of that year more comment appeared with the publication of the White Paper, Cmnd. 3799. In 1969 the exercises on the Parliament (No. 2) Bill offered further material and, in the summer, the Peers' activities on the Seats Bill provided more journalistic fodder. Such items are too numerous to mention here.

The autobiographies and biographies of individual Peers themselves and those involved with them (including Prime Ministers and civil servants) are naturally of considerable assistance. The most recent and fascinating observations are those in Richard Crossman's unpublished Cabinet Diaries. These suggest how inquiries into Lords' reform should be directed and provoke questions to which, ultimately, official records will give the answers.

INDEX